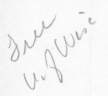
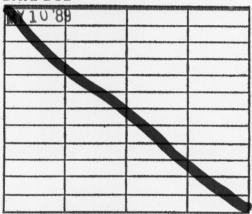

PATHWAYS TO PARLIAMENT

PATHWAYS *to* PARLIAMENT

CANDIDATE SELECTION IN BRITAIN

AUSTIN RANNEY

Madison and Milwaukee · 1965

THE UNIVERSITY OF WISCONSIN PRESS

Published by the University of Wisconsin Press
Madison and Milwaukee
P.O. Box 1379, Madison, Wisconsin 53701

Copyright © 1965 by the
Regents of the University of Wisconsin

Printed in the United States of America by the
George Banta Company, Inc., Menasha, Wisconsin

Library of Congress Catalog Card Number 65-16364

To David Butler

PREFACE

THE STUDY OF NOMINATIONS
AND CANDIDATE SELECTION

The free election of public officials has long been the western democracies' basic device for guaranteeing popular control over government. To be sure, it has been supplemented by various contrivances for sounding public opinion on particular issues between elections. But in a modern mass democracy the ultimate political decisions concern not what the rulers shall do but who the rulers shall be. Determining who shall rule through periodic elections of public officials remains the sovereign people's weapon-of-last-resort for influencing what government does.

Most free elections involve voters choosing among competing candidates whose names are printed on official ballots.[1] Accordingly, most elections are preceded by the making of *nominations*— that is, by legal proceedings in which eligible persons are formally designated "candidates" and have their names accepted by public authorities for printing on the election ballots. The legal procedures

---

[1] Since write-in votes are, in effect, additions by the voters to the names printed on the ballot, they are consistent with the statements in the text.

vii

vary widely in detail, but in one significant respect all nominations are alike: in elections for all but the most minor offices, the formal nominating proceedings are preceded and dominated by extralegal activities of political parties generally known as *candidate selection*. By these activities each party decides whom it will support. Having settled upon someone, the party publicly proclaims him to be its standard-bearer, helps finance and conduct his campaign, and, if he wins, enrolls him in its legislative conference, parliamentary party, or other intragovernmental party organizations.

The question of how elections are or should be conducted has deservedly received much attention from students of democracy. Some have emphasized problems of organization and administration.[2] Others have focused on the attitudes and behavior of voters.[3] Only a few, however, have given more than passing notice to nominations and candidate selection, and they have concentrated upon national nominating conventions and direct primary elections in the United States.[4] Thus the literature of political science provides few empirical descriptions of candidate selection outside the United States, and even fewer efforts to build a general comparative theory

---

[2] A small but representative sample of such works includes: David E. Butler, *The Electoral System in Britain Since 1918*, 2nd ed. (Oxford: at the Clarendon Press, 1963); Enid Lakeman and J. D. Lambert, *Voting in Democracies* (London: Faber & Faber, Ltd., 1955); Joseph P. Harris, *Election Administration in the United States* (Washington, D.C.: The Brookings Institution, 1934); Ferdinand A. Hermens, *Democracy or Anarchy? A Study of Proportional Representation* (Notre Dame, Ind.: The Review of Politics, 1941); W. J. M. Mackenzie, *Free Elections* (New York: Rinehart & Company, 1958); and J. F. S. Ross, *Elections and Electors* (London: Eyre & Spottiswoode, 1955).

[3] The literature on voting behavior is even more voluminous than that on election organization and administration. For bibliographical reviews, see Angus Campbell, "Recent Developments in Survey Studies of Political Behavior," in Austin Ranney, ed., *Essays on the Behavioral Study of Politics* (Urbana: University of Illinois Press, 1962), pp. 31–46; and Austin Ranney, "The Utility and Limitations of Aggregate Data in the Study of Electoral Behavior," *ibid.*, pp. 91–102.

[4] See, for example, Paul T. David, Ralph M. Goldman, and Richard C. Bain, *The Politics of National Nominating Conventions* (Washington, D.C.: The Brookings Institution, 1960); C. E. Merriam and Louise Overacker, *Primary Elections*, rev. ed. (Chicago: University of Chicago Press, 1928); V. O. Key, Jr., *Politics, Parties, and Pressure Groups*, 5th ed. (New York: Thomas Y. Crowell Company, 1964), Chs. 14–16; Julius Turner, "Primary Elections as the Alternatives to Party Competition in 'Safe' Districts," *Journal of Politics*, XV (May, 1953), 197–210; and C. A. M. Ewing, *Primary Elections in the South* (Norman: University of Oklahoma Press, 1953). Frank Sorauf has written a study of the selection of candidates for the Pennsylvania House of Representatives: *Party and Representation* (New York: Atherton Press, 1963).

from such descriptions. This constitutes a major lacuna in our knowledge of the institutions and problems of modern democracies.

CANDIDATE SELECTION
IN BRITISH PARTIES

Ever since the pioneering studies by M. I. Ostrogorski and A. Lawrence Lowell in the late nineteenth century, the British party system has attracted special attention from students of politics in many lands. There are good reasons for this interest. Britain has one of the oldest and most stable of all democratic party systems. British parties have long played a leading role in the nation's much admired and widely imitated version of cabinet government. And, as we shall see in Chapter 1, for almost a century now an influential school of American political scientists has held Britain's party system to be the model which should be followed by all democracies, especially the United States.

Hence it is not surprising that a number of studies of British parties have been written, some by scholars from other nations. But while some short descriptions are available, no comprehensive study of candidate selection exists comparable to David Butler's study of the electoral system.[5]

This book is intended to fill the gap. In addition to the available secondary literature, it employs three main bodies of data: (1) the author's interviews during 1961–1962 with a number of national party leaders and workers, regional organizers, constituency association officers, agents, and activists, M.P.s, prospective candidates, and aspirants for candidature; (2) accounts in the national and local press of controversies over candidate selection; and (3) information about the candidates adopted and the constituencies in which they were adopted for the general elections of 1951, 1955, 1959, and 1964, and for by-elections from 1951 to 1964.

Some reference will be made to candidate selection prior to the

---

[5] The principal descriptions to date are: Robert T. McKenzie, *British Political Parties,* 2nd. ed. (London: Mercury Books, 1964), pp. 241–53, 549–58; Peter G. Richards, *Honourable Members* (London: Faber & Faber, Ltd., 1959), Ch. 1; R. L. Leonard, *Guide to the General Election* (London: Pan Books, Ltd., 1964), Ch. 7; Martin Harrison, *Trade Unions and the Labour Party since 1945* (London: George Allen & Unwin, Ltd., 1960), pp. 80–88, Ch. 6; and articles on "The Selection of Parliamentary Candidates" in *Political Quarterly,* XXX (July–September, 1959) by William Rees-Mogg (Conservatives), T. E. M. McKitterick (Labour), and Philip Skelsey (Liberals).

Second World War, but the book is mainly concerned with events in the period between the general elections of 1945 and 1964. While no historical period is "typical" or "normal," certain of this period's special characteristics directly affecting candidate selection should be noted. First, the substantial reorganization of the Conservative party directed by Lord Woolton and R. A. Butler in the late 1940's both altered selection procedures and affected the kinds of candidates adopted. Second, the Conservatives' electoral fortunes steadily improved from 1945 to 1959 and thereby furnished them an ever-increasing number of constituencies presumed to be especially attractive to aspiring candidates: in 1950 the national average swing from Labour to the Conservatives (i.e., the average of the Conservative gain and the Labour loss in percentage of votes wherever both put forward candidates) was 3 per cent; in the succeeding three general elections it was, respectively, 1.1 per cent, 1.8 per cent, and 1.1 per cent.[6] In 1964 the swing was in the other direction by 3.1 per cent. In 1950 the Conservatives gained a net of 80 seats; in 1951, 23 seats; in 1955, 22 seats; and in 1959, 24 seats.[7] In 1964 they lost a net of 62 seats. And third, the often-bitter fight between Left and Right which characterized the Labour party's internal politics during most of the period affected candidate selection as well as the annual conferences and controversies over the national leadership.

Whether any or all of these conditions will persist in the 1960's and beyond is a question outside the scope of this book. Our task is to try to answer, in the political context of 1945–1964, the following questions:

What powers have each party's national officers and committees to induce local organizations to select particular persons or kinds of persons? How often and in what circumstances have they been used?

What powers have the national leaders to prevent the local organizations from selecting particular persons? How often and in what circumstances have they been used?

How do the local organizations select candidates? Who are the local "influentials"? What kinds of persons have they selected? Why?

---

[6] Cf. David E. Butler and Richard Rose, *The British General Election of 1959* (London: Macmillan & Co., Ltd., 1960), p. 235.

[7] David E. Butler and Jennie Freeman, *British Political Facts, 1900–1960* (London: Macmillan & Co., Ltd., 1963), p. 126.

What are the differences in these matters from one kind of constituency to another within each party and among the three parties?

I hope the answers to these questions will illuminate the part candidate selection plays in making British parties what they are. They may also provide some basis for estimating the extent to which British practices are exportable and constitute a model other democracies should follow.

ACKNOWLEDGMENTS

The Social Science Research Council, by granting a Senior Research Award in Governmental Affairs, enabled me to spend the academic year 1961–1962 in Great Britain collecting data for this book. I am deeply grateful for their generous support and hasten to absolve them of any blame for what I have done with it. I also wish to thank the Graduate Research Committee of the University of Wisconsin for providing research assistance and machine time for the analysis of candidate and constituency characteristics.

A succession of research assistants, Simon Sheridan, Clara V. Wall, Norman Adler, Madeleine Wing, and John Horsfield, performed their unexciting but demanding chores of coding and checking competently and cheerfully.

To the Warden and Fellows of Nuffield College, Oxford, go my warmest thanks for extending me the privileges of their Senior Common Room, their library resources, and their friendship. I am also grateful to the staff of the British Museum Newspaper Library, Colindale, for their many courtesies.

I am particularly indebted to the many national and local leaders of the Conservative, Labour, and Liberal parties who received me so cordially, talked to me so frankly, and often insisted on entertaining me as well. Since the use I have made of what they told me might embarrass them if they were publicly identified, I shall here thank all of them anonymously but most warmly.

The customary brief acknowledgments seem poor rewards for the considerable labors and valuable contributions of colleagues on both sides of the Atlantic, but such is the coin in which academics deal. Robert T. McKenzie of the London School of Economics and Political Science and Richard Rose of the University of Manchester devoted many hours to initiating me into the mysteries of the British way of politics. Hugh Berrington of the University of Keele generously supplied me with material for classifying constituencies and many leads to controversies over candidatures from his inexhaustible store of anecdotes about local politics. Martin Harrison of the University of Manchester, Peter G. Richards of the University of Southampton, and Jorgen S. Rasmussen of the University of Arizona read particular chapters and made valuable suggestions. Warren E. Miller of the University of Michigan, Executive Director of the Inter-University Consortium for Political Research, not only read several chapters but used his great skills as a teacher to grapple with my illiteracy in quantitative analysis.

Leon D. Epstein of the University of Wisconsin and Anthony S. King of Magdalen College, Oxford, read the entire manuscript. Most of their criticisms and suggestions are incorporated in what follows, and while I cannot blame them for the book's deficiencies, they deserve much of the credit for whatever virtues it may have.

I shall not offer the conventional thanks to my wife, my American sons, or my English son: after all, they had just as good a time as I.

Finally, the dedication of the book is an inadequate but deeply felt acknowledgment of my personal and scholarly debt to David E. Butler of Nuffield College, Oxford.

AUSTIN RANNEY

Madison
January 10, 1965

CONTENTS

PATHWAYS TO PARLIAMENT

Chapter 1 | Introduction

The selection of parliamentary candidates is one of the least discussed and most recondite of the interlocking mysteries that make up the British system of government. In Anthony Howard's apt phrase, it is "the secret garden of British politics."[1] Contests between the parties' candidates in general elections and by-elections are for the most part fully reported in the national and local press, and the ordinary voter can readily learn a great deal about the choices before him and the case being made for each. But accounts of the contests within the parties over the selection of candidates are usually confined to bare formal announcements that so-and-so has been adopted by the thus-and-such constituency party association. In most instances the voter cannot even find out who besides so-and-so was under consideration, let alone why he was chosen over them.

There is no great mystery about why this is so. The most obvious reason is the insistence of the activists in all three political parties that candidate selection is strictly a private affair and no business of the general public. They wish public disclosure of only the final result, and take great pains to erect a wall of secrecy between the public and whatever politicking leads to that result.

[1] "Candidates and the Closed Door," *Town* (April, 1962), p. 40.

3

Occasionally, of course, a party official lets slip or an enterprising journalist ferrets out the names on a "short list" (see below).[2] A few struggles over candidatures have grown so intense that total secrecy became impossible, and the press was able to report at least part of what happened.[3] In short, the garden is secret partly because its wardens keep the gates locked and patrol the walls to keep outsiders from peeping over.

It is also secret, however, because outsiders rarely think it worth the bother to try to see what is going on inside. Apparently neither the British press nor their readers consider candidate selection news to anything like the degree that election campaigns and results are news. No doubt candidate selection, being strictly a private party affair, has for many a faintly disreputable air.[4] Then, too, most people know that the British voter votes for a party and a government, not for the personal attractions of a local candidate. They know, also, that the destiny awaiting most of the election winners is to troop dutifully in and out of the lobbies as the whips direct. It is therefore not surprising that so many voters feel that when all is said and done it really does not matter very much what candidates either party selects.

This book proceeds from the very different conviction that candidate selection plays a vital role in the British system of government. So it seems appropriate to begin by outlining some of the principal aspects of that role.

Some Consequences of Candidate Selection

In Safe Seats, Selection Is Election

One striking characteristic of British politics in the post-war era has been the high stability of most voters' preferences for a particu-

---

[2] The present writer reviewed accounts in the national and local press of some 400 candidate selections between 1945 and 1964. He found only 26 published short lists.

[3] As, for example, in the long struggle between the Bournemouth East and Christchurch Conservative Association and Nigel Nicolson over the latter's readoption for the 1959 general election (see Chapter 3). A good part, though not all, of the illustrative material in this book is drawn from contests like this which did manage to break through the secrecy barrier.

[4] Professor W. J. M. MacKenzie, for example, holds that ". . . there is no doubt that the process of selecting candidates is one of the less open and admirable parts of British democracy": *Free Elections* (New York: Rinehart and Company, 1958), p. 43.

lar political party—preferences so deeply rooted in family tradition, social status, economic position, and the like that the voters have rarely considered voting for another party and even more rarely have actually done so.[5] This becomes evident when one surveys the small amount of electoral swing—meaning the average of the Conservative percentage gain or loss and the Labour percentage gain or loss—in post-war elections, as shown in Table 1.1.

TABLE 1.1

ELECTORAL SWING IN POST-WAR ELECTIONS*

Election	Median National Swing to Con.	Greatest Single Swing to Con.	No. of Seats with Swings over 5 per cent	No. of Seats with Swings over 10 per cent	Greatest Single Swing to Lab.
1950	+3.3%	11.5%	34	2	2.0%
1951	+1.1	7.8	11	1	11.8
1955	+1.8	6.2	15	0	5.1
1959	+1.1	7.3	19	3	13.4
1964	−3.1	7.2	153	7	17.0
By-elections, 1951–1964	—	5.1	40	9	13.7

* Some of the data for this table are drawn from the Nuffield election studies: Herbert G. Nicholas, *The British General Election of 1950* (London: Macmillan & Co., Ltd., 1951), p. 320; David E. Butler, *The British General Election of 1951* (London: Macmillan & Co., Ltd., 1952), pp. 267–75; David E. Butler, *The British General Election of 1955* (London: Macmillan & Co., Ltd., 1955), pp. 185–97, 210–11; and David E. Butler and Richard Rose, *The British General Election of 1959* (London: Macmillan & Co., Ltd., 1960), pp. 219–31, 235–39, 282–84. The other data are taken from reports of election results in the *Times* (London).

An inspection of the seats which changed hands in post-war general elections confirms the high stability of the voters' preferences suggested by the data in Table 1.1. In the 1950 general election, despite a national swing of only 3.3 per cent to the Conservatives, the Labour party had a net loss of 76 seats. Most of their losses, however, resulted from the redrawing of constituency boundaries in the 1948 redis-

[5] See the evidence presented in Mark Benney, A. P. Gray, and R. H. Pear, *How People Vote* (London: Routledge & Kegan Paul, 1956); and in John Bonham, *The Middle Class Vote* (London: Faber & Faber, Ltd., 1954).

tribution, not from the massive switching of Labour voters to Conservative candidates.

In the general elections of 1951, 1955, and 1959 the Conservatives lost a total of seven seats, six of which had been previously won by margins ranging from 0.6 per cent to 2.2 per cent of the popular vote, and the seventh by 14.6 per cent. Labour lost fifty-eight seats, which had been previously won by margins ranging from 0.2 per cent to 8.8 per cent. In the general election of 1964 the Conservatives lost sixty-three seats, of which fifty-eight had been previously won by margins of less than 10 per cent, four by margins of less than 13 per cent, and one (the Pollok division of Glasgow) by 17.5 per cent. Labour lost five seats, four of which had been won by margins from 0.2 per cent to 1.7 per cent, and the fifth (Smethwick, lost by Patrick Gordon Walker in the famous "white backlash" election) by 9.4 per cent.

In these four elections, accordingly, a margin of ten points (i.e., 55 per cent to 45 per cent in a straight fight) was enough to hold over 98 per cent of the seats for both parties, and a margin of five points (i.e., 52.5 per cent to 47.5 per cent) was enough to hold 95 per cent of the seats.

In by-elections, particularly those held between the 1959 and 1964 general elections, the voters have been more volatile. A margin of 5 percentage points was enough to hold the seat in only 77 per cent of by-elections between the 1951 and 1959 general elections, 10 per cent was enough in 96 per cent of the by-elections, and 14 per cent was enough to hold any seat. Of the by-elections held between 1959 and 1964 that permit direct comparison, the Conservatives lost seats previously held by majorities of 34.4 per cent (Orpington), 15.5 per cent (Middlesbrough West), 10.2 per cent (Luton), 6.3 per cent (Glasgow Woodside), and 4.1 per cent (Rutherglen). Labour lost only Brighouse and Spenborough, won in 1959 by a bare forty-seven votes.

Most students of British politics believe, for reasons we shall note below, that while British voters may occasionally vote abnormally in by-elections, they usually support the party of their longstanding choice in general elections. If, then, we define a safe Conservative seat in this period as one won by the Conservatives by 4.0 per cent or more in the preceding general election and a safe Labour seat as one won by Labour by 9.0 per cent or more, we discover that *almost two-thirds of all parliamentary constituencies are safe for one party or the other.*[6] And this, in turn, means that the effective choice of almost two-thirds of all M.P.s is made, not openly by the voters in elections, but secretly by the persons who select the parties' candidates.

IN MARGINAL SEATS AND IN BY-ELECTIONS
SELECTION MAY MAKE THE DIFFERENCE

In 1961–1962 the author interviewed several score parliamentary candidates, M.P.s, and local and national party officials. One question always put was, "Does it really make any difference in the election outcome what kinds of candidates are selected?" The answers varied considerably from one respondent to another. The parties' "civil servants"—the local agents, area agents, and officials at headquarters—usually replied that a candidate's personal qualities have very little influence on the result (five hundred votes one way or the other was the maximum often suggested). General elections, they declared, are decided partly by the relative efficiency of the parties' organizations but mainly by the voters' feelings about current national economic and social conditions and issues. The personalities of local candidates are scarcely, if at all, a factor.

On the other hand, the parties' local militants—the constituency organizations' officers and active supporters, and the candidates themselves—usually declared that a candidate's personal qualities can make a great deal of difference (up to two or three thousand votes some said). Many pointed out that in their particular constituencies it is of the highest importance to select the right kind of candidate—one whose record, bearing, accent, and social position are right for those constituencies. As one local chairman said, "Take old Colonel X, for instance; he might be splendid for some rural seat, but there's a bit of the parade ground in his manner, and that just won't do for a working-class constituency like this one. I don't care what Central Office says, he'd lose us thousands of votes!"

Probably the most reasonable view is that in general elections the candidates' personal qualities affect the results very little, but in by-

---

[6] See the Appendix. Richard Rose estimates that "from two-thirds to three-quarters of the seats in Parliament are 'safe'; that is, unlikely to be lost by a sitting member . . .": *Politics in England* (Boston: Little, Brown and Company, 1964), p. 149. See also R. L. Leonard, *Guide to the General Election* (London: Pan Books, Ltd., 1964), p. 42.

elections they can become a factor of some significance. The Benney study of the Greenwich electorate in the 1950 general election, for example, showed that 80 to 90 per cent of the voters knew the name of their party's candidate, but only 30 per cent could say anything at all about what kind of a person he was—and most of what even this minority knew consisted of "snippets of biographical information."[7]

This is perfectly understandable. A general election, after all, is a national referendum on the question of which party shall form the government. However little one may know about his party's local candidate, and however he may feel about what he does know, what matters is that the candidate will, if elected, cast his votes in the House to sustain the party's leaders as the government. However one may admire the appearance or eloquence or public record of the opposition party's candidate, he will, if elected, cast his votes to discomfit and, if possible, displace that government. And in any case the contest in any particular constituency in a general election is only one of 630, and local campaigning is bound to feature national policy and the personalities of the national party leaders. So the most sensible course in general elections is to vote for the party, not the man. This is precisely what most British voters do.

By-elections are different. Correctly or not, they are widely regarded as important indicators of the government's current state of political health. Only a few are held at a time, and so local candidates and campaigns receive a degree of national publicity and attention far beyond what is possible for them in general elections. Then, too, the fate of a government is seldom directly at stake, and so many voters may feel it is safe and even salutary to abandon temporarily their normal party loyalties in order to emphasize their dissatisfactions with the current state of affairs.

For these reasons, candidates in by-elections are far more visible than most of those standing in general elections. That is why party leaders generally believe that a particularly attractive candidate can materially boost his party's vote, and a particularly unattractive one can substantially depress it. That is why the national offices of all three parties, as we shall see, take a considerably more active part in selecting candidates for by-elections than for general elections.[8]

---

[7] Benney, Gray, and Pear, *How People Vote*, pp. 158–59.

[8] Cf. Peter G. Richards, *Honourable Members* (London: Faber & Faber, Ltd., 1959), p. 14.

IN ALL SEATS AND ELECTIONS
SELECTION SUSTAINS PARTY COHESION

One of the best-known traits of British politics is the fact that in almost all divisions in Parliament all, or nearly all, of the members of each of the three parliamentary parties vote as their whips direct. The resulting party solidarity (or "cohesion" as political scientists call it) is as high in the House of Commons as in any modern democratic legislature and far higher than in the American Congress, where it is very rare for all the Democrats to vote one way on a bill and all the Republicans to vote the other.[9]

An eminent and influential school of American scholars has long argued a thesis first advanced by Woodrow Wilson in 1879: that only cohesive, disciplined, and centrally controlled political parties can provide a modern mass democracy with effective yet responsible government. They find both American parties woefully deficient in these respects, and urge that they be reformed as soon and as thoroughly as possible. Most of them regard the modern British Conservative and Labour parties as true working models of "responsible party government," and cite them as proof that parties can conduct their affairs properly.[10]

Whether or not one accepts this view, there can be no doubt that the high cohesion of the parliamentary parties is one of the principal piers supporting the contemporary British structure of parliamentary government. The causes of that cohesion are, therefore, a prime subject for scholarly investigation, and a number of writers have studied them. Robert McKenzie, for example, has documented the power of both parties' national leaders over both their parliamentary parties and the mass organizations outside Parliament. Leon Epstein

---

[9] For information on the relative degrees of party cohesion in various nations, see Julius Turner, *Party and Constituency* (Baltimore: The Johns Hopkins Press, 1951), Tables 1 and 2, pp. 24, 27.

[10] This point of view is summarized and analyzed in Austin Ranney, *The Doctrine of Responsible Party Government* (Urbana: University of Illinois Press, 1954 and 1962). Its most recent expositions are: E. E. Schattschneider, *Party Government* (New York: Farrar and Rinehart, Inc., 1942); E. E. Schattschneider *et al.*, *Toward a More Responsible Two-party System* (New York: Rinehart and Co., Inc., 1950); Stephen K. Bailey, *The Condition of Our National Parties* (New York: Fund for the Republic, 1959); and James MacGregor Burns, *The Deadlock of Democracy* (Englewood Cliffs, N.J.: Prentice-Hall, Inc., 1963).

emphasizes the demands of parliamentary government, the relative absence of localism in British political attitudes, and the relative sharpness of ideological conflict among certain segments of British society.[11]

Some observers believe that the process of selecting parliamentary candidates also plays a leading role in sustaining the cohesion of the parliamentary parties. They point to the fact that the national agencies of both the Conservative and Labour parties (but not of the Liberal party) enjoy the power to veto any candidate selected by a constituency organization. Such a veto deprives the candidate of the official party label, without which his chances of being elected are slim. They conclude that the ever-present possibility of having his readoption vetoed keeps many an incipient rebel from ignoring or flouting his party whip's directions on how to vote.

As we shall see, however, this veto power has rarely been exercised in the post-war period. A sanction far more frequently imposed on actual or potential rebel M.P.s has been the local party associations' refusal to readopt them as candidates. Many local activists, as we shall observe, are fiercely loyal to their parties' ideals and leadership, and are often eager to punish rebellious candidates and M.P.s more rapidly and ruthlessly than the national party leaders attempt or sometimes even approve. "More Tory (or Socialist) than the Leader" they often are, and their role in disciplining M.P.s will be considered in some detail in later chapters.

WHO CONTROLS SELECTIONS CONTROLS THE PARTY

Finally, the selection of parliamentary candidates is one of the highest stakes in any internal struggle for control of a party's leadership and policy. The candidates selected fix the programmatic and human image the party presents to the public; they constitute the roster from which its officeholders and leaders are drawn; and they do much to determine the degree to which it can act cohesively in the conduct of government.

The post-war contest between the Left and the Right for control of the Labour party offers an instructive British example of this general rule. Much of this contest has been fought in annual conferences

---

[11] Robert T. McKenzie, *British Political Parties,* 2nd. ed. (London: Mercury Books, 1964); and Leon D. Epstein, "Cohesion of British Parliamentary Parties," *American Political Science Review,* L (June, 1956), 360–77.

over resolutions about party policy. Yet, as McKenzie argues, victories or defeats in conference appear to have had little effect upon the Parliamentary Labour Party's stands in the House, the security of the leadership, or any other major stake of power.[12]

Properly understood, selection conferences that pick parliamentary candidates constitute far more significant battlegrounds than annual conferences that adopt resolutions. After all, the Parliamentary Labour Party (PLP) is made up of persons initially adopted as candidates by constituency Labour parties, and even in the constituencies dominated by the Conservatives the prospective Labour parliamentary candidate plays a major role in local party affairs. If over a period of years the Left controlled most local candidate selections, they would surely win a majority in the PLP, dominate the leadership, and force the party's policies inside Parliament and out at last into the paths that the Left's spokesmen have urged for so long.[13] By the same token, the Right's primary line of defense is getting sympathetic candidates selected, particularly in winnable seats. In Chapters 5 and 6 we shall consider the extent to which the two factions have been aware of the importance of candidate selection, and what, if anything, they have done about it.

THE LEGAL FRAMEWORK

This book is concerned mainly with the political, social, and psychological forces that bear upon the selection of parliamentary candidates in Great Britain. In the chapters to come we shall deal with such matters as the power of the parties' national organizations to place particular candidates in particular constituencies, the conditions under which they exercise their powers to veto local selections, the sorts of persons who do the selecting in the local associations, the criteria they apply in making their choices, how these matters vary from one sort of constituency to another, and so on.

These extralegal party processes must operate within boundaries set by Britain's legal rules governing the making of nominations and the conduct of elections. Accordingly, we shall devote the re-

---

[12] McKenzie, *British Political Parties,* Chs. VIII and X.

[13] Leon Epstein has recently suggested that the PLP has in fact shifted leftward in recent years because of the replacement of retiring right-wing M.P.s by new left-wing Members: "New M.P.s and the Politics of the PLP," *Political Studies,* X (June, 1962), 121–29.

mainder of this introductory chapter to a brief outline of the rules that bear most directly upon candidate selection.

"PROSPECTIVE CANDIDATE" TO "CANDIDATE"

The typical constituency party organization selects its standard-bearer well in advance of the general election in which he is intended to stand. The local leaders reason that the more time their man has to learn the constituency's peculiarities and become known to its voters, the better will be his chances of winning. Moreover, choosing early saves them from having to scramble for a candidate at the last minute if a snap general election should be called or the seat unexpectedly vacated and a by-election ordered.

When they have adopted their man, however, they are careful not to refer to him as the party's official candidate for the constituency until after a writ for a by-election has been issued or a general election called. If they did, money spent on "nursing the constituency"—e.g., for his travel, public meetings at which he spoke, newspaper advertisements mentioning his name, and the like—would be legally chargeable to his election expenses. And these have a legal ceiling: his unaccounted-for personal expenses cannot exceed a maxi- of £100 for any one election; for any amount in excess he must provide a detailed accounting and justification. Moreover, his election expenses cannot exceed a maximum sum of £450 plus 2d. for each registered voter in a county constituency or £450 plus 1½d. for each voter in a borough constituency.[14] Most local parties regard these sums as barely adequate for effective work in the four weeks or so of the official campaign and toally inadequate for the "nursing" period of two or three years before the official campaign.

According, each local party publicly refers to its standard-bearer as its "prospective" candidate. Shortly after the writ for a by-election is issued or a general election called, the appropriate party agency (see Chapters 3, 6, and 9) holds an adoption meeting at which the prospective candidate is formally adopted as the party's candidate for the election, and the word "prospective" is thereafter dropped from his title.[15]

---

[14] A. N. Schofield, *Parliamentary Elections*, 2nd. ed. (London: Shaw & Sons, Ltd., 1955), pp. 170–78.

[15] Cf. Leonard, *Guide to the General Election*, p. 74.

DISQUALIFICATIONS FOR CANDIDATURE[16]

A leading authority on the law of parliamentary elections states that "any person, male or female, who is a British subject of full age and not otherwise disqualified, may be elected to Parliament."[17] Hence the simplest way to describe who is legally eligible for parliamentary candidature is to identify those disqualified to sit in the House of Commons and to assume that all other adults are eligible.

The disqualifications fall into the following five main clauses:

1. *Nationality*

Aliens cannot serve in Parliament, but naturalized citizens, citizens of Commonwealth countries,[18] and even citizens of the Republic of Ireland can do so.

2. *Age*

No one under twenty-one years of age is eligible.

3. *Disabilities*

Persons under any one of a number of disabilities are barred from seats in the House of Commons. The principal types are: certified lunatics; deaf mutes; English and Scottish peers, unless they have renounced their peerages for their lifetimes under the Peerage Act of 1963; ordained priests or ministers of the Church of England, Church of Ireland, Church of Scotland, and Roman Catholic Church (although clergy of the Church of Wales and of the nonconformist denominations are eligible); undischarged bankrupts; and members of the armed forces.

This last type of disability led to a minor crisis in 1962. It had long been customary to discharge servicemen who sought parliamentary candidatures so that they would be eligible to stand. In 1962 a growing number in the forces saw this custom as a way of leaving the service before their terms of enlistment had expired. By the end

---

[16] This topic is covered exhaustively in Schofield, *Parliamentary Elections,* pp. 78–118. A shorter and less technical account is given in Leonard, *Guide to the General Election,* pp. 80–84.

[17] Schofield, *Parliamentary Elections,* p. 79.

[18] Clearly including citizens of Canada, Australia, and New Zealand; the eligibility of citizens of the newer Commonwealth countries (e.g., India, Pakistan, Ghana, Nigeria, Kenya, Tanzania) is less clear.

of the year no fewer than 174 servicemen had applied for nomination papers for the by-election at Colne Valley, and 493 for the by-election at Rotherham. To dam the flood, the government established an eight-man advisory committee, appointed by the Home Secretary, to interview the applicants and identify the bona fide candidates among them. The committee recommended only one of the 667 for discharge —but after demobilization he announced that he had changed his mind and would not stand after all! Most observers regard the screening-committee device as only a temporary palliative for a knotty legal problem, but it served to discourage all but a trickle of service applications thereafter.[19]

4. *Misconduct*

Convicted felons are disqualified until they have served their sentences or received full pardons. Persons convicted of corrupt or illegal election practices—e.g., bribery, false declaration of election expenses, or knowingly appointing an election agent who commits corrupt or illegal practices—are also disqualified.

5. *Holding Offices of Profit Under the Crown*

Other than aliens and minors, the largest number of persons disqualified as M.P.s are those holding certain "offices of profit under the Crown." A jumble of statutes going back to the fourteenth century has put a wide variety of offices in this class. The best-known instances are sheriffs, judges, returning officers (see below), and members of many government corporations.[20]

As the political journalist R. L. Leonard points out, there is no formal way of preventing a disqualified person from standing; indeed, some have stood in recent years. If elected, however, he will not be allowed to take his seat, which will be declared vacant. If this happens, his defeated opponent can apply to the High Court to have the election declared void. If the Court decides that the facts leading

---

[19] Cf. Leonard, *Guide to the General Election*, pp. 82–83.

[20] A complete list is given in Schofield, *Parliamentary Elections*, pp. 97–107. This disability also provides M.P.s their only opportunity to resign their seats. Strictly speaking, an M.P. may not directly resign his seat at all. But he can apply for appointment to one of two ancient sinecure offices: Bailiff of the Manor of Northstead, or Steward of the Chiltern Hundreds. Such applications are always granted, and since appointment gives the M.P. an office of profit under the Crown he automatically forfeits his seat in the House: see Richards, *Honourable Members*, p. 53.

to the disqualification were generally known to the voters at the time of the election, all those who voted for the disqualified candidate are deemed to have thrown away their votes, and the candidate with the next highest poll is declared elected.[21] The most celebrated instance of this in recent years occurred in 1961. Anthony Wedgwood Benn, who was re-elected Labour M.P. for Bristol South-East in 1959, became Viscount Stansgate upon the death of his father in 1961. He tried to renounce his peerage and retain his seat in Commons, but the government and the courts ruled that he could not and declared the seat vacant. Nevertheless he stood again in the ensuing by-election, and defeated his Conservative opponent, Malcolm St. Clair, with 69 per cent of the votes. St. Clair appealed to the High Court, which ruled Lord Stansgate ineligible and declared St. Clair elected. Two years later Lord Stansgate was the first to take advantage of the Peerage Act and renounced his title. Thereupon St. Clair redeemed an earlier pledge by immediately applying for the Chiltern Hundreds. Neither the Conservatives nor the Liberals contested the ensuing by-election, and Wedgwood Benn won overwhelmingly against token independent opposition.

ENTERING THE NOMINATION PAPER

Any eligible person, whether previously selected by a political party or not, becomes an official candidate for Parliament by entering a properly-completed nomination paper with the returning officer for the constituency. The principal steps are:

1. *The Returning Officer*

Each constituency has a returning officer legally charged with supervising the conduct of its parliamentary elections. He usually acquires the office by virtue of holding another: in England and Wales he is usually the sheriff of a county, the mayor of a borough, or the chairman of an urban district council (depending upon the relation of the constituency's boundaries to those of the local government districts it overlaps); in Scotland he is the sheriff of the county; and in Northern Ireland the undersheriff. He appoints a deputy returning officer, who usually does most of the work.[22]

---

[21] Leonard, *Guide to the General Election*, p. 84.

[22] For the details, see Schofield, *Parliamentary Elections*, Ch. VII.

2. *Fixing the Period for Entering Nomination Papers*

The returning officer fixes the period for entering nomination papers, but it cannot begin earlier than the day after the publication of the notice of the election nor later than eight days after the date of the proclamation summoning the new Parliament (the ranges of choice for by-elections differ slightly).[23] In practice this usually means five days after the publication of the notice of the election, and nomination papers may be entered at any time during a ten-day period which ends ten days before the date of the election.

3. *Filling in the Nomination Paper*

The nomination paper must state the candidate's full name, place of residence, and description—i.e., ordinary occupation in most instances or station in life in a few.

4. *Subscriptions of the Nomination Paper*

The nomination paper must also bear the signatures and numbers on the electoral roll of ten qualified voters registered in the constituency: one proposer, one seconder, and eight assentors. The returning officer must examine the paper to make sure these conditions are satisfied.

5. *Consent to Nomination*

The nomination becomes valid only when the returning officer receives a written statement from the nominee, attested by one witness, that he consents to the nomination; or when he is otherwise satisfied that the nominee is willing to stand.

THE DEPOSIT

One requirement remains: at the time of entering his nomination paper the candidate must deposit with the returning officer cash or a bank draft of the sum of £150. If he wins more than one-eighth of the votes cast in the election, the deposit is returned to him shortly after the result is declared. If he wins only one-eighth or less, however, the deposit is automatically forfeited to the Treasury.[24] This

---

[23] *Ibid.*, pp. 124–25.
[24] *Ibid.*, pp. 141–42.

requirement was imposed by the Representation of the People Act of 1918 for the purpose of discouraging freak and propaganda candidatures. While it has not succeeded altogether, the leading student of British elections declares that "there can be little doubt that in recent years there would have been many more candidatures but for this limitation."[25]

NOMINATION AND CANDIDATE SELECTION

Britain's legal requirements for parliamentary candidature are among the simplest in the democratic world, and greatly less demanding than their counterparts in most states of the United States.[26] Yet in recent years very few persons have entered nomination papers and put down deposits without first having been selected by one of the three leading political parties: in the general elections from 1950 to 1964 there were a total of 3,140 constituency contests, only 95 of which (3 per cent) were contested by independents—that is, by candidates not publicly backed by any organization calling itself a political party. The only independents elected were the Speakers of the House of Commons, and Sir David Robertson, who was elected Conservative M.P. for Caithness and Sutherland in 1950, resigned the whip in January, 1959, won re-election in October with *de facto* local Conservative support, and retired in 1964. Minor parties (e.g., the Communists, Sinn Fein, Welsh Nationalists, etc.) fought 322 contests (10 per cent of the total), and won 7, all in Northern Ireland.[27]

In short, despite the simplicity of the formal nominating procedures and the leniency of their requirements, the great majority of British parliamentary elections have been fought exclusively by candidates previously selected by the Conservative and Labour parties, and, to a lesser degree, by the Liberals. Hence in Britain as in other

---

[25] David E. Butler, *The Electoral System in Britain Since 1918*, 2nd. ed. (Oxford: at the Clarendon Press, 1963), p. 167.

[26] American requirements and procedures are summarized in *The Book of the States*, published periodically by the Council of State Governments, and are analyzed in Austin Ranney and Willmoore Kendall, *Democracy and the American Party System* (New York: Harcourt, Brace and Company, Inc., 1956), Ch. 12; and V. O. Key, Jr., *Politics, Parties, and Pressure Groups*, 5th ed. (New York: Thomas Y. Crowell Company, 1964), Chs. 14 and 16.

[27] For a summary of the situation between 1919 and 1959, see Butler, *The Electoral System in Britain Since 1918*, 2nd ed., pp. 153–67.

western democracies the party processes of candidate selection rather than the legal processes of entering nomination papers and making deposits have set the alternatives for the voters.

How those processes have operated and the kinds of candidates they have produced constitute the subject matter of the rest of this book. Let us begin with the Conservatives.

Chapter 2	*The Role of the Conservatives' National Union and Central Office*

The area with the highest specific gravity in the political world is probably Smith Square in Westiminister, S.W. 1. At the southwest corner stands Transport House, owned by the Transport and General Workers' Union and housing the national headquarters of the Labour party. At the northwest corner stands No. 32, which shelters the Conservative party's national extraparliamentary organizations.

It is here, according to popular legend, that the Conservative Leader's lieutenants decide which of many applicants will be granted the party's unoccupied safe seats, and which will be sent forth to do hopeless battle in Socialist strongholds. It is here that Central Office is supposed to quash unsuitable candidates adopted by thoughtless or rebellious constituency associations.

In the present chapter we shall describe the activities and impact of the Conservatives' national officials and committees concerned with candidatures, and compare the legend with reality.

THE NATIONAL ORGANIZATIONS
CONCERNED WITH CANDIDATURES

The formal structure of the Conservative party's national organizations is graphically shown in Figure 1.

FIGURE 1

THE ORGANIZATION OF THE CONSERVATIVE PARTY*

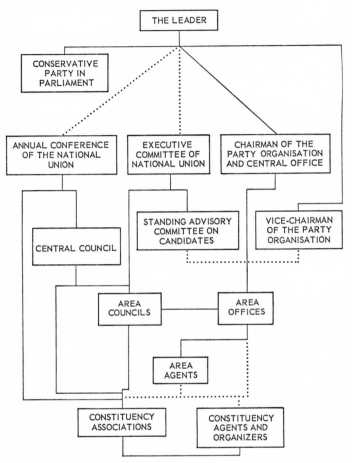

* Adapted from Robert T. McKenzie, *British Political Parties,* 2nd ed. (London: Mercury Books, 1964), p. 186.

The selection of Conservative parliamentary candidates in England and Wales is supervised by three national agencies. One, the Standing Advisory Committee on Candidates (SACC),[1] is attached to the National Union, and therefore to the national federation of the party's local activists. The second, the Vice-Chairman of the Party Organi-

---

[1] This agency is sometimes referred to as the Standing Advisory Committee on Parliamentary Candidates, but the form given in the text is the more common.

sation* responsible for candidatures, is an officer of the party's top national management. The third, the various Central Office area agents are employees of Central Office, and therefore belong to the party's "civil service."

Let us examine the role of each in candidate selection.

THE STANDING ADVISORY COMMITTEE ON CANDIDATES[2]

1. *Origins*

In the early 1930's a number of Conservative leaders grew concerned over the frequency with which Conservative constituency associations "sold" their parliamentary candidatures to wealthy men in return for large contributions to association coffers. This practice, the leaders felt, not only made the party appear the exclusive property of the rich, but also ensured that in many cases the best candidate was not adopted. The quality of the parliamentary party was felt to be deteriorating as a result.

At the sixty-first annual conference at Bristol in 1934, accordingly, a resolution was introduced

> That every effort ought to be made to broaden the representative and financial basis of the party organisations in constituencies in order that they may be able to avail themselves of the best and where possible local candidates, and that every effort ought to be made to avoid dependence upon the personal resources of members and candidates.

An amendment was moved

> That the National Union should arrange that a small committee, representative both of the Central Organisation and of the provincial area affected, should be established with which the constituency organisation in each area should consult before any individual is selected as the official candidate of the party.[3]

Both motion and amendment were referred to the Executive Committee of the National Union. In the following March, Colonel

---

* Formal titles of party offices and agencies are given in their British spelling throughout the book.

[2] For useful short descriptions of the SACC's composition, powers, and functions, see *Notes on Procedure for the Adoption of Conservative Candidates in England and Wales*, a pamphlet published by the Conservative and Unionist Central Office in July, 1960, pp. 2–3 (hereafter cited as *Notes on Procedure*); *Final Report of the Committee on Party Organisation* (London: The National Union of Conservative and Unionist Associations, 1949), pp. 18, 31–33; and Robert T. McKenzie, *British Political Parties*, 2nd ed. (London: Mercury Books, 1964), pp. 216–19.

[3] *Times* (London), October 6, 1934, p. 7.

George Herbert presented the committee's report to the National Union's Central Council. The committee recommended that a national standing advisory committee be established for consultation by constituency associations when selecting their candidates. It was particularly important, the report said,

that before the final selection of any candidate, not previously approved by the party organisation, was completed, the chairman of the constituency organisation should get into touch with the standing advisory committee in order to ensure that the proposed candidate would receive the full support of the party, which otherwise it might be necessary to withhold.

The council accepted the report and established the committee. They took great pains, however, to reassure the constituency associations that the new committee was not intended to deprive the associations of their longstanding and unchallenged right to select their own candidates. The SACC, the council said, would be merely a convenient device for central-local consultation, not a weapon for central control of candidatures:

The committee realised that it was the job of the constituencies to choose their own candidates, but they hoped that constituency chairman and committees appointed to select candidates would keep in close touch with the chairman of the party and the central office in doing so. There were times when a constituency and the central office did not see eye to eye, but the committee suggested that there was a means of bridging over any differences by the appointment of a standing advisory committee.[4]

2. *Purpose*

No one at that time challenged either the propriety or the wisdom of the council's action, and the SACC was little noticed during the 1935 general election campaign and in the years immediately following. The ferment of party reform generated by defeat in the 1945 general election and by the efforts of Lord Woolton and R. A. Butler to modernize the party's machinery and attitudes again brought candidate selection under scrutiny. The 1948 annual conference at Brighton formally endorsed the SACC, and also established the now-famous Committee on Party Organisation under the chairmanship

---

[4] This and the preceding quotation are taken from the *Times* (London), March 28, 1935, p. 8.

of Sir David Maxwell Fyfe (later Lord Kilmuir). This committee's report in 1949 described the SACC's purpose in terms considerably more ambitious than those used by Colonel Herbert in 1935:

The purpose of the Committee is to assess on broadest grounds the suitability of men and women who are desirous of becoming approved Candidates. A list of approved Candidates, together with brief biographies, is sent on request to Constituency Associations which are selecting a Prospective Candidate. When one of these Candidates is subsequently adopted by a Constituency Association, he or she becomes an official Conservative Prospective Candidate.

The aims of the Committee may be broadly summarised as follows:—

(a) To protect the good name of the Party by ensuring that no candidate is adopted unless the Committee is previously satisfied as to:—

     (i) Personal character
     (ii) Party loyalty
     (iii) Past record and experience
     (iv) Political knowledge
     (v) Speaking ability
     (vi) Financial arrangements

(b) To avoid coming to adverse conclusions unless it is abundantly clear that they are not based on personal prejudice or on insufficient evidence.[5]

3. *Structure*

The SACC has nine members, all ex officio. Five represent the National Union: the Chairman of its Central Council, who is also ex officio Chairman of the SACC; the Chairman of the Executive Committee of the National Union; the Chairman of the Women's Advisory Committee of the National Union; the Chairman of the Conservative Trade Unionists National Advisory Committee of the National Union; and the Chairman of the Young Conservative and Unionist National Advisory Committee of the National Union. Three members represent Central Office: the Chairman and Deputy Chairman of the Party Organisation, and the Honorary Secretary of the National Union (a post always occupied by the General Director of Central Office). And one, the Chief Whip of the party in the House of Commons, represents the parliamentary party.[6]

The SACC accomplishes its purpose "to assess on broadest grounds the suitability of men and women who are desirous of becoming

---

[5] *Final Report of the Committee on Party Organisation*, p. 31.
[6] *Notes on Procedure*, p. 3.

approved candidates" in three ways. First, it specifies in some detail the procedures[7] and criteria constituency associations should use in selecting their candidates. Second, it mantains a List of Approved Candidates, which constituency associations are urged to consult. And third, it is empowered to withhold or withdraw approval from any locally adopted candidate whom it finds unsuitable.

The SACC, accordingly, would appear to be the most powerful national agency supervising candidatures, and the fact that it advises the Executive Committee of the National Union would seem to suggest that the party's voluntary mass organization holds the whip hand in this field.

The appearance, however, is not the reality: the SACC is a ratifying not an initiating body. Although he is not formally a member, the Vice-Chairman of the Party Organisation (or his deputy) always meets with the committee, fixes its agenda, makes the suggestions on which it acts, and furnishes most of the information it considers. The List of Approved Candidates consists of names suggested by the Vice-Chairman and accepted by the committee. On those very rare occasions when the committee has considered withholding approval from a candidate adopted locally, it has done so at the Vice-Chairman's suggestion reinforced by the wishes of the Chairman of the Party Organisation and the Leader.

The SACC has, of course, the formal power to turn down any or all of the Vice-Chairman's suggestions, but it almost never does so. The committee, after all, meets only occasionally and considers only matters on its agenda. The Vice-Chairman's duties require him to keep well informed of the names and backgrounds of the persons seeking inclusion in the approved list. Thus he is bound to know a great deal more than the committee about the persons under consideration. And, as usually happens when a full-time professional confronts part-time amateurs, the committee accepts his proposals without question most of the time and, on those rare occasions when its members object, he is powerfully armed with arguments and evidence to persuade them he is right.

Despite its formal powers, in short, the Standing Advisory Com-

---

[7] These are given in *ibid.*, pp. 4–10.

mittee on Candidates has far less actual influence on candidate selection than does the Vice-Chairman.

THE VICE-CHAIRMAN OF THE PARTY ORGANISATION

1. *The Office and its Occupants*

Conservative Central Office is the party's national professional organization for supervising and co-ordinating national and local organization, finance, publicity, research, electioneering, and selection of candidates. Entirely separate from the National Union, it is directly responsible to the Leader, who personally appoints its top officers, the Chairman, Deputy Chairman, and two Vice-Chairmen of the Party Organisation.[8]

One of the vice-chairmen is usually a woman, charged with supervising women's activities in the party. The other, a man, supervises the Candidates' Department and is usually referred to as the "Vice-Chairman for candidatures." In recent years this post has been held by M.P.s of junior ministerial standing. The Vice-Chairman in 1945 was Harold Mitchell, Member for Brentford and Chiswick, who resigned after losing his seat in the general election because he felt that only an M.P. should hold the office. He was succeeded by J. P. L. Thomas, Member for Hereford since 1931, who had been parliamentary private secretary to Anthony Eden, an assistant whip, and Financial Secretary to the Admiralty. He resigned in 1951 on being named First Lord of the Admiralty, and was succeeded by John Hare, Member for Woodbridge from 1945 to 1950 and Member for Sudbury and Woodbridge since 1950. Hare, in turn, resigned in 1955 on being made Minister of State for Colonial Affairs, and he was followed by Donald Kaberry, Member for North-West Leeds since 1950, a former assistant whip, and Parliamentary Secretary to the Board of Trade. Kaberry resigned in 1961 "to take a more active role in the affairs of the House." He was succeeded by the present Vice-Chairman, Paul Bryan, Member for Howden since 1955 and a former assistant whip.

---

[8] See McKenzie, *British Political Parties*, Ch. V, for an account of Central Office's history and present organization. In 1963 it employed a total of 48 administrative and 98 clerical personnel: R. L. Leonard, *Guide to the General Election* (London: Pan Books, Ltd., 1964), Table 6, p. 47.

2. *The List of Approved Candidates*[9]

The Vice-Chairman has two main duties: to suggest to the SACC who should be included in the List of Approved Candidates; and to consult with constituency association officers about persons they should consider when selecting their candidates. He also keeps an eye on the associations' selection proceedings with a view to warning any about to choose someone unacceptable—or, in the extreme case, to advise the SACC to withhold its approval.

The List of Approved Candidates is compiled as follows. Anyone who wishes to be included notifies the Vice-Chairman or has his name called to the Vice-Chairman's attention by someone else in the party. The Vice-Chairman then asks the applicant to fill out the standard candidate's form. The sorts of questions asked on the form suggest a good deal about the criteria applied in compiling the List. They may be categorized thus:

(1) *Basic personal data:* name, address, date and place of birth, marital status.

(2) *Social position:* "rank, title, decorations," nationality, religion, where educated.

(3) *Nonpolitical experience:* present profession or occupation, details of past career, particulars of social service previously undertaken; "if a member of a Trade Union please state name of Union."

(4) *Political experience:* public offices and appointments held; details of political work, speaking experience, membership and offices in Conservative associations.

(5) *Political views:* "Do you fully support the Official Policy of the Party? If not, on what points do you differ?"

(6) *Attitude toward candidature:* "Type of Constituency preferred; What part of England or Wales?", "How much time are you in a position to give to any Constituency for which you may be selected? Will you undertake personal canvassing as well as addressing public meetings? Are you pre-

---

[9] The material in the text is drawn mainly from an interview with Paul Bryan in London in December, 1961, and from several interviews with applicants for the List. For an illuminating general discussion, see Victor Black, "Selecting for Safe Seats," *Crossbow*, IV (Autumn, 1960), 41–42.

pared to devote all the time that may be necessary to enable you to perform your duties, both in and out of Parliament, as a Member for a Constituency for which you may be elected?"

Finally, the applicant is asked to give the names and addresses of "3 responsible persons who will support your candidature . . . . These should include, if possible, one M.P. and a Constituency chairman. (Permission to use their names must first be obtained from those given as sponsors.)" He is also given to understand that the third referee might well be the agent for the constituency or area in which he lives.

The Vice-Chairman receives confidential reports from the three referees, and invites the applicant to come to London for an interview. From a panel of ten to twelve M.P.s, the Vice-Chairman chooses two or three to join him in interviewing the applicant for some thirty minutes to an hour. According to the accounts of participants, questions of party ideology or program are rarely raised. As one interviewer put it to the author, "We take the fact that a chap has applied to mean that he is a Conservative—and being a Conservative covers a rather wide bracket."

The questioners are far more concerned with the applicant's personal qualities. Is he a man of solid character? Is he articulate without seeming glib? Is his social, educational, and occupational background the sort that will add strength and representativeness to the List? How much and what kind of party service has he rendered?[10]

On the basis of the panels' and the referees' answers to these and similar questions, the Vice-Chairman recommends to the SACC at its periodic meetings that certain applicants be placed on the list forthwith, while others be asked to try again later. And, as we have seen, the SACC almost always accepts his suggestions.

How difficult are these hurdles? Journalist David Watt's view is probably correct:

This looks on paper like a formidable process, but in fact any man who is a Conservative of even moderate education or achievement will almost inevitably

---

[10] Inclusion in the list is in no sense a reward for past party service, but the latter is regarded as a useful index of the applicant's knowledgeability about and commitment to politics and the Conservative cause.

pass unless he is hopelessly young, inexperienced or uncouth. The fact that there are at present about 800 names on the list shows it is not wildly exclusive.[11]

THE CENTRAL OFFICE AREA AGENTS

"To facilitate the work of the Party," England and Wales are divided by the Conservatives into twelve areas.[12] In each area the party maintains two parallel sets of agencies. One consists of various bodies representing the area's constituency associations: the area chairman, area council, area executive committee, and various area advisory committees. The area chairman, according to the party's official pamphlet on organization, "advises the Standing Advisory Committee on Parliamentary Candidates when requested in particularly difficult cases,"[13] but a far more active role in candidate selection is played by the Central Office area agents.

The other set of agencies operates from the "area office" maintained in each of the twelve areas by Central Office. This office is headed by the area agent, who is an employee of Central Office and responsible to it for overseeing the financial, propaganda, election-

---

[11] "Picking and Choosing," *The Spectator* (May 1, 1964), p. 573.

[12] For more complete descriptions of the area organizations, see McKenzie, *British Political Parties*, pp. 231–41; and *The Party Organisation*, Pamphlet No. 1 of the Organisation Series, published in January, 1961, by the Conservative and Unionist Central Office, Ch. 8.

The twelve areas are as follows: (1) London (The City of London and all London boroughs), 43 constituencies; (2) Northern (Cumberland, Durham, Northumberland, and Middlesbrough), 34 constituencies; (3) North-Western (Lancashire, Cheshire, and Westmorland), 80 constituencies; (4) Yorkshire (excluding Middlesbrough), 56 constituencies; (5) East Midlands (Derbyshire, Leicestershire, Lincolnshire, Nottinghamshire, Northamptonshire, Rutland), 42 constituencies; (6) West Midlands (Gloucestershire excluding Bristol, Herefordshire, Shropshire, Staffordshire, Warwickshire, Worcestershire), 58 constituencies; (7) Eastern (Bedfordshire, Cambridgeshire, Hertfordshire, Huntingdonshire, Norfolk, Suffolk), 28 Constituencies; (8) Home Counties North (Essex and Middlesex), 52 constituencies; (9) Home Counties South-East (Kent, Surrey, Sussex), 48 constituencies; (10) Wessex (Berkshire, Buckinghamshire, Dorsetshire, Hampshire, Isle of Wight, Oxfordshire, Wiltshire), 37 constituencies; (11) Western (Cornwall, Devonshire, Somersetshire, and Bristol), 28 constituencies; (12) Wales and Monmouthshire, 36 constituencies: McKenzie, *British Political Parties*, p. 232, n. 4.

The Unionist party of Scotland and the Ulster Unionist party of Northern Ireland are, strictly speaking, allied with but entirely independent of the Conservative and Unionist party of England and Wales. Consequently, as the latter's pamphlet on candidate selection states, "neither the Vice-Chairman nor the [Standing Advisory] Committee has any jurisdiction over candidates in Scotland or Northern Ireland": *Notes on Procedure*, p. 2.

[13] *The Party Organisation*, p. 20.

eering, and other activities of the area's constituency associations.[14] He also regularly takes some part in the selection of parliamentary candidates in his area. He usually accompanies his constituencies' selection committee chairmen when they go to London to consult the Vice-Chairman. He also, as a matter of routine, attends the selection conferences in his area, answers questions about the party's rules and procedures, and reports any peculiarities in the procedures or results to Central Office. As noted before, he often acts as one of the three referees for an applicant from his area for the SACC's List of Approved Candidates, and his comments are given considerable weight.

So much is routine for all area agents. But the agents vary greatly, of course, in ability and effectiveness. The ablest establish close confidential relationships with association officers and have a good deal to say about when the associations start looking for candidates,[15] and a lot more about which "possibles" should be seriously considered and which should be dropped early in the screening.

He is, in short, Central Office's main pipeline to the local associations, and thus an important device for trying to place favored candidates in safe or winnable seats.

THE PLACEMENT POWER

One widespread belief about candidate selection is the notion that the central agencies of both the Conservative and Labour parties can at will place particular candidates in particular constituencies. For example, one often hears it said of a defeated M.P., "Don't worry about him; Central Office will find him another seat"; or, of a minister with a small majority, "Why doesn't Central Office get him a better seat?" Some of the most distinguished commentators on British institutions perpetuate the legend. Professor Herman Finer, for example, declares:

Now since the party must, for its very life's sake, have a minimum number of experts of different kinds—good debaters, able committeemen, financial experts, some especially expert in each great branch of social and economic legis-

---

[14] *Ibid.*, p. 22.

[15] One area agent testified, "I don't want the hopeless seats in my area tying up the best candidates before the winnable seats have had a chance at them, so I never let them start looking seriously until six months or less before the general election is expected."

lation and in international affairs—headquarters seizes every opportunity that offers to claim a comparatively safe seat for such candidates, *and local caucuses rarely dispute such claims.*[16]

In any ideal system of "responsible party government" (see Chapter 1), the parties' national agencies clearly would have this kind of placement power. The question here is, do the Conservatives' national agencies actually have it?

CENTRAL-LOCAL CONSULTATION[17]

The normal procedure requires that, shortly after a constituency association has appointed its selection committee, its chairman goes to Smith Square to consult with the Vice-Chairman about possible names. He is usually accompanied by the Central Office agent for his area.

The conversation typically begins with a discussion of the special character of the constituency, and the sort of candidate best suited to it. The local chairman often announces a number of qualifications previously stipulated by his committee: e.g., the candidate must be under fifty, a man, not a Jew, with a solid business background and strong connections in the constituency. The Vice-Chairman usually responds by urging the chairman not to insist on such limitations, but to aim at getting the best possible person available.

The Candidates' Department maintains a file in which the characteristics of those on the List of Approved Candidates are cross-indexed in several ways: e.g., farmers, proprietors of small businesses, persons holding office in local government, persons willing to stand in Wales, and so on. From this file the Vice-Chairman and his staff prepare a list of ten to twenty persons whom they consider especially suitable for the constituency in question. He presents them to the local chairman and recommends that his selection committee consider them. The chairman usually takes some or all of

---

[16] *The Theory and Practice of Modern Government*, rev. ed. (New York: Henry Holt and Company, 1949), p. 243, emphasis added. Finer adds that "England is more earnest and rational in this respect than either France or the United States": *ibid.* For a similar view, see E. E. Schattschneider, *Party Government* (New York: Farrar and Rinehart, Inc., 1942), pp. 99–100.

[17] The information in the text is drawn mainly from the previously cited interview with Paul Bryan, from an interview with C. F. R. Bagnall, Chief Agent of the Conservative and Unionist party, and from an interview with Anthony Garner, Central Office agent for the London area.

the suggested names back with him, and the selection committee "puts them in the hopper" along with those volunteered and suggested locally.

CENTRAL OFFICE'S PLACEMENT OBJECTIVES

In making his suggestions, the Vice-Chairman usually seeks to accomplish one or both of two main objectives:

1. *Placing Particular Persons*

The Candidates' Department always has in mind the names of several individuals whom it would especially like to see adopted: for example, promising young men without electoral experience; able Central Office employees lacking strong local connections; and, of course, former M.P.s and even ministers who have lost their seats and look to Central Office to help them back to Westminster. The newcomers to politics often seem appropriate for safe Labour seats where they will have a chance to prove their electioneering mettle. The Central Office employees regarded as potential ministerial material may be suggested for winnable or even safe Conservative constituencies.[18]

When the Vice-Chairman, often on the advice of the area agent, judges that an association would be right for this or that person on his preferred list, he will include his name in the ten or twenty suggested. If he is confident that it will not be resented, he may even put in a special word for him. But this, as we shall see, can be dangerous and is usually done indirectly and with great circumspection.

2. *Making the Party More Representative*

The central agencies of all three parties feel strongly that their rosters of adopted candidates should be as broadly representative as possible. By this they mean that the rosters should include respectable numbers of candidates identified with each substantial

---

[18] Two recent examples are: John Biffen, an employee of the research department, who fought hopeless Coventry East in 1959 and then was adopted for the safe Conservative seat of Oswestry, which he won in the 1961 by-election; and Peter Goldman, director of the Conservative political center, who fought hopeless West Ham South in 1959 and was adopted for the presumably safe Conservative seat of Orpington in 1961, but lost the by-election to the Liberal candidate.

stratum or interest in British society: i.e., women as well as men, Jews and Roman Catholics as well as Protestants, trade unionists as well as businessmen, and so on. This notion is a more general version of the American (ethnically) balanced ticket, which guarantees that Irish Catholics will be nominated by both parties in Massachusetts, Jews in New York, and Scandinavian Lutherans in North Dakota and Minnesota. In both countries the desire for representative candidates rests in part upon the self-serving calculation that excluding any major segment of the population might arouse its hostility at election time. It rests in part also upon the loftier belief that a democratic party has a moral duty to contribute to national unity and human dignity by including in its councils and rewards men and women from all segments of society.

All three parties' central offices, we repeat, take this view. But Conservative Central Office has for some time been particularly concerned by what it regards as the unwarranted under-representation among Conservative candidates of women, trade unionists, and members of minority religious groups. This is evidenced by statements such as these in the official pamphlet on candidatures:

Religious prejudices should in no circumstances be allowed to sway the judgement of a selection committee. . . . From time to time the Party has passed resolutions urging the need for more women and more trade unionists to be adopted. There is no doubt that our Party wants more women M.P.s and more trade unionist M.P.s.[19]

These, then, are the national officers' chief objectives. What success have they had?

CENTRAL OFFICE'S PLACEMENT POWER

In 1947, J. P. L. Thomas, then Vice-Chairman for candidatures, told the party's annual conference at Brighton:

We find it very difficult from the Candidates' Department to make certain people—certain sections of the Press—understand that in the long run it is always the Constituency Association and not Central Office which makes the final choice of candidate. But you know this is the case.[20]

Thomas's successors will tell anyone who cares to listen that their "placement power" is very limited. With rare exceptions, the

---

[19] *Notes on Procedure*, p. 8.

[20] *Proceedings of the 68th Annual Conference of the National Union of Conservative and Unionist Associations, 1947*, p. 86.

Vice-Chairman and the area agent can do only two things: in general terms urge local selection committees to give full consideration to able women and trade unionists; and see to it that the selection committees at least consider particular names on the approved list.

In most cases, to try to do more is likely to be not only ineffective but downright dangerous. As Victor Black puts it:

> Outside pressure on a selection committee is resented and will sometimes, as a result, tend to harm the very candidate it seeks to help. Any erosion of local autonomy would in any case give rise to other problems. . . . The proposition that "Central Office knows best" is difficult to defend in a constituency association and is guaranteed to raise the blood pressure of the executive committee faster than almost any other issue.[21]

Evidence for the truth of Black's statement is Central Office's failure to find seats for such luminaries as Randolph Churchill and Leslie Hore-Belisha in the late 1940's and 1950's. Even more striking is the nearly complete failure of Central Office's long and earnest effort to get more trade unionists adopted in winnable constituencies.

The party's leadership has long been embarrassed by the paucity of Conservative trade unionist candidates and M.P.s. From 33 to 43 per cent of manual workers support the Conservatives,[22] and Central Office feels this should be recognized and sustained by having a respectable number of trade unionists among the party's candidates. Moreover, when matters affecting trade unions are debated in Parliament, it is highly embarrassing to have all the expertise on the other side.

Accordingly, since the late 1940's Central Office has lost few opportunities to urge selection committees to give the most earnest consideration to adopting trade unionists. What has happened? This answer was given the author by a high Central Office official:

> Every time I attend a meeting of a local selection committee I tell them how much the party needs more trade unionists in the House and how a truly national party like ours should have *all* kinds of people among its candidates. Every time I do I get loud applause, and several members come up to me after the meeting and tell me how much they agree with what I said. Then they proceed to adopt someone who is not a trade unionist. When I ask why, they

---

[21] *Crossbow*, IV (Autumn, 1960), pp. 41–42.

[22] R. R. Alford, *Party and Society* (Chicago: Rand McNally & Company, 1963), Table 6–5, pp. 146–47.

say, "None of those trade union chaps we considered are the right sort for this constituency—they just don't sound right or look right, and they really don't have the kind of background we expect here. I'm sure they'll do well in some other constituency!"

The record bears him out. Since 1945 the Conservatives have had a few trade unionist candidates, but only two have been adopted for Conservative-held seats. One was Ray Mawby, of the Electrical Trades Union, who was elected Member for Totnes in 1955. The other was Sir Edward Brown, a laboratory technician, chairman of the Enfield branch of the Association of Supervisory Staffs, Executives and Technicians, and chairman of the National Union of Conservative and Unionist Associations in 1958-1959. Sir Edward is reported to have gone before no fewer than twenty-nine constituency selection committees between 1954 and 1963 without being able to get a winnable seat.[23] Finally, in June, 1963, he was adopted for Bath, and his election in 1964 doubled the number of trade unionists on the Conservative back benches.

Central Office's efforts at making Conservative candidates more representative in other respects have been equally fruitless. For example, in 1951 women filled 7 per cent of Conservative candidatures by non-incumbents; the figure rose to 8 per cent in 1955, but fell to 5 per cent in 1959, and went to 4 per cent in 1964. For another example, 46 per cent of Conservative non-incumbent candidates in 1951 had attended public schools; the proportion rose to 48 per cent in 1955, 49 per cent in 1959, and 56 per cent in 1964.

These data confirm what Central Office officials have long said: that under ordinary circumstances their power to place even general types of candidates, let alone particular individuals, is very weak. It is perhaps the least of the weapons by which the Leader maintains control of the party. For explanations of the high cohesion and discipline of the Conservatives in Parliament we must look elsewhere.[24]

---

[23] Christopher Driver, "The Men They Choose," *Guardian* (London), March 18, 1964, p. 10.

[24] The point is developed at some length in Austin Ranney, "Central Guidance of Parliamentary Candidate Selection in Britain," mimeo., a paper presented at the Sixth World Congress of the International Political Science Association, Geneva, 1964. For similar evaluations, see Peter G. Richards, *Honourable Members* (London: Faber & Faber, Ltd., 1959), p. 20; Ivor Bulmer-Thomas, *The Party System in Great Britain*

THE SPECIAL CASE OF BY-ELECTIONS

1. *The Context*

For reasons outlined in Chapter 1, in almost any constituency a by-election attracts far more national publicity than when it is merely one-630th part of a general election. The national agencies of each party are well aware that a by-election result will be widely regarded as an indication of the party's current popularity. They also know that the constituency's voters are more likely to stray from their regular party loyalties in by-elections than in general elections. So they want their by-election candidates to be especially attractive to win whatever additional votes personal qualities can win.

Accordingly, the national party agencies are commonly said to pay special heed to the selection of candidates for by-elections. To be sure, neither Conservative Central Office nor the SACC has special formal powers like those of the Labour party's National Executive Committee to suspend the normal procedures and intervene directly in such selections (see Chapter 5); but they are equally concerned with the quality of the persons adopted.

Of course, by-election candidatures are not always open. If the seat vacated was previously held by another party, and if the vacancy occurs two or three years after a general election, the chances are that the local association will already have selected its prospective candidate, and rarely will he be asked to stand down in someone else's favor.[25]

(London: Phoenix House, Ltd., 1953), pp. 207–8; and William Rees-Mogg, "The Selection of Parliamentary Candidates: The Conservative Party," *Political Quarterly*, XXX (July–September, 1959), 215–19.

[25] One well-publicized exception to this rule came in 1963. When the Earl of Home became the Conservative party's new Leader and Prime Minister in early October, it became imperative that he disclaim his peerage and get a seat in the House of Commons as soon as possible. Lord Home preferred a seat in Scotland near his home; for obvious reasons it had to be a safe seat and one in which a by-election was imminent. The only constituency meeting all these conditions was Kinross and West Perthshire, which had been vacated by the death of its Unionist Member, Gilmour Leburn. But there was a problem: the constituency association had already adopted as its prospective candidate George K. H. Younger. Two weeks after Lord Home had kissed hands as Prime Minister, however, Younger announced that he would withdraw in favor of the new Leader. Lord Home accepted the candidature, disclaimed his

If the seat is vacated by the death or resignation or elevation to the peerage of a Conservative M.P., however, not only is the Conservative candidature usually open but everyone understands that in all probability the local association will select not merely a candidate but a member.[26] And even in hopeless seats the national agencies want to get the best possible candidate, for reducing a Labour majority may give party morale at least as big a lift as holding a Conservative seat by a reduced majority.

2. *Differences in Candidates*

The special atmosphere in which by-elections take place may affect candidate selection in one or both of two ways. It may enhance Central Office's placement power by impelling it to try harder than usual to place particular persons and by lowering the constituency associations' normal resistance to central pressure. Or, without any direct Central Office pressure, the local associations may be more inclined than usual to select persons of the sort Central Office desires.[27] If either or both of these factors operate, we would expect

peerage, and, as Sir Alec Douglas-Home, was elected in early November: *Times* (London), October 21, 1963, p. 10; November 9, 1963, p. 8. There is no evidence of any pressure from Smith Square on either Younger or the Kinross Association, but Younger's withdrawal greatly eased matters for Sir Alec and Central Office. He was rewarded for his team spirit by being adopted and elected for Ayr, another safe Scottish seat, in 1964.

[26] Although there have been, as we have seen, greater fluctuations in by-elections than in general elections, only a small fraction of by-elections have shifted seats from one party to another. For example, from the 1945 general election to the end of 1964 there were a total of 213 by-elections, and in only 15 (7 per cent) did seats change hands.

[27] One prominent instance of this occurred in the course of the maneuvers over the leadership succession in October, 1963. When Harold Macmillan announced his intention to resign during the annual conference, Viscount Hailsham—a leading candidate for party Leader—declared his intention to disclaim his peerage and re-enter the House of Commons. Almost immediately two Conservative M.P.s in safe seats, Rupert Speir in Hexham and Sir Cyril Black in Wimbledon, publicly stated that they would be willing to resign so that Lord Hailsham could be returned in an early by-election. The local association in a third safe constituency, Morecambe and Lonsdale, invited Lord Hailsham to confer with them about the possibility of replacing their incumbent Member, Basil de Ferranti, who had previously announced his intention to retire at the next general election. The selection of Lord Home as the new Leader did not weaken Lord Hailsham's resolve to move to the Commons. On November 2 a barony was announced for Sir Wavell Wakefield, Member for the safe London borough of St. Marylebone. On November 8 the local executive adopted Lord Hailsham as their prospective candidate. On November 20 he disclaimed his peerage, and on December 5, as Mr. Quintin Hogg, he was elected: *Times* (London), October 12, 1963, p. 8; November 2, 1963, p. 6; November 19, 1963, p. 9; December 6, 1963.

the characteristics of persons given candidatures for by-elections to differ significantly from those of persons given candidatures for general elections.

In order to test this hypothesis, we have compared the characteristics of persons given the 120 Conservative by-election candidatures between the general election of 1951 and the end of 1961 with those of persons given the 997 candidatures by non-incumbents in the general elections of 1951, 1955, and 1959.[28] The principal findings are as follows.

Local Connections. In Chapter 4 we shall consider at some length the controversy among Conservative activists over the questions of to what extent parliamentary candidates are and/or should be local men. Clearly if there is any pressure for picking local candidates it must come from local activists, not from Central Office. Local people tend to emphasize a candidate's potential local performance—e.g., his ability to poll the maximum possible vote in the particular constituency, his willingness to nurse the constituency assiduously and to support the local association's activities, and the like (see Chapter 3). Central Office, on the other hand, emphasizes the candidate's national potential—e.g., his ability to contribute to the party's operations in the House, and his contribution to the "representativeness" of the party's roster of candidates (see above).

If this is correct and if Central Office's placement power is significantly stronger in by-elections than in general elections, we would expect a smaller proportion of locally-connected persons in by-election candidatures than in general election candidatures, especially in the safe seats. But, as Table 2.1 shows, this was not the case.

The overall totals in Table 2.1 show that 30 per cent of both the by-election and general election candidatures went to persons with some local connections. The table also shows, however, that in the most winnable constituencies a significantly higher proportion of candidatures were given to locally-connected persons than to outsiders. The reverse tendency appears in the candidatures for the least winnable constituencies. Both tendencies are inconsistent with

---

[28] Note that the basic unit of analysis in this discussion is the *candidature*, not the individual candidate. Any non-incumbent who stood more than once in this period in either by-elections or general elections appears more than once in the relevant tables.

TABLE 2.1

CONSERVATIVE GENERAL ELECTION AND BY-ELECTION NON-INCUMBENT CANDIDATURES
RELATED TO PERSONAL CONNECTIONS IN CONSTITUENCY,* BY
WINNABILITY OF CONSTITUENCY †

Local Connections	Winnability of Constituency					
	High		Medium		Low	
	Gen. Elect.	By-Elect.	Gen. Elect.	By-Elect.	Gen. Elect.	By-Elect.
Some	16%	35%	32%	(46%)‡	32%	15%
None	84	65	68	(54)	68	85
	100%	100%	100%	100%	100%	100%
Number of cases	85	72	317	13	559	33

* This includes having been educated in the constituency, making a living there, holding a trade union or trade association office there, holding a local government office there, or being the child or spouse of the present or former M.P. for the constituency.
 † For the definitions of the categories of winnability, see the Appendix.
 ‡ Figures are in parentheses because of the small number of cases.

the notion that Central Office's placement power is higher in by-elections than in general elections.

Previous Electoral Experience. We observed earlier that the Vice-Chairman always has in mind a number of persons he would like adopted in particular kinds of seats: promising young novices in hopeless seats, where they can prove their electoral mettle, and more experienced candidates in the winnable seats. If his placement power is greater in by-elections than in general elections, we would expect to see these objectives reflected in the distribution of candidatures according to previous electoral experience. But this is not what the data in Table 2.2 show.

The overall totals in Table 2.2 indicate that persons with no previous contests received a lower proportion of by-election than of general election candidatures (42 per cent and 59 per cent respectively). But when we divide the constituencies according to winnability, we see that this tendency is reversed: 44 per cent of the by-election candidatures in the high-winnability constituencies went to new candidates, as compared with only 33 per cent of the general election candidates in comparable constituencies. This too is inconsistent with increased central placement power in by-elections.

TABLE 2.2

<small>Conservative General Election and By-Election Non-Incumbent Candidatures
Related to Previous Electoral Experience, by
Winnability of Constituency</small>

Previous Electoral Experience	Winnability of Constituency					
	High		Medium		Low	
	Gen. Elect.	By- Elect.	Gen. Elect.	By- Elect.	Gen. Elect.	By- Elect.
First contest	33%	44%	44%	(23%)*	69%	46%
One previous loss	34	32	34	(54)	24	36
Two or more previous losses	25	21	18	(23)	6	18
Former M.P.s	8	3	4	0	1	0
	100%	100%	100%	100%	100%	100%
Number of cases	85	72	317	13	559	33

* Figures are in parentheses because of the small number of cases.

Age. Why should a higher proportion of by-election candidatures in the most desirable constituencies than of their counterparts in general elections go to new candidates? One possible explanation is that a higher proportion of promising but inexperienced young persons are picked for by-elections than for general elections in the winnable seats because of Central Office's desire to get them started toward the front bench as soon as possible. This hypothesis receives some support from the fact that more of the by-election candidatures than of the general election candidatures went to young persons (47 per cent under the age of forty compared with 40 per cent under forty). Once more, however, when we divide the candidatures according to the winnability of the constituencies, as in Table 2.3, we find that this relationship disappears.

Table 2.3 shows that the only significant difference in age distribution appears in the low-winnability constituencies (56 per cent of general election candidatures and 76 per cent of by-election candidatures went to persons under forty). But in the high-winnability constituencies the by-election candidatures went to slightly higher proportions of persons at both ends of the scale: 47 per cent under forty compared to 42 per cent for general election candidatures, but 22 per cent over fifty as compared with 12 per cent for

TABLE 2.3

CONSERVATIVE GENERAL ELECTION AND BY-ELECTION NON-INCUMBENT CANDIDATURES
RELATED TO AGE, BY WINNABILITY OF CONSTITUENCY

Age	Winnability of Constituency					
	High		Medium		Low	
	Gen. Elect.	By-Elect.	Gen. Elect.	By-Elect.	Gen. Elect.	By-Elect.
21–29	6%	10%	9%	(8%)*	17%	36%
30–39	36	37	36	(54)	39	40
40–49	46	31	33	(30)	26	21
50–59	12	18	20	(8)	14	3
60 and over	0	4	2	0	4	0
	100%	100%	100%	100%	100%	100%
Number of cases	85	72	317	13	559	33

* Figures are in parentheses because of the small number of cases.

general elections. So the differences in electoral experience shown in Table 2.2 cannot be explained as mere reflections of age differentials.

Education. In Chapter 4 we shall see that attendance at public schools was highly correlated with the allocation of the most desirable constituencies in general election candidatures, and that candidatures given to those who had gone on to Oxford or Cambridge from public school were no better than those given to persons who had no schooling after public school.

We mentioned earlier that many Conservative national leaders are disturbed by the image of their party as an exclusive club for the aristocracy of birth and wealth. The predominance of public school products among the candidates in the winnable seats tends to perpetuate this image, and a number of Central Office officials have testified that they would like to see it altered. Table 2.4 suggests that the educational backgrounds of persons named for by-elections have given them more reason to rejoice than those of the general election candidates. Table 2.4 shows that in the high-winnability constituencies a slightly smaller proportion of by-election than of general election candidates went to persons who had attended public schools (74 per cent to 79 per cent), and in the low-

TABLE 2.4

CONSERVATIVE GENERAL ELECTION AND BY-ELECTION NON-INCUMBENT CANDIDATURES RELATED TO SECONDARY-UNIVERSITY COMBINATIONS, BY WINNABILITY OF CONSTITUENCY

Secondary-University Combination	Winnability of Constituency					
	High		Medium		Low	
	Gen. Elect.	By-Elect.	Gen. Elect.	By-Elect.	Gen. Elect.	By-Elect.
Secondary only	12%	11%	31%	(22%)*	37%	27%
Secondary and univ. other than Oxbridge	4	5	14	(8)	15	6
Secondary and Oxbridge	5	10	6	(8)	6	3
Public school only	37	17	24	(31)	16	27
Public school and univ. other than Oxbridge	5	7	2	0	6	6
Public school and Oxbridge	37	50	23	31	20	31
	100%	100%	100%	100%	100%	100%
Number of cases	85	72	317	13	559	33

* Figures are in parentheses because of the small number of cases.

winnability constituencies the reverse was true (64 per cent to 42 per cent). But the significant difference was the substantially lower proportion of high-winnability candidatures going to the public-school-only group in by-elections (17 per cent) than in general elections (37 per cent), and the reverse proportions going to public-school-and-university (57 per cent to 42 per cent). In the best seats, in short, those who had attended universities after public schools did better than those who did not, but in both sets of candidatures public school attendance was highly correlated with getting winnable constituencies.

3. Conclusion

We have no systematic evidence about how often the Conservative party's national agencies have tried to place particular persons or types of persons in particular constituencies either for by-elections or for general elections. The characteristics of the candidates actually selected, however, are in no way inconsistent with the testimony of most Central Office officials that their placement power in both types of elections is almost nil.

THE VETO POWER

THE FORMAL POWER

Since the establishment of the Standing Advisory Committee on Candidates in 1935, the national agencies of the Conservative party have had the explicit formal authority to veto any candidate adopted by a constituency association.[29] The official pamphlet on candidate selection states:

> The Standing Advisory Committee . . . is empowered to withhold or with-draw approval from any candidate or would-be candidate who is not considered suitable, or in cases where the financial rules are being broken or there have been serious irregularities in the adoption procedure.
>
> If the endorsement of the Standing Advisory Committee is refused and the constituency adopts him in spite of this, the candidate will not be regarded as an official Party candidate at the next election. He will not receive the usual letter from the Leader of the Party commending his candidature to the elec-torate, nor will he be eligible for help from Central Office in the way of speakers or publications. If elected he will not receive the Party Whip.[30]

The formal decision to veto is made by the SACC, but as in other matters, the initiative and preponderant influence belong to the Vice-Chairman.

Formalities aside, however, does the veto power constitute a pow-erful weapon of central control, or is it as weak and ineffective as the placement power?

THE POWER EXERCISED

Since 1945, the SACC has directly vetoed only one locally adopted candidate and indirectly vetoed another. The circumstances of each case tell much about the nature and limitations of the veto power. We shall relate them in some detail.

1. *Direct Veto: The Chorley Case, 1949—1950*

The distinction of being the only Conservative candidate directly vetoed by the SACC since 1945 belongs to Andrew Fountaine of King's Lynn. Fountaine first became active in Conservative politics

---

[29] *Final Report of the Committee on Party Organisation,* p. 32.

[30] *Notes on Procedure,* pp. 3–4.

immediately after the war. His credentials were excellent. The son of Admiral Charles Fountaine, he attended Stowe School and Cambridge; he served for six years in the Royal Navy, rising to the rank of Lieutenant; and, at the age of thirty, he became Chairman of the South-West Norfolk Young Conservatives.[31] He first achieved national prominence at the Brighton Annual Conference in 1947, when in the course of an otherwise unremarkable speech on Israel he asserted:

In Palestine, twenty British soldiers a month are murdered, and the only concern of our British Socialist Government is that there shall be no undue anti-Semitic outbreaks in England.[32]

At the Llandudno Conference the following year he caused a sensation when he proclaimed:

The first defensive step in the war against Russia, which is being fought with ever-increasing bitterness today, is for you to get rid of this Socialist Government, because today we are faced with the situation that, if we have a military war with Russia—and face this, a large section of our trade union population will be actively fighting on the other side....

The rest of his sentence was drowned by shouts of protest, and the chairman asked him to retire.[33] But Fountaine had become a minor celebrity.

Chorley, a semi-rural mining constituency in Lancashire, had been narrowly won by Labour in 1945, and the local Conservatives believed they had an excellent chance of winning it back. After the usual screening, their selection committee in January, 1949 recommended a short list of four local aspirants and Fountaine. According to the local press, Fountaine delivered a rousing attack on the Labour government at the selection conference, and was adopted despite the general knowledge that he had not yet received SACC approval. Afterwards, a reporter for the local newspaper asked the association chairman, Tom Hargreaves, whether the rumors of a possible Central Office veto had had any effect on the deliberations. Hargreaves' reply set the tone for much of what was to follow, and the press's summary of it is worth quoting at some length:

---

[31] *Chorley Guardian,* January 14, 1949, p. 8.

[32] *Proceedings of the 68th Annual Conference,* p. 69.

[33] *Proceedings of the 69th Annual Conference of the National Union of Conservative and Unionist Associations, 1948,* p. 103.

If the Conservative Central Office had any designs on this seat, they must have dropped them by now. Indignation of local Tories at the very thought of interference can hardly have been overlooked. . . . That he was not on the Central Office list was not . . . likely to have counted against Mr. Fountaine when he came for consideration in Chorley. On the contrary, it might have been in his favour! . . . Disciplinary measures against Chorley Divisional Conservative Association, should Mr. Fountaine be adopted, would be hard to reconcile with the much vaunted claim of the Conservative Party that there is no interference with local associations. It would then appear that one result of speculations which have animated Chorley's political scene this week has been to make doubly sure of Mr. Fountaine's adoption when he comes before the general meeting of the Divisional Conservative Association.[34]

While thus breathing defiance in public, the association's officers privately sought SACC approval. Hargreaves and Lord Hacking, the association's President and former Member for Chorley, met in London with the Vice-Chairman. They were apparently told that Fountaine would not be approved unless he publicly repudiated his by-now notorious remarks at Llandudno and gave a firm undertaking to restrain his future utterances.

In March, 1949, at a general meeting of the association called for his formal adoption, Fountaine replied. Asked from the floor why Central Office had not approved his candidature, he responded by playing a gramophone record of his Brighton speech. Fountaine refused to comment further, but most of those present took him to mean that he attributed the Central Office stand to general Jewish hostility to him, presumably for his remarks at the Brighton Conference, and perhaps even to Jewish influence in Smith Square.[35]

This episode hardened the attitude of Central Office, and the breach with the Chorley association was made public two weeks later when Fountaine at a press conference announced that the SACC had definitely vetoed his candidature. "I cannot bring myself to feel the least bit alarmed," he said: he could get along quite well without Central Office speakers or literature or financial help. The only point that mattered was the possible withholding of the whip, and he was sure that he would in fact receive it once he had won Chorley back from the Socialists.[36]

Lord Hacking and Chairman Hargreaves renewed their efforts

---

[34] *Chorley Guardian,* January 28, 1949, p. 4.

[35] *Ibid.,* March 11, 1949, p. 4.

[36] *Ibid.,* March 18, 1949, p. 5.

to get Central Office to relent, but to no avail. In December Central Office took the unusual step of making public a letter to Hargreaves from S. H. Pierssene, the Secretary of the SACC, explaining that Fountaine had been vetoed for refusing to withdraw the sentiments he had expressed at Llandudno, which were so completely at variance with the party's views.[37]

Lord Hacking told a meeting of the Chorley association the next day that, while he and the other officers regretted the disagreement with Central Office, an important matter of principle was involved, and the association could not in honor back down. He continued:

I must make it quite clear that the National Union has never taken, and I hope it never will take away the right of any constituency association to choose and to adopt its own candidate. . . . I want to assert tonight that as Mr. Fountaine is the Conservative Candidate for Chorley, it is the duty of all Conservatives to support him now, and if and when he is adopted as our official candidate for the General Election.[38]

With the announcement of the general election for February 23, 1950, the association met and formally adopted Fountaine as its candidate. Chairman Hargreaves described him as "the official Conservative Candidate," and was asked from the floor whether this phrase meant that Central Office had, after all, approved Fountaine. "No," Hargreaves replied, "he is the official *Chorley* Conservative Candidate."[39] Subsequently local Conservative advertisements did not refer to him as "The Conservative Candidate." A typical notice in the local newspaper read:

Conservative Public Meeting
THE RT. HON. THE LORD HACKING
O.B.E., P.C., D.L., and
MR. ANDREW FOUNTAINE
will speak.[40]

Presumably this format was intended to make the rather subtle point that the meeting was sponsored by a body in good standing with the National Union but that the second speaker was not an

---

[37] *Daily Telegraph* (London), December 17, 1949, p. 1.
[38] *Chorley Guardian*, December 16, 1949, p. 6.
[39] *Ibid.*, February 10, 1950, p. 4, emphasis in the original.
[40] This advertisement appeared in *ibid.*, February 17, 1950, p. 4.

official Conservative candidate. In any event, the result in Chorley, with 88.6 per cent of the eligible voters going to the polls, was:

> Kenyon, Labour: 23,233 (47.6%)
> Fountaine: 22,872 (46.9%)
> Adams, Liberal: 2,706 (5.5%)

Vetoed or not, Fountaine missed winning by a mere 361 votes.

Technically, the holding of an election cancels all candidatures. But with another election seemingly not far off the matter of selecting a new candidate for Chorley immediately arose. Fountaine's showing at the polls had impressed many in the association, and Hargreaves went to London to plead his cause with Lord Woolton, Chairman of the Party Organisation. Lord Woolton impressed upon him that Fountaine would not be approved, adding that the Chorley association would have to choose between their candidate and continued membership in the National Union.[41] This ultimatum apparently impressed a number on the Chorley executive, because at their next meeting they insisted that the new candidate should be on the SACC approved list. Fountaine's friends, alarmed, warned him of what was happening. Immediately, and without notifying the association's officers, he called a secret meeting to rally his supporters.

This action so angered the association's officers that they determined to drop Fountaine once and for all. A general meeting of the association was called for May, and for a time it looked as though the Fountaine faction would force a final show-down—a show-down many believed the Fountaine group would win. Lord Hacking, however, managed to persuade Fountaine that he should not precipitate a fight which could only split the association and deliver the seat permanently to Labour. At the May meeting he read a letter from Fountaine announcing his withdrawal from the list of possible candidates because he "conceived it to be in the national interest that the breach amongst Chorley Conservatives should be closed." Lord Hacking then moved that Fountaine's withdrawal be accepted, but, after a bitter debate filled with references to "knuckling under to Central Office dictation," a majority voted

---

[41] *Ibid.*, April 28, 1950, p. 6.

him down and instructed the selection committee to retain Fountaine's name among those still under consideration.[42]

After this set-back, the executive council left things alone for awhile. They stretched out the screening process until the end of August, when they selected a new prospective candidate from the List of Approved Candidates: Alfred Hall-Davis, 26, director of a family brewery, Vice-Chairman of the North-West Young Conservatives, a member of the National Union's executive, and a candidate at nearby St. Helens in the 1950 election.

The council presented Hall-Davis to a general meeting of the association in late October, which Fountaine attended despite the express wish of the officers that he stay away. The angry atmosphere of the meeting is suggested by the fact that an opening motion declaring that "the Chorley Association is and should remain a member of the National Union of Conservative and Unionist Associations" carried by only 493 votes to 393. A petition that Fountaine be adopted as prospective candidate was brought forth, but the chairman ruled it out of order amid loud protests. Then Hall-Davis gave a speech which was well received by most in the hall. When the motion to adopt him was made, the chairman ignored a number of calls for a show of hands, and called for a voice vote. A great many "No's" were heard, but the chairman declared the motion carried, and Hall-Davis officially replaced Fountaine as Chorley's prospective candidate.[43]

For a time rumors persisted that Fountaine would stand in Chorley as "National and Empire Candidate" and that a good many local Conservatives would support him. Finally, however, he decided not to. Despite the long factional struggle and despite Central Office's full support of the new candidate, the Chorley results in 1951 were almost identical with those in 1950: the turnout was 88.2 per cent of the eligible voters, and they divided:

> Kenyon, Labour: 24,771 (50.6%)
> Hall-Davis, Conservative: 24,188 (49.4%)

The rest of the story is soon told. Fountaine abandoned his ambitions in Chorley, and the association readopted Hall-Davis. La-

---

[42] *Ibid.*, May 26, 1950, pp. 1, 5.
[43] *Ibid.*, October 27, 1950, pp. 5, 7.

bour held the seat in the 1955 election with 51.4 per cent of the vote. The association then dropped Hall-Davis and adopted a well-known adherent of the party's right wing, Frank Taylor, who lost to Labour's 51.2 per cent of the vote in 1959.[44]

Fountaine drifted out of the party into right-wing splinter politics. He stood as an independent in the South-West Norfolk by-election in 1959, and lost his deposit. In 1962 he became president of the British National party, a group dedicated to preserving Nordic Supremacy in Britain by "combatting Jewish domination of British life" and barring all colored immigrants.[45] He retains, however, the distinction of being the only locally adopted Conservative parliamentary candidate directly vetoed by the SACC since 1945.

2. *Indirect Veto: The Newcastle-upon-Tyne North Case, 1951*

When Lord Woolton told Tom Hargreaves of Chorley that the association would be expelled from the National Union if they re-adopted Fountaine, he uttered no idle threat. As McKenzie points out, "The associations are admitted to membership of the National Union in the first instance subject to the approval of the Executive Committee. The latter reserves the right to withdraw that approval, an action which is of course equivalent to expulsion from the National Union."[46]

The most recent instance of such an expulsion came in 1951 as the result of a controversy over a candidature. Briefly told, the story is this:

In the late 1940's, a split developed in the Newcastle-upon-Tyne North Conservative association over the future of their seventy-three-year-old Member Sir Cuthbert Headlam. One faction, headed by the association chairman, Alderman Temple, wished to drop Sir Cuthbert and replace him with a local man (some said Alderman Temple himself). The other wanted to retain Sir Cuthbert until he wished to retire, and then replace him with a prominent

---

[44] Taylor was elected Member for the Moss Side division of Manchester in the 1961 by-election. Hall-Davis was elected Member for Morecambe and Lonsdale in 1964.

[45] *Observer* (London), July 1, 1962, section 2, pp. 3, 7.

[46] McKenzie, *British Political Parties*, p. 242.

national figure rather than a local man (and especially rather than Alderman Temple).[47]

The quarrel flared into the open in November, 1949, when the Temple-controlled executive council proposed to a general meeting of the association that Sir Cuthbert not be readopted for the next general election. The motion lost by 481 votes to 301.[48] The Temple faction accepted their set-back, Sir Cuthbert was readopted and held the seat in the 1950 general election with 25,323 votes (53.8%) to Labour's 16,858 (35.8%) and the Liberals' 4,839 (10.4%).

After the election the Temple faction renewed their efforts to drop Sir Cuthbert. The anti-Temple group decided that, rather than fight an increasingly difficult battle within the existing association, they should secede, form a new association, and seek affiliation with the National Union. On receiving their application, the National Union's Executive Committee appointed a three-man board of inquiry to look into the merits of the controversy. After receiving its report, the National Union officially recognized the new association and informed Alderman Temple that they were withdrawing approval from the old.

The latter's executive council declared that the National Union's action was "a departure from the fundamental principles of democracy" and "one that cannot go unchallenged."[49] They determined to carry on, and adopted as their candidate, not Alderman Temple, but Colin Gray, a twenty-four-year-old schoolmaster who was vice-chairman of the Conservative association in neighboring Wallsend.

Sir Cuthbert shortly thereafter issued a statement announcing his retirement before the next general election. He declared his full support for the new association, which in August, 1950, adopted as prospective Liberal and Conservative candidate Major Gwilym Lloyd-George, Liberal M.P. for Pembroke from 1929 to 1950, and Minister of Fuel in the wartime National government. He received the Leader's official letter of endorsement and full support from Central Office. No one was surprised when he won the seat in the 1951 general election with 23,930 votes (51.1%) to Labour's 17,005

---

[47] For the background of the conflict, see the *Newcastle Journal and North Mail*, August 13, 1951, p. 3.

[48] *Times* (London), November 21, 1949, p. 2.

[49] *Newcastle Journal and North Mail*, July 24, 1951, p. 1.

(36.3%). Gray, standing as an Independent Conservative, received 5,904 votes (12.6%). Lloyd-George became Minister of Works in the new Conservative government.

Soon after the election the old association recognized the futility of carrying on the fight, and decided to name no more parliamentary candidates. No disciplinary action was brought by the party against Gray for opposing its official candidate. But it is perhaps worth noting that no Conservative association has since seen fit to adopt him as its parliamentary candidate.

THE IMPACT OF THE VETO POWER

What, then, has been the impact of the SACC's formal veto power? On the evidence, very slight.

As we have seen, the national agencies have used their veto power directly only once and indirectly only once—surely an exceedingly sparing use of this presumably powerful weapon. Even in these two instances, be it noted, Central Office dealt with constituency associations which were divided over the issues and personalities in dispute, not united in a determination to stick by their candidates whatever the consequences. And in both cases the ultimate weapon was not the veto or even threat of veto of the candidate, but rather the expulsion or threat of expulsion of the association from the National Union.

It is conceivable, of course, that the deliberations of Conservative selection committees are shaped by the knowledge that Big Brother is watching from Smith Square and that they voluntarily eliminate any candidate who might be vetoed. The present writer, however, has not come across a single unequivocal instance in which a selection committee or executive council has dropped a candidate they wanted because they had been informed, or had surmised, that the SACC would veto him.

A more frequent and vigorous exercise of the SACC's veto power would, indeed, be quite out of keeping with the Conservative party's long-established understanding about the ideological obligations of its members and about the proper and improper ways of disciplining party rebels. It is clear, for one thing, that the party's central agencies are far more reluctant than Labour's to impose sanctions on members who defy the whip. Since 1945, for example, the party's leadership has itself withdrawn the whip from none of its rebel M.P.s, although a number of the latter have voluntarily resigned the whip.[50] Moreover, not only has Central Office not taken any disciplinary action against those who have resigned the whip, but it has refrained from doing so *as a matter of principle.* And the principle involved appears to be that, except in most unusual circumstances, the disciplining of M.P.s—and, by extension, of parliamentary candidates—is a matter for the constituency associations, not for Central Office.

This was made clear in a statement made by the Chairman of the Party Organisation, Oliver Poole (now Lord Poole), in 1957. When asked what Central Office intended to do about Paul Williams and the other Suez-rebel M.P.s who had resigned the whip, Poole replied that Williams's resignation meant only that he "will not have, and he does not want, any help or support from us. I am ready to give my advice, but I have no other comment to make on Mr. Williams's position at the present time. *It is a matter between the member and his association.*"

When asked what Central Office would do if the local associations continued to support and readopt the rebels, Poole replied, "As I have said, it is a matter for each association, *which is entirely autonomous,* to deal with, and for each of these particular members to decide whether to remain outside the party or rejoin."[51]

THE FINANCIAL RULES

The SACC's veto power, then, has at most been a reserve weapon for control of candidate selection. A far more significant form of central regulation has been provided by the "Maxwell Fyfe rules," which since 1949 have strictly limited the nature and amount of financial contributions by candidates and M.P.s to their constituency associations.

THE "PURCHASE" OF CANDIDATURES
BEFORE 1949

Prior to World War II there was no restriction upon how much money an individual could contribute to a Conservative constitu-

---

[50] Cf. Richards, *Honourable Members,* pp. 151–53.
[51] *Times* (London), May 20, 1957, p. 4, emphasis added.

ency association. It was not uncommon for wealthy men who wished to be M.P.s to approach the association officers in safe Conservative constituencies and offer substantial and continuing financial contributions in return for being adopted as their parliamentary candidates. According to one Conservative politician, indeed, this practice was so widespread and taken for granted that the candidates could be graded according to how much they were good for. He wrote in 1939:

> There are roughly three categories of candidates:
> Class "A": those who are willing to pay all their election expenses (anything between £400 and £1,200) and to subscribe between £500 and £1,000 a year to the local Association.
> Class "B": those who are willing to pay at least half their election expenses and to subscribe between £250 and £400 a year to the local Association.
> Class "C": those who are unable to pay anything towards their election expenses and only able to subscribe £100 or less to the local Association.
> According to present standards, "A" class have always an excellent chance of being adopted, "B" class a reasonable one, and "C" class hardly any chance at all. These standards are set up not, as is usually alleged, by Central Office, but by the local Associations themselves.[52]

And Henry Brooke told the annual conference of the party in 1948 that

> Having studied the evidence, I have to tell you that there are still too many constituencies—not by any means a majority, but still too many—which do not summon for interview with the selection committee anyone who does not promise in advance to contribute half the election expenses—that means a sum of perhaps £400—and to pay £100 a year towards the association. Or if they do interview him they make it all too clear to him early in the interview that money counts.[53]

---

[52] Extracts from a memorandum (dated 1st January 1939) by Mr. Ian Harvey, "Facts Regarding the selection and adoption of candidates for Parliament in the Conservative Interest," quoted in J. F. S. Ross, *Parliamentary Representation* (New Haven: Yale University Press, 1944), pp. 236–38. For other testimony on the same point: "In the days when he was in the habit of making ritual descents on the Carlton Club Mr. [Harold] Macmillan was fond of regaling younger members with an account of a selection committee he attended in the Twenties at which the chairman simply asked each applicant to write his name on a piece of paper together with the amount he was prepared to donate to the Association's funds. The highest bidder was adopted forthwith": David Watt, "Picking and Choosing," *The Spectator* (May 1, 1964), p. 573.

[53] *Proceedings of the 69th Annual Conference*, p. 36.

THE MAXWELL FYFE REFORMS

After the startling Conservative defeat in the 1945 general election (which in a number of ways is the watershed in the party's recent history), the team of Lord Woolton and R. A. Butler set about rebuilding the party's machinery and reforming its procedures. One of their first concerns was the purchase of candidatures, both because of the image of the party as a rich men's club and because, as Lord Woolton put it in his memoirs, "I noticed that the organisation of the party was weakest in those places where a wealthy candidate had made it unnecessary for the members to trouble to collect small subscriptions."[54]

Aided by a resolution proposed by Gerald Nabarro in the Central Council of the National Union in 1946[55] and another proposed by Nigel Fisher to the annual conference of 1947, a fourteen-man committee on Party Organisation was established under the chairmanship of one of the party's most respected lawyers, Sir David Maxwell Fyfe, who, as Lord Kilmuir, was later to become Lord Chancellor. A year later the committee reported to the 1948 annual conference, and proposed, among other things, the following three new rules regulating contributions to constituency associations by candidates and M.P.s:

1. Constituency associations must henceforth assume all election expenses, to which neither a candidate nor an M.P. may make any contribution whatever.
2. Annual contributions to a constituency association's general funds may not exceed £25 by its prospective parliamentary candidate or £50 by its M.P.
3. Under no circumstances may an association raise the question of financial contributions with any aspirant for its candidature until after the candidate has been selected.[56]

After some debate (see below), the report was adopted, and the rules have remained in force since the beginning of January, 1949.

EFFECTS OF THE REFORMS

The Maxwell Fyfe rules have been scrupulously enforced by Central Office and its area agents, and there is no doubt that Conserva-

---

[54] The Rt. Hon. the Earl of Woolton, *Memoirs* (London: Cassell & Company, Ltd., 1959), p. 345.

[55] *Times* (London), March 15, 1947, p. 2.

[56] *Ibid.*, October 4, 1947, p. 8; *Final Report of the Committee on Party Organisation*, Appendix A, p. 42.

tive candidatures can no longer be "bought" in the old manner. There is some disagreement about what effects this has had upon candidate selection and the party in general, but most observers would agree at least upon the following.

In the first place, many Conservative associations have responded to being made entirely dependent upon their own money-raising efforts by becoming far more active. They have enlarged their subscription-paying memberships; they have held whist parties, bazaars, casinos, and the like; and not only have the majority of the associations raised adequate funds, but there has been a noticeable revival in their vigor and pride in their place in the party.[57]

In the second place, when the Maxwell Fyfe reforms were being debated several Conservative leaders expressed the fear that increasing the associations' independence of their candidates and M.P.s might mean decreasing the independence of the latter. Nigel Fisher, then Member for Hitchin, told the 1947 annual conference:

It is regrettably true that in the bad old days many Conservative candidates were expected to pay up regularly and to attend in their Divisions perhaps once a month. But now we work three or four or even seven nights in our Divisions, and we pay very little.[58]

And Aubrey Jones, then prospective candidate for Acocks Green, made this plea to the 1948 annual conference:

. . . in making this change, do not let us throw away this quality of independence which has been brought down to us from other days. When our Members and candidates paid the piper they were able to some extent to whistle their own tune. Now the Constituency Associations and the Central Office are going to pay the piper, may I ask them very solemnly to declare this afternoon that in this matter of calling the tune they will exercise a very proper restraint?[59]

Have these fears been realized? McKenzie concludes that, to a degree, they have. The Maxwell Fyfe reforms, he contends, have tended to make the local Conservative activists more possessive about their rights as well as their obligations to the party. As a

---

[57] Lord Woolton's judgment to this effect, *Memoirs*, p. 346, is supported by Richards, *Honourable Members*, p. 23. See also J. D. Hoffman, *The Conservative Party in Opposition* (London: MacGibbon & Kee, Ltd., 1964), pp. 45–46.

[58] *Proceedings of the 68th Annual Conference*, p. 83.

[59] *Proceedings of the 69th Annual Conference*, p. 118.

result they are now more prone to feel that it is not only their right but their duty to discipline a candidate or an M.P. when he fails to measure up to their standards of ideological purity, personal propriety, or service to the association and the constituency.[60] In Chapter 3 we shall review in detail some evidence bearing on this question.

Finally, while it is difficult to say precisely what effects the Maxwell Fyfe rules have had on the kinds of persons adopted as candidates,[61] most observers believe that they have made some difference. There have been fewer rich eccentrics and fewer corporation "barons" than before, and more able young men going straight to Parliament from Central Office,[62] more lawyers, and more professional men in general. Yet, without denying any of these impressions, the evidence we shall review in Chapter 4 seems to support Allen Potter's view that

> The constituency associations have not, as a consequence of these reforms, chosen a markedly different kind of candidate. On the whole, the safe and marginal Conservative seats continue to send well-to-do and well-connected men to Parliament. In any case a parliamentary career usually requires either an outside source of income compatible with the heavy demands put on a Member's or "prospective" candidate's time or the financial support of a patron or pressure group. . . .[63]

CONCLUSION

Since 1935, the Conservative National Union and Central Office have together enjoyed considerable formal power over the selection of parliamentary candidates. The local selectors' obligation to consult with the Vice-Chairman and the SACC's control of the List of

---

[60] Robert T. McKenzie, "The 'Political Activists' and Some Problems of 'Inner Party Democracy' in Britain," mimeo., a paper delivered at the Fifth World Congress of the International Political Science Association, Paris, September, 1961. Lord Kilmuir comes to much the same conclusion in his memoirs, where he comments that the new independence of the local associations has led many to select mediocre local men rather than outsiders of ability: *Political Adventure: The Memoirs of the Earl of Kilmuir* (London: Weidenfeld and Nicolson, 1964), pp. 157–60.

[61] Chapter 4 of the present book offers information about the kinds of persons adopted since 1945, but the author has only impressionistic evidence of the candidates before 1945. The most exhaustive study, P. W. Buck, *Amateurs and Professionals in British Politics, 1918–59* (Chicago: University of Chicago Press, 1963), does not categorize the data by different periods of time.

[62] Such as, for example, Iain MacLeod, Reginald Maudling, and John Biffen.

[63] A. M. Potter, "The English Conservative Constituency Associations," *Western Political Quarterly*, IX (June, 1956), 363–75, at p. 367.

Approved Candidates provide ample opportunities for positive central influence over local selections; and the SACC's power to withhold and threaten to withhold approval of any locally adopted candidate constitutes a major negative weapon to prevent and correct local mistakes. Taken together, these formal powers appear to provide exactly the sort of machinery that, according to the advocates of responsible party government, political parties should have to maintain their national cohesion.[64]

As we have seen, however, these formal powers are little used—because they are not very usable. They were grafted upon the long-standing and much-admired Conservative tradition that candidate selection and the discipline of rebel M.P.s are matters for the constituency associations, not Central Office, to decide. They have not noticeably lessened the adherence to or reduced the impact of that tradition.

We cannot, therefore, escape the conclusion that central control of candidate selection makes, at most, only a minor contribution to the much-remarked cohesion of the Conservative party in Parliament. A much greater contribution is made by the attitudes and practices of the party's constituency associations. But that is a matter for the next chapter.

---

[64] See Chapter 1.

Chapter 3 | The Role of Conservative Constituency Associations

The Conservatives, unlike their Labour rivals, do not require contenders for parliamentary candidatures to be nominated by organizations affiliated with the party. Any individual party member may submit his name or have it submitted by someone else. Consequently, a Conservative constituency association known to be selecting a candidate receives applications from a variety of sources. Members of the association may suggest names. The Vice-Chairman of the Party Organisation, as we saw in Chapter 2, usually offers suggestions. The local officers and even the agent may invite persons they admire to let their names be put forth.

After all the applications are in, the selection process begins.

THE STAGES OF SELECTION

From the aspirant's point of view the local selection process has three critical stages.

DRAWING UP THE SHORT LIST

In the first stage some kind of screening committee sifts through the initial list of applicants and draws up a "short list." This is the most critical of the three stages, for most of the hopefuls are eliminated here. In safe or winnable Conservative seats it is not unusual for well over a hundred persons to apply, and even in hopeless seats there are usually at least fifteen or twenty applicants.[1] Since short lists rarely include more than three or four names, the odds against any particular aspirant are higher at this stage than at any other.

Usually the association's executive council appoints a special selection committee to screen the applicants, although occasionally the regular finance and general purposes committee does the job. The selection committees vary in size and composition from one association to the next, but they usually include the association's principal officers, the president, chairman, vice-chairmen, honorary treasurer, and chairmen of the executive council's chief committees. Sometimes this core of nine or ten is augmented by representatives elected by the ward branches and possibly also a trade union representative, bringing the total membership to eighteen or twenty. But, whatever its formal constitution, the screening committee invariably includes most of the association's most active and influential members.[2]

The selection committee begins by reviewing all the applicants. Understandably, at this stage it welcomes any valid reason for striking them off: A is too old, B is too young, C has too many local enemies, D is a woman, and so on.

When the committee has pruned its initial list to perhaps fifteen or twenty, it invites each of the survivors to appear for an interview. Committees often stipulate that the aspirants bring their wives as well (though feminine aspirants are seldom asked to bring their husbands!). The screening of wives—almost unknown in the Labour party—results from the expectation of many Conservative associations that their candidates and M.P.s will be prominent in local social as well as political affairs. We shall return to this point and its significance later.

After all the interviews are concluded, the committee draws up

---

[1] Although the exact number of applicants is, like other aspects of candidate selection, usually kept secret, the information does occasionally appear in the press. Some figures for recent selections in safe Conservative seats are: Torquay (1955), 71 applicants; Richmond and Barnes (1958), 135; Ealing South (1958), 150; St. Albans (1959), 78; Harrow West (1960), 164.

[2] Cf. Ivor Bulmer-Thomas, *The Party System in Great Britain* (London: Phoenix House, Ltd., 1953), pp. 204–6.

the short list[3] and submits it to the executive council. Councils have been known to reject their selection committees' short lists, however. A recent instance occurred at Chippenham in 1962. Sir David Eccles, Member for this safe Wiltshire seat since 1943, had been elevated to the peerage. In their search for a candidate for the ensuing by-election, the association's selection committee passed over all the local applicants and recommended a short list of four outsiders. But after a stormy meeting, the executive council rejected the entire list and instead adopted Daniel Awdrey, a local solicitor and former mayor.[4]

Usually, however, the executive council accepts the recommended short list and sets the date for the second stage of the process.

THE SELECTION CONFERENCE

A selection conference is a special meeting of the association's executive council called to select the prospective parliamentary candidate from the short list recommended by the selection committee. Usually from thirty to one hundred members attend.[5] On what information do they make their choice?

In the first place, it is clear that they are rarely influenced by any pre-conference lobbying on behalf of the contenders. Most Conservatives strongly disapprove of such maneuvers, and any suspicion that a particular aspirant or his supporters are violating this taboo, is likely to destroy his chances (the situation in the Labour party, as we shall see in Chapter 6, is quite different).[6] Accordingly, only

---

[3] Not all selection committees are as elaborately systematic as the Beckenham committee in 1957. In one of the rare public disclosures of a selection committee's procedures, the committee's chairman, Dr. J. B. Patrick, told the press why Philip Goodhart had been selected over all local aspirants for the 1957 by-election. His committee, he explained, had required all the applicants to address the committee on a specific and difficult topic "worthy of a Chancellor of the Exchequer." Committee members graded each aspirant's performance on a scale of 0 to 25. None of the local contenders did well, and one received an average score of 4! Among the final four contenders, Dr. Patrick said, "there was a vote of 14 to 1 in favour of Mr. Goodhart. We had no option but to place his name before the Executive Council": *Beckenham Journal,* March 9, 1957, pp. 3–4.

[4] *Sunday Times* (London), August 19, 1962, p. 5.

[5] David E. Butler and Richard Rose, *The British General Election of 1959* (London: Macmillan & Co., Ltd., 1960), p. 122.

[6] Samuel H. Beer in Sigmund Neumann, ed., *Modern Political Parties* (Chicago: University of Chicago Press, 1956), p. 25.

the members of the selection committee are likely to have any first-hand knowledge of all the contenders prior to the conference.

Before each aspirant speaks, the association's chairman, either orally or in writing, describes the speaker's background: his age, occupation, education, service record, party service and party offices, and previous candidatures, if any. This information is intended, as one association chairman put it to the author, "to let the members know what sort of stable the chap comes from."

Then each aspirant delivers a ten to fifteen minute speech on current political affairs and/or his qualifications, and answers questions for another ten to fifteen minutes. In some instances a particular contender is so well known and liked (or disliked) that his speech makes little difference. In most, however, the impressions the contenders make in their half-hour appearances constitute the main basis for the council's choice. Most aspirants who have undergone this ordeal by elocution would endorse Nigel Nicolson's description of how it feels:

> It is a gala occasion for the selectors; slow torture for the candidates. So great is the strain of maintaining an amicable conversation with his rivals and their wives, that it is a relief for the applicant to leave the ante-room and follow the agent into the main hall for the ten or twenty-minute interview which may alter the entire direction of his life. The audience already knows a great deal about him, but he cannot be sure quite what they know. Normally, a candidate makes the most of all favourable facts which are not likely to be contradicted by the more impartial summary of his life-story which the selectors hold in their hands. They do not want a speech about party policy. They want to discover what sort of person he is, or is capable of pretending to be, for most people can conceal the less agreeable sides of their natures for so short a period. If they cannot, they will not make good politicians, and deserve to lose.[7]

Nicolson's point that the decisive factor is the aspirant's character rather than his ideology is emphasized by almost everyone who has participated in a Conservative selection conference. A Central Office official who has attended hundreds of conferences told the author:

> What most associations want is a man of solid character. Not necessarily a brilliant man, you understand; in fact they may distrust a chap who seems too brilliant or flashy or glib. They want someone with the right sort of background, someone who looks and sounds right. They want someone they can

---

[7] *People and Parliament* (London: Weidenfeld and Nicolson, 1958), p. 40.

count on to do the right thing, whether as a campaigner or a leader in association affairs or a Member of Parliament. They want someone who, by his business career or his war record or his party service or his social standing, has
proved that he is this kind of man.[8]

ADOPTION BY THE ASSOCIATION

The third stage comes when the executive council recommends
its choice to a general meeting of the entire association. Usually
the association adopts the executive's recommendation without discussion, and the candidate, who has been waiting modestly in the
wings for the decision, comes forward to make his first official speech
as prospective parliamentary candidate.

Occasionally, however, an association has refused to accept its
executive's choice. One dramatic instance was the affair in Southport in 1952. This safe Conservative seat fell vacant when its Member, R. S. Hudson, was elevated to the peerage. From fifty-two applicants the association's finance and general purposes committee
drew up a short list of five, consisting of three outsiders and two
local men, Alderman William Bellis, the association's chairman,
and Councillor Roger Fleetwood-Hesketh. The selection conference met on a Friday evening and chose Alderman Bellis. The association's general meeting convened on the following Monday, and
the executive's motion to adopt Alderman Bellis was seconded by
Councillor Fleetwood-Hesketh. But a prominent member of the association moved from the floor that this motion be rejected and that

---

[8] On at least one occasion—in North Kensington in 1952—an executive council did
not rely solely on its own reactions to the contenders' speeches to determine their
vote-getting potentials. The Conservatives first lost North Kensington to Labour in
the 1945 general election, and lost again in 1950 and 1951 by majorities of 4,000
(around 8 per cent). The local executive council decided they needed a candidate who
could appeal effectively to the constituency's marginal Labour voters. So they invited
the four persons on their short list to speak, not to a private selection conference in
the usual way, but on a streetcorner in the Portobello Road with members of the
council mingling with the crowd to observe the reactions! The four consented, and
after the "streetcorner selection conference" had been held the council selected R. W.
("Bob") Bulbrook, a trench inspector for the South Metropolitan Gas Company, a
member of the National Union of General & Municipal Workers, and the model for
the posters of the Tory working man used in the 1951 general election: *Kensington
Post*, December 14, 1951, pp. 4, 6; January 11, 1952, p. 1. Bulbrook reduced the Labour
majority to 3,000 in 1955 (7 per cent) and to 877 (2 per cent) in 1959. This record
might seem to justify the North Kensington association's innovation in selection
procedures, but so far no other has copied it.

Fleetwood-Hesketh be adopted instead! A secret ballot was taken, and the motion carried. Alderman Bellis accepted the decision, commenting to the meeting that "Councillor Fleetwood-Hesketh's seconding of my nomination may now appear to be something technical." But, he added, the outcome resulted from "a clash of strength by two loyalties—not loyalties in any way relating to the question of party policy, but personal loyalty, which develops in the course of time as one moves among his fellows."[9] No schism seems to have developed from this rebellion; the Conservatives won the by-election with their usual majority, and Fleetwood-Hesketh held the seat until he voluntarily retired for the 1959 general election.[10]

CONSERVATIVE "DIRECT PRIMARIES"

The American institution of the direct primary, in which rank-and-file members of the parties select candidates by casting ballots in state-supervised secret elections, is unknown in Great Britain as in all other democratic nations. Yet on at least two occasions Conservative parliamentary candidates have been selected by procedures closely resembling primaries.

The Hampstead "Primary," 1949. Charles Challen had been elected Conservative Member for Hampstead in 1941, and re-elected in 1945. A number of the Hampstead association's officers, however, grew increasingly dissatisfied with what they regarded as Challen's lack of color, his failure to make a name for himself in the House or in national party affairs, and his reputation as an adamant opponent of social welfare measures. They told him in 1947 that his readoption for the next general election would not be automatic and that other names would be considered.

A deep split in the association ensued. The anti-Challen faction declared that they were looking for "an outstanding national figure," and settled upon Henry Brooke, a resident of Hampstead who had been Conservative M.P. for West Lewisham from 1938 until

---

[9] *Southport Visitor,* January 15, 1952, pp. 1, 6.

[10] Another instance was the episode in Dudley and Stourbridge in 1949. Despite last-minute pressure for Major Roy Farran, a hero of the Palestine war, the executive council chose another candidate. The association's general meeting, however, refused to adopt him and instructed the executive to consider a new short list including Major Farran. The executive did so, adopted Major Farran, and the association naturally accepted their recommendation: *Dudley Herald,* October 29, 1949 p. 5; November 5, 1949, p. 5; December 10, 1949, p. 3.

his defeat in the general election of 1945, and was currently serving as Conservative leader on the London County Council. The pro-Challen faction hotly contested what they regarded as an unwarranted effort to dismiss an M.P. who had never given offense or slighted his local duties and therefore was entitled to readoption. They managed to get Challen on the short list along with Brooke and two outsiders.

In July, 1949, the executive council heard speeches from the four contenders, and chose Brooke over Challen by a vote of 46 to 21.[11] But the Challen faction did not give up. They disputed the council's right to drop an M.P. in this summary fashion and claimed that a majority of the association's rank-and-file felt the same way. After protracted negotiations, the two factions agreed to let the association choose between Challen and Brooke by a novel procedure combining a regular association meeting with features of a direct primary. A circular to the association's 7,500 subscribing members notified them that a meeting was scheduled for the evening of August 15 at the Embassy Theatre in Swiss Cottage, at which members would be able to vote for a candidate. It also stated that any member unable to attend the meeting could come to the association's offices at any time during the day and vote by special ballot. The ballots listed Brooke and Challen in alphabetical order and provided a third space to permit a voter to reject both contenders. It was agreed that any member who cast a ballot prior to the evening meeting would be ineligible to vote at the meeting itself.

An estimated 450 ballots were cast during the day, and in the evening the theatre was packed to capacity. Following speeches by Challen and Brooke, the members present balloted. Their ballots were added to those cast during the day, and all were counted together. It was announced that Brooke had won the combined poll by 714 votes to 449. Some observers judged from the applause given the two speakers that there was a slight majority of Challen supporters at the meeting, and concluded that Brooke's margin must have come from the votes cast during the day.[12]

Challen's supporters—somewhat belatedly—protested the novel

---

[11] *Hampstead News*, December 8, 1949, p. 1.
[12] *Daily Express* (London), August 19, 1949, pp. 1, 3.

procedures and appealed to Central Office to set aside Brooke's candidature. But Lord Woolton, the Chairman of the Party Organisation, made public a letter to the local chairman stating that Brooke was now the party's official prospective candidate for Hampstead and implying that such procedures could be used if an association wished.[13] Brooke was elected in 1950 with a substantially increased majority and rose rapidly in the parliamentary party, becoming Home Secretary in 1962. Challen dropped out of active political life.

The Bournemouth East and Christchurch "Primary," 1959. The Hampstead "primary" was followed ten years later by another which climaxed the most publicized struggle over a Conservative candidature in recent history. The story of Nigel Nicolson's defiance of the whip during the Suez affair of 1956, of the alacrity with which his constituency association dropped him and adopted another candidate, and of Nicolson's efforts to reverse their decision has been told too often and too well to be repeated in detail here.[14] For our purposes the main events in this instructive story were the following:

Nicolson was adopted and elected in a by-election in 1952, and re-elected in 1955. In November, 1956, he abstained from a vote of confidence on the Eden government's handling of the Suez crisis, and even worse, publicly attacked the government in terms resembling those used by the Labour opposition. A few days later the Bournemouth East and Christchurch Conservative association's executive council issued a public statement supporting the government and condemning Nicolson's behavior. In early December a special meeting of the association passed, by a vote of 298 to 92, a resolution calling for the selection of a new candidate for the next general election. In February, 1957, the executive selected Major James Friend, and in March a general meeting of the association, by a vote of 569 to 176, accepted their recommendation.

Nicolson fought hard to reverse this decision. He asked that any

---

[13] *Hampstead News,* December 8, 1949, p. 1.

[14] The best accounts are Lawrence W. Martin, "The Bournemouth Affair: Britain's First Primary Election," *Journal of Politics,* XXII (November, 1960), 654–81; Leon D. Epstein, *British Politics in the Suez Crisis* (Urbana: University of Illinois Press, 1964), pp. 98–102; and Nicolson's own account in *People and Parliament,* cited above.

action on the status of his future candidature be delayed for two years, but the executive refused. He then asked that the association members vote for him or Major Friend on the Hampstead precedent, but again the executive refused. In 1958 he published his book *People and Parliament,* and his supporters in the association organized an effort to displace Major Friend and have Nicolson readopted.

Their cause appeared hopeless until, in December, 1958, Major Friend resigned as a result of criticism of his associations with the League of Empire Loyalists and other extreme right-wing groups. This reopened the Bournemouth candidature, and now Lord Hailsham, Chairman of the Party Organisation, prevailed upon the association's executive to agree to a postal vote of all the members on the question of whether Nicolson should be readopted.

Despite much adverse press comment about this "Americanisation" of British politics, the poll was conducted in February, 1959. A total of 9,724 ballots were mailed, of which 2,118 were not returned, and 173 were undelivered or spoiled. Of the remainder, 3,671 were cast in favor of Nicolson's readoption, and 3,762 were cast against. Thus by the tiny majority of 91 votes (50.6 per cent), Nicolson's candidature was permanently quashed. The association then proceeded in the usual fashion to select a new candidate, John Cordle, who was elected with a slightly reduced majority in the 1959 general election and re-elected in 1964.

The Brighton Kemptown "Primary," 1965. The Conservatives lost Brighton Kemptown by 7 votes in 1964. In early 1965 their Executive Council was given a short list of two outsiders, but a powerful group in the association demanded a local man be chosen. The executive ducked the issue by adding two former constituency M.P.s and leaving the final choice up to the whole association. In February, 1,000 of the 2,300 paid-up members attended a mass selection conference and heard speeches from the four contenders. On the second ballot they chose Andrew Bowden of London, former national chairman of the Young Conservatives, over David James, Member for Kemptown 1959–1964, by 346 votes to 253.[15]

---

[15] Jack Egremont, "Tory Fracas in Brighton," *New Statesman,* February 19, 1965; *Daily Telegraph* (London), February 20, 1965.

FROM "PROSPECTIVE CANDIDATE"
TO "CANDIDATE"

As we noted in Chapter 1, the candidate adopted by the association is technically only the prospective parliamentary candidate for
the time being. Presumably this gives the association the right to
remove him at any time. A formal adoption meeting of the whole
association is called after a general election has been announced or
a writ issued for a by-election. Only when this meeting has adopted
him does he become the constituency's full-fledged Conservative
candidate. In most instances the distinction is purely formal, and
the prospective candidate becomes the candidate automatically.
Yet the few exceptions should be briefly noted.

1. *Candidate Resignations*

Occasionally a prospective candidate will feel he can win a candidature in a constituency with better electoral prospects. Technically, he is entirely free to resign his current candidature and accept
another. If he does, the association may resent it; but if the seat he
leaves seems unwinnable, they know, as one Central Office official
put it, that "they are in no position to resent their candidate's moving on to better things. It is simply one of the penalties of manning
an association in a hopeless seat."[16]

2. *Candidate Dismissals*

From the moment of his adoption, the prospective candidate as-
sumes many obligations. He is expected to canvass, make speeches,
confer with party officers about campaign strategy, attend association fund-raising and social affairs, and in general plunge whole-
heartedly into the local party's affairs. Even if he does not satisfy
everyone he is usually retained at least until after the election, and

---

[16] If a candidate contemplates such a move, however, he is well advised to keep
both associations fully informed. In April, 1958, for example, the West Bromwich
Conservative association executive selected F. L. Morgan as their prospective candidate.
Three weeks later, before the association general meeting had met to adopt him, the
Montgomeryshire Conservative association announced that *they* had adopted Morgan.
C. D. Pawson, the chairman of the West Bromwich association, said that his group
had not been informed of Morgan's intentions, and viewed his move "with disappoint-
ment and dismay": *West Bromwich, Oldbury and Smethwick Midland Chronicle and
Free Press*, May 16, 1958, p. 1.

quietly dropped thereafter. Occasionally, however, some local activists become so dissatisfied that they try to secure his dismissal and replacement by a better man before the next election. Sometimes they succeed, sometimes not.

The Widnes Dismissal, 1954. In Widnes in 1954, for example, they succeeded. In May, 1953, the Conservative association in this marginal Labour seat adopted as its prospective candidate a thirty-eight-year-old barrister, C. J. I. Cunningham. The executive soon grew restive, however, at the infrequency of Cunningham's local appearances and his casual attitude toward his local duties. Finally, in September, 1954, they were reported to have passed a vote of no confidence in him. Interviewed about the report, Cunningham replied:

> The only reaction I have to it is one of humour because the only people I have met in Widnes who would do such a thing are a number of old women of both sexes who have neither the resolution nor the confidence in anything, least of all their own power to win the seat. . . . I am awaiting with pleasure the first official sign of this kindergarten caucus outbreak of spleen.[17]

This pronouncement did not improve the executive's opinion of Cunningham, and a month later he resigned his candidature.[18] He was not subsequently adopted by another association, though he remained in good standing on the Standing Advisory Committee's list of approved candidates.

The Colchester Dismissal, 1947–48. At Colchester in the winter of 1947–48, the executive passed a resolution of no confidence in their prospective candidate, Dr. Pearl Hulbert, on the ground that she was an ineffective canvasser and stump speaker. Dr. Hulbert's supporters claimed that the executive acted from anti-feminine prejudice, and announced their intention of attending in force the association meeting called to adopt the new candidate. At the last moment, however, Dr. Hulbert withdrew.[19]

Such dismissals are rare. For a number of reasons, most Conservative associations are reluctant to dismiss their candidates once they are adopted. For one, the candidate usually has enough supporters to precipitate a fight, and a fight lowers the association's morale and

---

[17] *Widnes Guardian,* September 27, 1954, p. 7.

[18] *Widnes Weekly News,* October 15, 1954, p. 1.

[19] *Colchester Gazette,* December 3, 1947, p. 1; *Essex County Standard,* February 6, 1948, pp. 1, 7.

damages its public reputation. For another, the candidate may have enough support to prevent his dismissal, and his opponents know that to start a fight and lose it is to risk the loss of all future local influence.[20] It therefore usually seems prudent to make do with an unsatisfactory candidate until after the election. If he loses, the association can take advantage of the technicality that an election automatically cancels all candidatures, and pass him over in their selection of a new candidate. If he should win, he may suddenly rise in their estimation. Even if they like him no better, he will be not merely an ex-prospective candidate but a Member of Parliament; and ousting him, as we shall see, will not be easy.

THE ASSOCIATIONS' "INFLUENTIALS"
INVOLVEMENT IN ASSOCIATION AFFAIRS

In local Conservative associations, as in all human groups, some members have more influence than others. And since those with influence derive much of their power from their greater involvement in the group's affairs, it is necessary to understand who are active in local Conservative affairs and to what extent.

1. *Subscribing Members*

According to the party's model rules, membership in a Conservative association is open to "any man or woman residing in or connected with the constituency who declares his or her support of [the party's] objects" and pays an annual subscription (2/6 is the usual rate).[21] Accounting practices vary so widely from one association to the next that official figures are notoriously misleading, but dividing the total number of party members by the number of associations produces an average membership of five thousand.

---

[20] Recent instances of unsuccessful efforts to dismiss prospective candidates include the controversy in Maldon in 1948 over the continuation of Aubrey Moody's candidature (see the *Essex County Standard*, November 26, 1948, p. 1); the reversal by the Southall and Hanwell association's general meeting of a no-confidence motion adopted by its executive on the candidature of Arthur Tickler in 1952 (see the *Middlesex County Times and West Middlesex Gazette*, November 22, 1952 p. 1); and J. C. Cobbold's survival of a struggle within the Ipswich association over his candidature in 1958–59 (see the *East Anglian Daily Times*, May 9, 1959, p. 7; and *ibid.*, August 22, 1959, p. 6).

[21] Conservative and Unionist Central Office, *Model Rules*, pamphlet No. 3 in the organisation series, pp. 3–4.

The association's power formally rests in all its members. They are empowered to adopt the constitution, choose the officers, and select the prospective parliamentary candidate, and they have the final word in all other association affairs. The model rules require that at least one general meeting of all members be held each year to receive and audit the accounts, receive and adopt the executive council's annual report, elect the association's officers, and transact any other business brought before it. Special meetings may be called at any time by the chairman of the association or at the written request of at least fifty members.[22]

2. *Activists*

As in most groups, only a fraction of the typical association's members actively participate in its affairs. In most constituencies, according to the testimony of party agents, only about 10 to 20 per cent of the members even attend the annual general meetings: attendances of over one thousand are rare. And most of these members confine their participation to attending the annual meetings: the Gallup Poll reported that only 7 per cent of their Conservative respondents claimed to have canvassed in the 1959 election, and Butler and Rose consider even this minimal figure probably too high.[23] McKenzie estimates that only about 1 to 3 per cent of most associations' members are continuously active, in the sense that they regularly canvass, attend all association meetings, and keep in close touch with what the officers are doing.[24]

These 50 to 150 members, then, are the association's activists. What are they like? How do they view candidate selection? Regrettably, there is no recent study of British local party operations comparable to McKenzie's comprehensive analysis of the national party organizations.[25] On the basis of interviews with area and constituency party leaders, journalists, and scholars, however, the author has formed the following impressions.

---

[22] *Ibid.*, pp. 12–13.

[23] *The British General Election of 1959*, p. 140.

[24] Cf. Robert T. McKenzie, "The 'Political Activists' and Some Problems of 'Inner Party Democracy' in Britain," mimeo., a paper delivered at the Fifth World Congress of the International Political Science Association, Paris, September, 1961.

[25] A useful though brief analysis is in Jean Blondel, *Voters, Parties, and Leaders* (London: Penguin Books, Ltd., 1963), pp. 90–108.

In most Conservative associations the activists constitute a cross-section of all segments of British society except the semi-skilled and unskilled workers; they are by no means all aristocrats or industrial tycoons or landowners.[26] The most visible types include middle-class women,[27] small tradesmen, junior company executives, white-collar workers, and retired military officers, with a sprinkling of the aristocracy and their offspring.

What are their characteristic political attitudes? Are they more extreme than the views of the inactive members or the party leaders? Richard Rose in his study of resolutions submitted by constituency associations to party conferences concludes that they are not—that "Attitudes on questions of policy are randomly distributed among constituency parties and, it may be tentatively assumed, among party activists as well."[28] McKenzie and Epstein, on the other hand, conclude from other kinds of evidence that the local activists are generally far more prone than the national party leaders to insist on unswerving loyalty to "the principles of true Conservatism."[29] Certainly the activists, as we shall see below, have been far more eager than the national leaders to punish M.P.s who have, in their view, departed from these principles.

Whatever their personal political views, however, most Conservative activists undoubtedly place great value on such virtues as loyalty to the national Leader, solidarity in the face of attacks by Labour, public silence about internal party conflict, and solid character and reliability rather than flashiness or brilliance as prime qualities for party leaders. Nigel Nicolson has written of one such activist:

---

[26] A. H. Birch suggests that the present broadly representative character of Conservative association activists is largely the product of the "opening up" of the party accomplished under the leadership of Lord Woolton and R. A. Butler after the defeat of 1945: *Small Town Politics* (London: Oxford University Press, 1959), p. 76.

[27] Cartoonists, comedians, and playwrights have by now given "the Tory woman," with her outrageous hat, shrill voice, and cowering husband, a seemingly permanent place in the nation's demonology.

[28] "Political Ideas of English Party Activists," *American Political Science Review,* LVI (June, 1962), 360–71, at p. 369. Blondel reaches the same conclusion: *Voters, Parties, and Leaders,* p. 92.

[29] McKenzie, "The 'Political Activists' "; and Epstein, *British Politics in the Suez Crisis,* pp. 204–05.

In my own constituency, there is a highly valued member who has beaten all regional records for enrolling new members . . . . A modest, though indefatigable man, he cannot believe that the leaders for whom he has worked so hard could ever be guilty of a serious error of judgement. So, faithful to a fault, *plus royaliste que le Roi,* he regards deviations within his own party as an enormity ten times more dreadful than forthright opposition to it from outside.[30]

3. Leaders

The officers of a Conservative association include: the president, a largely honorary office given a member of the association distinguished for his governmental service, military record, position in the aristocracy, or the like; the chairman, who is the association's presiding officer and usually its key figure; three or four vice-chairmen, including the chairman of the women's divisional advisory committee, the chairman of the Young Conservatives, the chairman of the divisional council of Conservative trade unionists, and one other member; and the honorary treasurer. All officers except the ex officio vice-chairmen are elected annually by the general meeting.

The composition of the executive council varies, but it usually includes the officers, the chairmen of committees,[31] two or more representatives elected by each ward branch, one representative named by each Young Conservative ward branch, two representatives named by the trade unionists' council, one representative picked by each subscribing Conservative club, and up to six co-opted members.[32] Executive councils usually number between eighty and one hundred members.

INFLUENCE OVER CANDIDATE SELECTION[33]

The selection committee undoubtedly has the greatest influence over candidate selection. The executive council, to be sure, formally

---

[30] *People and Parliament,* p. 33.

[31] Such as the Young Britons, political education, local government advisory, publicity, and teachers' advisory committees.

[32] *Model Rules,* pp. 6–7.

[33] The analysis in the text is a distillation of the author's impressions derived from interviews with national and local Conservative officials and activists. For similar conclusions, see Birch, *Small Town Politics, passim.;* Nicolson, *People and Parliament,* pp. 35 ff; and especially A. M. Potter, "The English Conservative Constituency Association," *Western Political Quarterly,* IX (June, 1956), 363–75.

recommends the candidate, and the association's general meeting officially adopts him; and on a few occasions, as we have seen, one or the other has rejected recommendations made to it. But in most cases the selection committee fixes the *range* of choices before the larger bodies. The executive council and general meeting are empowered to give the answers, so to speak, but the selection committee asks the questions. And in candidate selection as in any other variety of decision-making, the questions asked largely determine the answers given.

Most selection committees are dominated by a few members who take their lead from the chairman; he, in turn, is the key figure in the whole selection process. His association elects him because they feel he is the best person they have to direct the association's affairs. He usually sees to it that the selection committee includes a preponderance of members he regards as reasonable and co-operative. He calls the committee's meetings and prepares its agenda. He acts as the official channel of communications with the aspirants and with Central Office. He presides over the committee's meetings and manages its discussions.[34] As a by-product of his administrative tasks, he knows more about the strengths and weaknesses of the aspirants than do any of his committee. As a result of these factors, his opinions weigh heavily with them. He usually can veto any contender he finds unacceptable, and give crucial support to one he particularly favors. In short, although the chairman is no dictator, he is the nerve center of all the association's affairs, and as such he usually plays a critical role in the selection of candidates.

The constituency agent and Central Office area agent sometimes exercise considerable influence, especially when they enjoy the chairman's confidence. As "civil servants" they have no formal power beyond that of making suggestions, but they are often confidants of the chairman. When the chairman is weak or inactive or has withdrawn from the selection process because he is himself a contender,

---

[34] A skillful chairman who knows the weak points of aspirants he wishes to eliminate and also knows his committee plays a decisive role in the initial vetting. The chairman of a west-central London association told the author in an interview, "I know my committee and I'm frank to say I use it. I know, for example, that old Colonel X never has a good word to say for anyone, whereas Lady Y can't bear to say anything harsh about anyone. So when the name before us is someone I want to see kept off the short list, I call on Colonel X to make the first comment; and when it's someone I want to see on the list, I call on Lady Y first!"

either or both agents sit with the committee and guide its deliberations.

In most instances, however, the chairman is the key figure. What range of choice has he? Considerable but not unlimited is the answer: he cannot impose on his committee or association a candidate who outrages their sensibilities, nor can he deny them a candidate they greatly prefer. But the first and foremost factor limiting his choice is whether or not the association already has a sitting M.P. who wishes to be readopted.

The Member and His Association

the member's claim to readoption

Strictly speaking, a member of Parliament does not automatically become his association's candidate at each election. He must be formally readopted, and the association technically reserves the right to refuse readoption.[35] But there is a general presumption in favor of sitting members who wish to stand again. This presumption is so powerful that an M.P. usually need only indicate his desire to continue, and he will be readopted unanimously and without question.[36]

The practical consequences of this presumption are shown in Table 3.1.

The figures in Table 3.1 show that most incumbent Conservative M.P.s in recent years have been readopted. They also indicate that most of the few M.P.s who retired did so voluntarily and not because their associations forced them to. Consequently, in any general election, as we shall see in Chapter 4, most of the candidates adopted in the safest Conservative seats are incumbents seeking re-election.

Yet the doctrine of responsible party government outlined in

---

[35] Peter G. Richards, *Honourable Members* (London: Faber & Faber, Ltd., 1959), pp. 15–16.

[36] This presumption has long obtained. A. Lawrence Lowell remarked over a half-century ago that "nothing . . . impresses a foreign observer of British politics more than the universal recognition of the claim of a sitting member to renomination": *The Government of England* (New York: The Macmillan Company, 1908), I, 499. And M. I. Ostrogorski observed, "As a general rule the sitting member is *eo ipso* the candidate of the Association for the next election; it recognizes his vested rights": *Democracy and the Organization of Political Parties,* trans. Frederick Clarke (New York: The Macmillan Company, 1902), I, 449.

Chapter 1 holds that refusing and threatening to refuse readoption to rebel M.P.s should be a powerful weapon for the national party leaders to maintain party solidarity and responsibility. The doctrine aside, how often has the weapon actually been used in the Conservative Party in recent years, who has used it, under what conditions, and with what success? The answers to these questions

TABLE 3.1

READOPTION OF CONSERVATIVE INCUMBENTS, 1950–1964 *

Election	Number of Incumbents at Dissolution	Number of Incumbents Readopted	Number of Retirements	All Known Instances of Attempts to Force Retirements	Known Instances of Forced Retirements
1950	218	194	24	5	4
1951	296	280	16	1	1
1955	320	297	23	1	0
1959	365	323	42	7	5
1964	350	315	35	4	2

* The figures in columns 1–3 are taken from the *Times House of Commons* series; the figures in columns 4 and 5 were compiled by the author from the cases discussed in the text.

should tell us a great deal about how closely Conservative practice resembles the responsible-parties model.

CONFLICT OVER THE READOPTION OF M.P.S

Several scholars have recently suggested that, contrary to what is widely supposed, the strongest pressures bearing on Conservative M.P.s come not from the Leader or the whips or Central Office, but from the members' constituency associations.[37] Presumably the most powerful of all local pressures would be the denial or threat of denial of readoption, for to deny a member readoption is almost always to deny him his seat. The present writer has found eighteen instances since 1945 in which a Conservative M.P.'s claim to readoption has been seriously challenged by groups in his local association. They may be summarized under the following headings.

[37] This position is taken by Epstein, Martin, McKenzie, and Richards in the works cited previously.

1. *For Personal Failings*

Before every general election a number of M.P.s announce that they have decided not to stand for re-election. Usually the general public has no reason to believe that the retirement is other than truly voluntary: the member is ill, too old, or wishes to devote full time to his business or profession. Sometimes, however, the retirement is not voluntary: the member, facing strong opposition in his association, stands down rather than undertake an arduous and possibly losing struggle for readoption.

Some M.P.s retire because influential members of their association regard their personal behavior as improper, immoral, or ridiculous. Failure to pay bills, habital drunkenness, repeated lying, adultery, even divorce—each has been the cause for one or more forced retirements. No outsider can say, however, how many M.P.s have stood down for such reasons, for both members and associations take great pains to keep such matters private.[38]

Patrick Wolridge-Gordon and East Aberdeenshire, 1962. One well-publicized attempt to force a retirement for personal reasons took place in East Aberdeenshire in 1962. Patrick Wolridge-Gordon was elected Conservative member for this Scottish constituency at a 1958 by-election at the age of twenty-three while still an Oxford undergraduate, and was re-elected in 1959. A zealous member of the Moral Rearmament movement, Wolridge-Gordon devoted an increasing portion of his time to MRA activities until, in October, 1961, the association executive expressed the fear that he was neglecting his duties in the House. They made it clear that they objected to his participation in the MRA movement in particular. Wolridge-Gordon assured them he would devote full time to his parliamentary duties, but dissatisfaction spread with what the executive felt to be his failure to keep his promises. In March, 1962, the chairman was reported to have told him that, since the execu-

---

[38] One case in which this was not entirely successful was that of Nigel Fisher in Hitchin in 1952. Fisher was elected in 1950 and re-elected in 1951. In January, 1952, his wife brought suit for divorce, which Fisher did not contest. As soon as the suit was filed he reportedly went to the Hitchin association's executive and offered to stand down at the next election. The executive accepted the offer, and proceeded to select another candidate: cf. *Hertfordshire and Bedfordshire Express*, April 5, 1952, p. 4. Fisher was later adopted by the Surbiton association, and was elected for Surbiton in 1955 and re-elected in 1959 and 1964.

tive had lost confidence in him, he should take the gentleman's way out and announce his intention to retire. But Wolridge-Gordon refused, and soon the fight flared into the open.[39] In April the executive voted 22 to 15 to withdraw their support, and in effect recommended that he not be readopted.[40]

Wolridge-Gordon's response was prompt. A few days later he held a press conference in Westminster at which he announced, "I will not be bullied out of my seat. The chairman and his clique have met again. These minority McCarthys have issued a statement purporting to represent the whole executive."[41] In the following weeks he stumped the fishing villages and market towns of the constituency rallying rank-and-file Conservative support.

The executive, accepting the challenge, called a general meeting of the association for April 25 to settle the issue, which Wolridge-Gordon defined as "whether a member of Parliament is to be a lapdog for a few or a watchdog for all the people." Expecting an overflow attendance, the executive provided that members failing to gain entrance to the hall could vote by ballot. The meeting heard the Member defend his right to be active in MRA and the chairman and the president repeat their case against him. Then, by a vote of 463 to 185, they rejected the executive's recommendation and declared their confidence in the Member. Wolridge-Gordon subsequently demanded the resignation of his opponents on the executive, and by late June the East Aberdeenshire association had an entirely new slate of officers.[42] If there had been any doubt on the matter, the Wolridge-Gordon case made it clear that a sitting M.P. is far from helpless when his readoption is challenged.

Arthur Marsden and Chertsey, 1949. A member's readoption may be challenged, not because of immoral behavior or improper associations, but simply because his association feels he is ineffective. The Hampstead association's abandonment of Charles Challen in 1949 (see above) and the Newcastle-upon-Tyne North association's effort to drop Sir Cuthbert Headlam (see Chapter 2) are cases in point. Another case in 1949 involved Captain Arthur Marsden, R.N., who had been member for Chertsey since 1937 and was said

---

[39] *Times* (London), April 14, 1962, p. 5.
[40] *Ibid.,* April 9, 1962, p. 6.
[41] *Ibid.,* April 24, 1962, p. 6.
[42] *Ibid.,* April 26, 1962, p. 12; June 29, 1962, p. 7.

to have been a heavy contributor to association funds. The Maxwell Fyfe reforms in the late 1940's (see Chapter 2) prohibited any further such contributions, and when the 1948 redistribution split the Chertsey division into two seats, the Chertsey association invited Marsden to stand for Esher, the new seat. When Marsden refused to move, the Chertsey selection committee decided to consider him merely one of the seventy-nine applicants for the candidature. They included him in their short list of four, but the selection conference passed him over for L. F. Heald, K.C., by 132 votes to 55.[43]

Dr. Donald Johnson and Carlisle, 1963–64. Dr. Donald Johnson, a physician and former Liberal, won Carlisle from Labour in 1955 and held it by the slim majority of 1,998 in 1959. The association executive grew increasingly restive about what they regarded as his excessive personal eccentricities. However, they made no move against him until 1963, when his public criticism of the party Leader, Harold Macmillan, for his handling of the Profumo affair prompted them to act. They passed a vote of no confidence in him and announced that they would seek another candidate for the next general election. Fifty of his local supporters signed a petition demanding a meeting of the whole association to reconsider the decision. It was held in December, the executive announced that they would resign if their decision were overruled, and the meeting voted 138 to 31 to uphold them and seek a new candidate. Dr. Johnson's supporters then asked Central Office to hold a postal ballot of the entire association membership on the Bournemouth-Nicolson precedent (see above), but Central Office refused, and Carlisle chose a new candidate.[44] Dr. Johnson stood as an independent in 1964, but lost his deposit.

John Henderson and Glasgow Cathcart, 1964. John Henderson was elected for the safe Unionist Cathcart division of Glasgow at a by-election in 1946 at the age of fifty-seven and held it in successive general elections, though by decreasing majorities. In January, 1964, the association executive voted 20 to 16 to seek a new candidate younger than Henderson's seventy-five years. At first Henderson intimated that he would resist any effort to drop him, but even-

---

[43] *Surrey Herald,* January 7, 1949, p. 4; January 21, 1949, p. 4.
[44] *Daily Telegraph* (London), December 3, 1963, p. 1; December 31, 1963, p. 1; *Times* (London), January 7, 1964, p. 5.

tually he decided not to fight and announced his retirement to make way for a younger man.[45]

2. *For Inadequate Local Services*

The typical constituency association expects a great deal of strictly local service from its M.P. It counts on him, for example, to "nurse the constituency": to hold periodic "surgeries" at which constituents can meet him personally and tell him their troubles, to bring meritorious complaints to the attention of relevant ministries, to make speeches at charitable and sporting events, to greet constituents who visit Westminster and find them tickets to the Strangers' Gallery, to speak up for local and regional interests in the House, and so on.[46]

The typical association expects its member to "nurse the association" as well. They expect him to grace with his presence the association's social and fund-raising dances, whist drives, and the like. They count on him to speak to association and ward meetings. They expect him to canvass personally during an election campaign and to help out in local elections as well.

The typical Conservative association feels it has every right to insist that its member perform his local duties. The Maxwell Fyfe reforms prevent him from making any substantial financial contributions, and since 1921 the Treasury has furnished him limited funds for travel between Westminster and his constituency. So unless he is a senior minister he has no acceptable excuse for not spending many weekends in his constituency, and his association is likely to feel that he is duty-bound to do so. If they feel he is shirking his local duties, they may even challenge his readoption. Following are some cases in point.

Sir Gifford Fox and Henley, 1949. Sir Gifford Fox was elected Member for Henley in 1932 and re-elected in 1935 and 1945. After 1945, however, a number of the association's branches grew increasingly annoyed with the rarity of his local appearances. Several adopted resolutions urging the executive to consider other possible candidates for the next election. After some hesitation the executive agreed, and the selection committee recommended a short

---

[45] *Times* (London), January 11, 1964, p. 5; January 12, 1964, p. 5.
[46] See the account in Richards, *Honourable Members*, pp. 164–72.

list including Sir Gifford, Sir Walter Monckton, a former minister, and John Hay, a former national chairman of the Young Conservatives. The selection conference chose Hay, and Sir Gifford accepted his dismissal.[47]

E. E. Gates and Middleton and Prestwich, 1951. E. E. Gates was elected Member for Middleton and Prestwich in 1940, and re-elected in 1945 and 1950. In early 1951, the executive's long-standing feeling that he was shirking his constituency duties came to a head. The finance and general purposes committee voted that he not be readopted. Before the full executive could meet to act on this recommendation, the chairman met Gates and received assurances that he would mend his ways.[48] The day after the 1951 general election was announced, however, Gates publicly stated that he would stand down. In a letter to the chairman he said:

> The only possible circumstance under which I could offer myself for selection as your Conservative candidate to contest the next election would be if I had full confidence in your Finance and General Purposes Committee and could enjoy their unanimous recommendation to the Selection Committee. I must now assume, unless I hear from you immediately to the contrary, that the Prime Minister's abrupt announcement of a General Election, in only five weeks from now, has left an insufficient margin of time in which to win such unanimous support. I am therefore writing this letter so that you can proceed with the selection and adoption of another candidate.[49]

The association agreed with alacrity, and adopted a new candidate.

Colin Turner and West Woolwich, 1962–63. Sir William Steward was elected Member for West Woolwich in 1950 and re-elected in 1951 and 1955, but stood down in 1959 because of ill health. His successor, Colin Turner, was elected with a slightly increased majority. Soon, however, elements in the association grew dissatisfied with Turner's local services, and determined to press for his replacement by Sir William, who had now recovered from his illness. In July, 1962, the executive instructed its selection committee to consider other possibilities as well as Turner. From thirty-three applicants the committee recommended a short list of four, including both Turner and Sir William. In December, the selection con-

---

[47] *Henley and South Oxfordshire Standard*, April 15, 1949, pp. 4–5.

[48] *Prestwich and Whitefield Guide*, July 20, 1951, p. 4; *Middleton Guardian*, July 28, 1951, p. 5; September 22, 1951, p. 5.

[49] Quoted in the *Middleton Guardian*, September 29, 1951, p. 7.

ference chose Sir William over Turner by 52 votes to 31. The pro-Turner faction determined to carry the fight to the association's general meeting. They mobilized the Young Conservatives, sent each association member a copy of a letter praising Turner signed by thirty-six Conservative M.P.s, and urged all members to support Turner at the meeting. The association met in January, 1963, and voted by 274 votes to 184 to reject the executive's recommendation. Turner was, in effect, readopted,[50] but lost the seat in the 1964 election.

E. L. Gander Dower and Caithness and Sutherland, 1946–48. This case differs somewhat from the others in that it involved a conflict between the Member's conception of his obligation to the voters and the association's conception of his obligations to the association. In his election address in 1945, E. L. Gander Dower promised to resign after the surrender of Japan and fight a by-election to protest the breakup of the wartime coalition. He was elected by the razor-thin margin of 5,564 votes to Labour's 5,558 and the Liberals' 5,503. Japan surrendered in August, 1945, and in December, 1946, after being twitted publicly about his failure to keep his promise, Gander Dower asked the executive's permission to apply for the Chiltern Hundreds. They prevailed upon him to wait until local electoral prospects improved. During the next two years he periodically pressed them to let him redeem his pledge, but they continued to find the time inopportune. Finally, in September, 1948, he made public a letter he had sent the executive requesting permission to resign. The executive met the following day in Wick and resolved "That the executive committee strongly disapproves of a by-election being fought, and if it is fought will recommend to a special general meeting that the support of the association be not given Mr. Gander Dower."[51] Gander Dower requested that the membership of the association be polled, but the executive refused.[52] They proceeded with the selection of a new candidate and excluded Gander Dower from the names considered. In November they adopted Sir David Robertson, then Member for Wandsworth Streatham. At this Gander Dower resigned the whip, saying that

---

[50] *Guardian* (London), December 12, 1962, p. 1; January 14, 1963, p. 1; *Times* (London), January 4, 1963, p. 4.

[51] *Times* (London), September 16, 1948, p. 3.

[52] *Caithness Courier*, October 6, 1948, p. 3.

since he had been forced out of his constituency association he might as well resign from the party altogether.[53]

3. For Parliamentary Deviations

A majority of the recent cases in which an M.P.'s readoption has been publicly challenged stemmed from associations' objections to their members' votes or speeches in the House. Since these cases are the most significant from the standpoint of the responsible-parties ideal, we shall review them in some detail.

Viscount Hinchingbrooke and South Dorset, 1952. Lord Hinchingbrooke, Earl of Sandwich from 1962 to 1964, and now Mr. Victor Montagu, played the leading part in two well-publicized cases of member-association conflict. He was elected for South Dorset in 1941 and re-elected in 1950 and 1951. In early 1952 he supported the Bevanite rebels in the Labour party by voting and speaking against the Conservative government's policy of rearming Germany. The South Dorset executive regarded this as outrageous disloyalty to the national party leaders, and in September adopted, by 46 to 9, a vote of no confidence in Hinchingbrooke. Their reasons, later made public, are revealing:

(1) Repeated publicly-expressed opinions of the Member on foreign affairs and repeated attacks on party leaders has gradually built up a position which in the opinion of the Executive would make a present of the seat to a Socialist if our Member were again the candidate; (2) complete disregard of the advice and suggestions given to the Member by the officers of the Association; (3) He stated once at an Executive meeting, and we feel it is continually in his mind, that once elected to Parliament he claims the right to express and act on his own opinions . . . .[54]

The executive invited Hinchingbrooke to appear before them and defend his actions, but he refused. It was, he said, a matter for the whole association to decide. The executive accordingly called a special general meeting for late October. An overflow crowd heard the member, sounding like the very reincarnation of Edmund Burke, proclaim his right and duty to speak and vote as he saw fit. The association chairman, W. R. Machin, put the executive's position but was overmatched. The meeting adopted, by 836

---

[53] *Ibid.,* December 1, 1948, p. 2.
[54] Quoted in the *Dorset Daily Echo and Weymouth Dispatch,* October 9, 1952, p. 1.

votes to 468, a resolution of confidence in Hinchingbrooke and of no confidence in the executive. The officers resigned and Hinching-brooke returned triumphantly to Westminster. He was re-elected in 1955, and, after another display of independence (see below), again in 1959.

Even after his elevation to the peerage in 1962 he managed to make trouble for the association officers: his active support of the anti-Common Market independent candidate in the ensuing by-election threw the seat to Labour.

His independence had its penalties. In 1964 he decided to renounce his peerage and re-enter the House of Commons as Mr. Victor Montagu. He was rejected, however, by the selection committees in the three Conservative-held constituencies of Winchester, Bromley, and Southampton Test before he was finally adopted for the Labour-held seat of Accrington, which he was unable to win in the 1964 general election.

The Left-Wing Suez Rebels, 1956. The story of the Suez rebels has been fully told elsewhere, and only its essentials need be repeated here.[55] The Eden government's military intervention in Egypt in November, 1956, produced two types of dissidents among Conservative M.P.s: left-wing rebels who opposed the government on grounds similar to those of the Labour party, and right-wing rebels who favored the intervention but later attacked the government for its withdrawal and acceptance of President Nasser's control of the Canal.

The left-wing rebels included ten Conservative M.P.s publicly identified as opposed to the intervention, although not all actually abstained from voting on Labour's no-confidence motion of November 8. Each of the ten encountered substantial criticism from his association and the readoption of each was called into question. Four actually lost their seats: Nigel Nicolson, as we saw earlier, was denied readoption by the Bournemouth East and Christchurch association; Sir Frank Medlicott was so effectively frozen out by the Central Norfolk association that, after several unavailing attempts to get a hearing for his position, he stood down rather than fight a

---

[55] See especially Leon D. Epstein, "British M.P.s and Their Local Parties: The Suez Cases," *American Political Science Review,* LIV (June, 1960), 374–90; Epstein, *British Politics in the Suez Crisis,* Ch. vi; and Martin, *Jour. of Politics,* XXII, 654–81.

foredoomed battle for readoption;[56] Anthony Nutting resigned his ministerial post and, after ascertaining that the Melton association strongly disapproved of his position, resigned his seat as well;[57] Cyril Banks resigned the whip, and his Pudsey association adopted a new candidate without even considering him (indeed, even after he resumed the whip in 1958, he never regained contact with the Pudsey association). A fifth, J. J. Astor, had already announced his intention to stand down at the next general election, so the Plymouth Sutton association took no action beyond issuing a public statement opposing his stand.

Three left-wing abstainers retained their candidatures. Sir Edward Boyle, who had resigned his junior ministerial post in protest, was blessed with excellent relations with his local officers. He met with the executive of the Birmingham Handsworth association and explained his action. The executive afterward declared their support for the Eden policy, but took no punitive action against Sir Edward. William Yates, a popular M.P. in a very marginal seat, explained his position to the Wrekin association, which supported both Eden's policy and Yates's right to disagree with it. Sir Robert Boothby explained his position to his East Aberdeenshire association, and while they publicly differed with him, his candidature was never seriously challenged (on his elevation to the peerage in 1958 he was succeeded by Patrick Wolridge-Gordon, of whom we have spoken previously). Since the other two known left-wing rebels, Sir Alexander Spearman and Peter Kirk, did not go so far as to defy the whip, neither's readoption was frontally challenged, and both were readopted in 1959.

The Right-Wing Suez Rebels, 1957–58. In May, 1957, Prime Minister Macmillan announced that the government would no longer advise British shipowners to refrain from using the Suez Canal, thereby tacitly accepting complete defeat for the Eden policy. In protest eight right-wing Conservative M.P.s resigned the

[56] In 1962, Sir Frank announced that he had joined the Liberal party and would be prepared to stand as a Liberal candidate: *Daily Telegraph* (London), June 6, 1962, p. 13. He received no candidature, however.

[57] In January, 1962, Nutting was adopted as prospective parliamentary candidate for Oldham East—the only English seat the Conservatives had lost to Labour in the 1959 general election: *Times* (London), January 20, 1962, p. 6. However, he failed to recapture it in the 1964 election.

whip. Their subsequent treatment by their constituency associations provides an instructive contrast with that meted out to the left-wing rebels.

Lord Hinchingbrooke, the group's leader, appeared before a general meeting of the South Dorset association, repeated the substance of his highly successful Burkean oration of five years before, and received a vote of confidence by the overwhelming margin of 495 to 6.[58]

John Biggs-Davison met with the officers of the Chigwell association and explained his position. They took no action other than issue a statement that "the situation has been discussed to the satisfaction of the members."[59]

Paul Williams appeared before the executive of the Sunderland South association, which afterward issued a statement that "The Council upholds the right of an M.P. to disagree with the Government on any issue and to abstain from voting if he so wishes."[60]

Lawrence Turner met with the executive of the Oxford association, which afterward unanimously adopted a resolution expressing appreciation for his past services and giving him "full support as Oxford's Member."[61]

Anthony Fell appeared before a general meeting of the Yarmouth association. In introducing him the chairman, Major-General R. T. O'Cary, said, "We don't hamstring our candidates. They are entitled to give views they hold personally." The meeting voted full confidence in Fell.[62]

Angus Maude spoke to a general meeting of his Ealing South

---

[58] *Dorset Daily Echo*, May 18, 1957, pp. 1, 7. After the vote, Hinchingbrooke drew laughter and applause with the remark that "I really thought when I entered this hall tonight that this massive demonstration had assembled for another purpose. The size of the audience reminded me of another meeting some years ago!"

[59] *Chigwell Times and West Essex Star*, May 17, 1957, pp. 1, 16.

[60] *Sunderland Echo and Shipping Gazette*, May 22, 1957, p. 8.

[61] *Oxford Mail*, June 12, 1957, p. 1.

[62] *Yarmouth Mercury*, May 17, 1957, p. 1. It should be noted that after being re-elected in 1959, Fell did get into some trouble with his association because of his strong speeches against the Conservative government's policy of attempting to join the Common Market. Mrs. L. K. Barfield resigned her chairmanship of the association because she felt she could no longer support Fell's activities, but no serious effort was made to challenge his readoption: *Times* (London). October 23, 1962, p. 14; October 24, 1962, p. 5. He was re-elected in 1964.

association, defended his position, and received a vote of confidence by the margin of 572 to 28.[63]

Two of the eight right-wing rebels did not even bother to return to their constituencies to justify their actions. The chairman of Sir Victor Raikes's Liverpool Garston association said there would be no special request that he return and defend himself. "Sir Victor," he said, "is still a 100 per cent Conservative."[64] The chairman of Patrick Maitland's Lanark association told the press, "The local party were well aware of Mr. Maitland's attitude regarding Suez, and at our recent association general meeting when he said that he might have to take other action which might prove unpopular, no demur was made." The honorary secretary added, "I don't regard this as an emergency, and I don't expect a special meeting will be called to consider Mr. Maitland's action."[65]

Angus Maude later resigned his seat to accept the editorship of a Sydney newspaper. Sir Victor Raikes resigned to take a business position. In neither case is there any reason to believe that any kind of local pressure was involved.[66] The other six applied for a restoration of the whip (Maitland in December, 1957, and the others in June, 1958), and received it. Lawrence Turner decided not to stand again in 1959 because of failing personal health.[67] The other five were readopted and four were re-elected. Only Patrick Maitland, defeated in Lanark by a bare 540 votes, after several new housing developments had brought in more Labour voters, clearly retired from Parliament other than voluntarily. And he was later adopted for Caithness and Sutherland, but lost in the 1964 election.

Montgomery Hyde and North Belfast, 1959. The last case to be noted involves a mixture of personal and doctrinal differences.

---

[63] *Middlesex County Times and County Gazette,* June 1, 1957, p. 10.

[64] *Liverpool Echo,* May 14, 1957, p. 5.

[65] *Lanark and Upperward Gazette,* May 17, 1957, p. 3.

[66] Maude, indeed, returned from Australia and was adopted by the South Dorset association for Hinchingbrooke's old seat in the 1962 by-election, which he lost mainly because of the opposition of his old comrade-in-rebellion (see above). He was later adopted and elected for Stratford in the 1963 by-election necessitated by John Profumo's resignation.

[67] There are persistent rumors, which the author has been unable to verify or disprove, that Turner was in fact asked to stand down by his association executive, not because of his Suez rebellion but because he was regarded as an ineffective M.P.

Montgomery Hyde was elected Unionist Member for North Belfast in 1950 and re-elected in 1951 and 1955. He was a member of the right-wing Suez rebel group, and abstained from two votes of confidence. What the activists in his constituency association objected to, however, was his support of the abolition of capital punishment, his approval of the Wolfenden Report's proposals for relaxing laws against homosexual offenses, and his recommendation that a legally-disputed set of pictures be returned from a London to a Dublin gallery.

Recognizing the considerable opposition to his readoption, the selection committee in early 1959 placed Hyde on their short list along with three other names, and the executive chose him over his nearest rival by a margin of only 77 votes to 72. His opponents carried the fight to the association's adoption meeting, and, by a vote of 171 to 152, secured the adoption of a resolution rejecting Hyde's candidature and stipulating that "the general body of the Unionist association having refused to ratify the selection, Mr. Hyde's name cannot be submitted again to the selection committee for further consideration."[68] Hyde asked the association officers to conduct a postal vote of the membership on the Bournemouth East and Christchurch model (see above), but by a vote of 25 to 1 they refused. He then appealed to Unionist headquarters to force the association to conduct a vote, but they refused to intervene. The executive named another candidate, who was unanimously approved by a general association meeting, and Hyde finally admitted defeat.[69]

THE READOPTION OF MEMBERS: A SUMMARY

The foregoing twenty cases do not constitute a scientifically-drawn sample. We can discuss them only because they were reported in the press, and that in itself indicates an abnormal degree of tension and/or indiscretion in the associations involved. Yet the following summary of what took place and why should tell us something about the strength and limitations of Conservative M.P.s' claims to readoption.

---

[68] *Belfast News-Letter*, February 14, 1959, p. 5.
[69] *Ibid.*, April 4, 1959, p. 5.

The first thing to note is that nearly all Conservative M.P.s in this period were in fact readopted, most of them apparently without question. This confirms the general view that a Conservative M.P.'s claim to readoption is very strong, rarely challenged, and even more rarely challenged successfully.

Second, all the challenges reported came from constituency associations, not from Central Office. In at least two instances (the Headlam and Nicolson cases) Central Office even made some effort to soften the associations' harsh actions. On several other occasions (e.g., in the Challen, Hyde, and Williams cases) Central Office officially stated that candidate selection—including the readoption of M.P.s—is entirely up to the constituency associations, and that Central Office has neither the inclination nor the right to intervene.[70] For a Conservative M.P., then, the first law of political survival is to cultivate and maintain the support of his association—a law publicly recognized by Harold Macmillan:

In a television interview on November 23, 1958, Macmillan replied to a question about the Bournemouth affair by pointing out that, although he had been a rebel in his time, he had never quarrelled with his association. "Then it does not matter, falling out with the Party leaders if you keep in with your constituency association?", asked the interviewer. "Of course," replied Macmillan, "that is the right tradition."[71]

Third, speaking—even voting—against official party policy in Parliament does not invariably jeopardize a member's readoption. Of the seven left-wing Suez rebels who defied the whip but wished to stand again, five were subjected to severe criticism by their associations, and four were not readopted. But of the eight right-wing rebels who defied and then resigned the whip, not one was even criticized by his association for his parliamentary deviation, let alone refused readoption. This suggests that Conservative local activists do not necessarily demand that their member follow the party Leader wherever the Leader goes; rather they insist that he adhere faithfully to what they regard as the true principles of Conservatism. If the local activists feel that the Leader has, as in the 1957 "retreat from Suez," abandoned those principles while the

---

[70] See, for example, the statements of the Chairman of the Party Organisation quoted above, p. 51.

[71] Quoted in Martin, *Jour. of Politics*, XXII, at p. 670. See also *ibid.*, at pp. 680–81.

member, by his defiance of the whip, remains faithful to them, they may well support the member rather than the Leader. But if they feel the member's defection is a defiance of basic principles *and* the Leader's authority as well, they are far more likely to refuse him readoption. The critical point, in short, appears to be not the act of disobeying the Leader in itself but rather the reasons for the disobedience.

This is not to dispute McKenzie's general observation that:

. . . the traditional Conservative concepts of leadership and discipline have tended to discourage (although not to eliminate) the possibilities of rebellion. In any event, in all normal circumstances, revolt against their leaders is furthest from the minds even of the activists among Conservative party workers. Subtle considerations of social deference towards their leading parliamentarians (especially when they are the Queen's ministers, as they tend to be most of the time) reinforce the Party's own view that it is the prime duty of "followers" to sustain rather than to attempt to dominate their leaders.[72]

The lesson of the right-wing Suez rebels is that when circumstances are not normal—when the M.P. seems to his association more faithful to true Conservatism than the Leader—the attitudes McKenzie describes do not operate to endanger his readoption. As Martin puts it:

. . . constituency organizations, embodying a purer form of party doctrine, are doomed to chronic frustration by the need of party leaders to compromise with facts and with the moderate voter, a frustration the more poignant if the constituency's own Member is a conspicuous symbol of moderation. Within wide bounds the anonymity of discipline in the Commons affords a Member great protection against attack by constituents who set great store by loyalty to the party, for he cannot be condemned outright without damning the leaders. But a Member who openly registers his deviation from the party line exposes himself to attack in the very name of loyalty. The occasions on which constituencies fall on their Members with an outwardly sudden ferocity, though infrequent, are thus not unnatural but rather an understandable product of the system.[73]

Fourth, holding a marginal seat is helpful but no guarantee of readoption. The eight right-wing Suez rebels were evenly divided between safe and marginal seats. Of the ten M.P.s whose readoption was challenged on personal grounds, six held safe seats and

---

[72] "The 'Political Activists,'" at p. 5. Cf. Lowell, *The Government of England*, I, 499–500 for an earlier statement of this point of view.

[73] *Jour. of Politics*, XXII, at p. 676.

four held marginal seats. Of the four left-wing Suez rebels whose readoption was challenged, all held safe seats; and of the five whose readoption was not challenged, two held safe seats and three held marginal seats. It appears, then, that if the association is sufficiently angered by the member's action (or inaction), it will get rid of him, but if he is a popular M.P. in a marginal seat they are likely to try harder to control their anger.

Finally, an M.P. whose readoption is challenged can look to Central Office for little or no help, but he may be able to rally support among the association's rank-and-file even if the officers are against him. Wolridge-Gordon, Colin Turner, Headlam, and Hinchingbrooke all managed to get general meetings of their associations to reverse their executives' decisions not to readopt, while Challen, Hyde, Nicolson, and Dr. Johnson tried but failed.

CONCLUSION

Adherents of the doctrine of responsible party government, as we have seen, often defend its feasibility by pointing to what they presume to be British party practices. The worst political sin an M.P. can commit, they suggest, is to vote in the House contrary to what his party's leaders have officially prescribed. The leaders' main weapon for preventing such defections is their control of candidate selection: they can deny any rebel readoption and thus his seat in Parliament. The mere threat of such retaliation, we are told, should be enough to keep the incipient rebel in line.[74]

This idealized picture of British practices only faintly resembles what actually happens in the Conservative party. Central Office has declared repeatedly that the adoption and readoption of candidates is a matter for the constituency associations, and in no case since 1945 have they made any visible attempt to induce any association to refuse readoption to an M.P. who has defied or resigned the whip.

The constituency associations and not Central Office, then, are the true guardians of the orthodoxy of Conservative M.P.s And their view of what is proper Conservative behavior in Parliament has not always agreed with that of Central Office and the Leader. Of the twelve known instances since 1945 in which constituency associa-

[74] See the works cited in Chapter 1, footnote 10.

tions have denied M.P.s readoption, in four cases the associations objected to their members' defiant votes in Parliament but in eight they objected to the members' personal inadequacies. In the twelve other instances of M.P.s who defied the whip and whose readoptions, according to the responsible-parties view should have been denied, no serious question was even raised in eleven cases, and the member survived the challenge in the twelfth.

The Conservative M.P.'s claim to readoption is well summed up by Nigel Nicolson, who has good reason to know that it is not absolute:

> An Association cannot continue to support a man who has been found guilty of drunkenness in charge of a car, or has involved himself in a discreditable affair with one of his constituents' wives. If he becomes too old, or is too obviously inefficient to do his job, and refuses to take a hint, then he must be gently but firmly eased out of his seat. If it is a question of persistent disagreement with the party on fundamental points of principle, then again there is every reason for the Association to indicate to the Member that he is unlikely to be readopted at the next election . . . .
>
> Of one thing [the Association] can be quite certain, that the decision will be left to them. Central Office will not interfere. However esteemed the Member may be by his party leaders or his colleagues in the House, he depends for his seat on the goodwill, and on the subscriptions and hard work, of his voluntary workers in the constituency. If he offends them by opposing his party, he must discuss the matter with them beforehand, and afterwards make the best case he can for acting as he did. If he fails to persuade a majority, and if the final decision is to come after as much time as possible has been given to considering it, and without calumny or other discreditable tactics, then he must accept his dismissal.[75]

---

[75] *People and Parliament,* pp. 58–59.

Chapter 4 | *Conservative*
            | *Candidatures and Constituencies,*
            | *1951–1964*

To conclude our discussion of Conservative candidate selection, in this chapter we shall describe certain characteristics of Conservative candidates and the constituencies in which they stood in the general elections of 1951, 1955, 1959, and 1964.[1] Our object is to discover what kinds of persons Conservative associations in different kinds of constituencies chose, and we shall offer some speculations about why some traits seem to have been valued over others.

This exercise cannot, however, provide an exact and comprehensive description of the criteria applied by local selectors. For one thing, the raw material for our statistical analysis consists entirely of publicly-reported facts: e.g., each candidate's age, previous parliamentary contests, formal education, occupation, and his constituency's geographical location, population density, and previous electoral performance. We have no comprehensive or systematic information about each candidate's speaking ability, demeanor, character, accent, and other such subjectively-measured but highly important qualities. What follows is therefore only part of the story.

[1] See the Appendix for a description of the materials and methods used in this chapter and in Chapters 7, 8, and 9.

In addition, even our publicly-reported information is far from complete. We know some things about all aspirants who were adopted, but in only a few instances do we have comparable information about the other contenders on the short lists rejected in their favor. And we know even less about the aspirants rejected in the screening processes which produced the short lists.

Nevertheless, a first step is better than none, and we may hope that what follows will at least prove useful for more complete analyses to come.

CHARACTERISTICS OF CANDIDATES: THE PUBLIC RECORD

It seems reasonable to assume that the better a Conservative association's chances appear of electing its candidate in the next election, the greater will be the number and variety of aspirants for its candidature and the better the selectors' opportunity to pick just the kind of candidate they want. Conversely, if the association's chances appear dim, fewer contenders will come forth, the selectors' range of choice will be correspondingly limited, and they will have to settle for the best—or least bad—person they can get.

Most politicians assess a constitutency's "winnability" by relating its poll in the preceding general election to their estimate of current trends in public opinion.[2] Thus most Conservatives feel a seat they hold is more winnable than one held by Labour; and a seat won by a majority of 20,000 is more winnable than one won by a majority of 1,000.

What traits, then, were characteristic of Conservative candidatures in the more and less winnable seats during this period?

INCUMBENCY

In Chapter 3 we noted the general presumption that a Conservative M.P. who so desires will be readopted for the next general elec-

---

[2] This is not to say that politicians pay no attention whatever to by-election results. The point is that most feel that while voters behave normally in general elections, many behave abnormally in by-elections. Hence politicians are likely to regard the results in the most recent general election as a better base for assessing the winnability of a seat in the next general election, though the by-election results may be taken as an important indicator of current trends in opinion in the country.

tion. The powerful impact of this presumption on the nature of candidatures[3] is evident in Table 4.1.

TABLE 4.1

WINNABILITY OF CONSTITUENCY RELATED TO INCUMBENCY OF CONSERVATIVE CANDIDATES

Incumbency of Candidate	Winnability of Constituency*				All Candidates
	High	Medium	Low	Other	
Held seat contested	88%	28%	0%	0%	48%
Held another seat	†	†	†	8	†
Lost seat contested in previous election	†	15	19	0	9
Lost another seat in previous election	7	22	11	28	11
First contest	5	35	70	64	32
	100%	100%	100%	100%	100%
Number of cases	1,153	560	735	47	2,495

* For the definitions of these winnability categories, see the Appendix.
† Less than 0.5 per cent (all percentages rounded to the nearest whole number).

Table 4.1 shows that almost nine out of every ten seats held by the Conservatives in 1951–64 were contested by their incumbents. Incumbency, therefore, is easily the most powerful single correlate of Conservative candidatures in the winnable constituencies. It was overborne only under such exceptional circumstances as those described in Chapter 3. It is, indeed, so powerful that we can best observe the impact of other characteristics by controlling incumbency. This we shall do by eliminating incumbents from all future tables and analyses.

PREVIOUS CONTESTS

There was a total of 2,495 Conservative candidatures in the four general elections we are considering. Of these, 32 per cent went to

---

[3] It should be emphasized that, unless specified otherwise, the tables in this and later chapters were compiled by assembling information about all the candidates and their constituencies in each of the four general elections, and then combining all four elections so as to make the most general statements possible. Thus the basic unit of analysis is the *candidature,* not the individual candidate. Any person who stood in more than one of the general elections appears more than once in each of the tables.

candidates making their first fights, and 20 per cent to persons who had had only losing contests previously. How the new candidates and previous losers were distributed among the more and less winnable seats is shown in Table 4.2.

TABLE 4.2

WINNABILITY OF CONSTITUENCY RELATED TO PREVIOUS ELECTORAL EXPERIENCE OF
CONSERVATIVE NON-INCUMBENT CANDIDATES

Previous Electoral Experience	Winnability of Constituency			
	High	Medium	Low	Other
First contest	42%	53%	67%	70%
One previous loss	29	32	24	20
Two or more previous losses	23	12	8	5
Former M.P.s	6	3	1	5
	100%	100%	100%	100%
Number of cases	133	364	771	43

Sixty-one per cent of all Conservative candidatures by non-incumbents went to candidates fighting their first contests; 26 per cent went to candidates who had had one previous loss; 11 per cent went to candidates with two or more previous losses; and the remaining 2 per cent went to former M.P.s trying to return to Westminster. Table 4.2 shows that the more experienced candidates were more strongly represented in the winnable seats than the less experienced, and that former M.P.s did best of all. Previous electoral experience, then, was significantly related to the desirability of the constituencies in which the non-incumbents stood.

SEX

We noted in Chapter 2 that Conservative Central Office has long expressed concern with what it regards as the unduly small proportion of candidatures going to women. We saw that its representatives have missed few opportunities to urge constituency associations not to discriminate against women. As Table 4.3 shows, however, their efforts do not appear to have had any notable success.

Of the 1,311 Conservative candidatures by non-incumbents, 1,240 (95 per cent) went to men, and only 71 (5 per cent) to women. The

TABLE 4.3

CONSERVATIVE WOMEN CANDIDATES, 1951–1964

Election	Total Candidates	Women Candidates	Per Cent of Women	Total New Candidates	New Women Candidates	Per Cent of Women
1951	617	23	3.7	166	3	1.8
1955	624	32	5.1	202	17	8.4
1959	625	27	4.3	219	12	5.5
1964	629	24	3.8	210	4	1.9

women, moreover, were somewhat more concentrated in the less winnable seats, although the difference is not statistically significant.[4] The comparison also shows that the women were slightly older than the men, a somewhat higher proportion had held office in local government councils, and a slightly higher proportion had some prior personal connections in the constituencies adopting them, but none of these differences was very great.

Only one new woman candidate was adopted in a safe seat. Mrs. Evelyn Emmet (now Lady Emmet), 56, was adopted for East Grinstead in 1955. She had been educated at St. Margaret's School, Bushey, and Lady Margaret Hall, Oxford; she had been a member of the London County Council from 1925 to 1934, and the West Sussex County Council from 1946 on; she had been a member of the British delegation to the United Nations General Assembly in 1952 and 1953; and in 1955 she was chairman of the National Union of Conservative and Unionist Associations. Such, it seems, were the credentials necessary to qualify a new woman candidate for a safe seat!

But the question remains: *Why* are so few women adopted by Conservative associations? In Chapter 2 we noted the widespread belief that women do not make good candidates—that they are ineffective campaigners, weak association leaders, and unacceptable to the numerous voters who feel that women should tend to their families and stay out of politics and other kinds of men's business. According to Lucille Iremonger, who experienced it in several ap-

---

[4] The familiar chi-square test has been used throughout to test the significance of relationships suggested by the tables. The conventional .05 level has been used as the minimum level of confidence. In this particular case, a 2×4 table relating the proportions of men and women in each of the categories of winnability yields a chi-square of 5.3694; with three degrees of freedom, this is significant at the .20 level—well below the .05 level, and therefore not statistically significant.

pearances before Conservative selection committees and conferences, this attitude underlies many of the questions a woman aspirant is asked by local selectors:

> Married women are asked why they contemplate neglecting (a) their husbands and (b) their children and grandchildren and (c) their homes. But single women have faced a blunt "Why aren't you married? Isn't it rather odd?" . . . . It is perplexing to a robust woman who has achieved the equivalent of driving in the Monte Carlo rally or running in the Olympics to be asked if after a train journey of six hours she would be fit to "do things" next day.[5]

Of course this is not a uniquely Conservative or even British attitude. Students of political attitudes in other countries have encountered a belief widespread among both men and women that politics is a dirty business quite unsuitable for women. And plunging into the rough and tumble of politics by standing for office seems to some the most unwomanly activity imaginable.[6]

There is some evidence that a Conservative woman will not draw as many votes as a Conservative man, but this could not possibly cost the party a seat in any constitutency with a Conservative majority of, say, 15,000 or more.[7] There were many such seats in the 1950's, some of them at each election were not pre–empted by an incumbent, and the party's national leaders were continually urging the adoption of more women. Yet, with one lone exception, the

---

[5] "Women on Approval," *Sunday Times* (London), April 26, 1964. For attacks on this point of view by some Conservative M.P.s, see letters to the *Times* (London) by H. J. Hulbert, March 13, 1952, p. 5, and by Viscountess Davidson, Mrs. Eveline Hill, Lady Tweedsmuir, and Miss Irene Ward, March 7, 1952, p. 7. See also the analysis by the *Times* political correspondent: *Times* (London), May 28, 1962, p. 5.

[6] Cf. Robert E. Lane, *Political Life* (Glencoe, Ill.: The Free Press, 1959), pp. 209–16; and Angus Campbell, Philip E. Converse, Warren E. Miller, and Donald E. Stokes, *The American Voter* (New York and London: John Wiley & Sons, Inc., 1960), pp. 484–85.

[7] The political journalist R. L. Leonard tabulated the results of the 1955 and 1959 general elections in every constituency where a woman candidate in 1955 was replaced by a man in 1959 and vice versa. He found no sex-related differences in the vote among Labour and Liberal candidates. However, in the constituencies where Conservative women replaced men the Conservative swing averaged 0.4 per cent against the national average swing of 1.2 per cent, while in those where Conservative men replaced women the swing averaged 1.6 per cent. He concludes, " . . . there is a small minority of normally Conservative voters who will not vote for a woman candidate," and "in the average constituency a women Conservative candidate might expect to receive about 300 votes less than a man": *Guide to the General Election* (London: Pan Books, Ltd., 1964), p. 97.

good seats were given to men. Why? A good part of the answer is provided by a member of the Bow Group, an association of young progressive Conservatives:

> Consisting, as it does, of people who give a great deal of their time to the association and in whose lives the association plays a large and emotional role, [a local executive council] is understandably preoccupied with results. An election is the culmination of years of work. Consequently, an increase in the majority is a triumph; a decrease is regarded as a failure.
>
> It follows, therefore, that the executive, even in a safe seat, will tend to select a good candidate rather than a promising Member. The applicant with the wrong accent or an unattractive wife, but with a brilliant organizing brain, is handicapped and may well be lost to Parliament because he appears unlikely to gain the extra (unnecessary) votes.[8]

If this is true, a woman applicant, however good an M.P. she might make, is likely to be passed over because many of the local executive council will believe she would cost them votes.

AGE

Conservative party workers generally testify that an aspirant's age affects his chances of adoption in several ways. If he is too young—say under thirty—he will not have had time to establish himself firmly in his business or profession, or to hold responsible positions in civic or party organizations, or to acquire the maturity and presence that comes when a man has won a respected place in the community. On the other hand, if he is too old—say in his late fifties or sixties—his health and energy are not likely to be equal to the demands of campaigning and providing other local services; and if elected his chances of playing a prominent role in Parliament are small.

Such considerations no doubt help explain the fact that only a few Conservative candidatures in the constituencies of high winnability went to persons under the age of thirty or over the age of fifty. Brief descriptions of the few so favored hint how they managed to overcome their age handicaps.

Those under thirty included:

Lord Balniel (28), adopted for the rural seat of Hertford in 1955; heir to the Earl of Crawford and Balcarres; educated at Eton and

---

[8] Victor Black, "Selecting for Safe Seats," *Crossbow*, IV (Autumn, 1960), 41–42.

Trinity College, Cambridge; former officer in the Grenadier Guards; employee of the Conservative Research Department, 1952–1955.

Robert Chichester-Clark (27), adopted for the Ulster seat of Londonderry in 1955; educated at the Royal Naval College, Dartmouth, and Magdalene College, Cambridge; his grandfather had been Member for Derry County and City; a journalist.

Timothy Kitson (28), adopted for the rural seat of Richmond (North Riding) in 1959; educated at Charterhouse and the Royal Agricultural College, Cirencester; member of the North Riding County Council and the Thirsk Rural District Council; an executive member of the National Farmers Union.

Stratton Mills (27), adopted for the Ulster seat of North Belfast in 1959; educated at Campbell College, Belfast, and Queen's University, Belfast; had been Vice-Chairman of the Federation of University Conservative and Unionist Associations; a solicitor.

Edward Taylor (27), adopted for the Cathcart division of Glasgow in 1964; educated at Glasgow High School and Glasgow University; President of the Glasgow Springburn Unionist Association; member of the Glasgow City Council since 1960.

Those over fifty included:

Mrs. Evelyn Emmet (56); see above.

Captain John Litchfield (56), adopted for the London borough of Chelsea in 1959; educated at the Royal Naval Colleges at Dartmouth and Osborne; Director of Naval Operations, 1953–1954; retired from the Royal Navy in 1955; member of the Kent County Council, 1955–1958.

Frank Lilley (52), adopted for Glasgow Kelvingrove in 1959; educated at Bellahouston Academy; elected to Glasgow Corporation in 1957; managing director of a firm of public works contractors.

Evelyn King (57), adopted for South Dorset in 1964; Labour M.P. for Penryn and Falmouth, 1945–1950; Parliamentary Secretary to the Ministry of Town and Country Planning; joined Conservatives in 1951; lost Southampton Itchen in 1959.

A. D. Dodds-Parker (55), adopted for Cheltenham in 1964; M.P. for Banbury, 1945–1959; did not stand in 1959; Undersecretary, Foreign Office, 1953–1954, 1955–1957; colonial civil service, 1930–1939.

The only non-incumbent candidate in his sixties adopted for a seat of high winnability was James Bias (60), who was chosen for the marginal seat of Glasgow Scotstoun (which he lost) in 1959; educated at Dobbie's Loan and St. George's Road schools, Glasgow; member of the Glasgow City Council since 1949; senior magistrate of Glasgow, 1958–1959; a personnel officer.

These miniature biographies suggest that each person overcame an age handicap of one sort or another to win a candidature in a safe seat. Chichester-Clark, Mills, Lilley, Bias, and Taylor all had strong connections in their constituencies. Kitson had been active in the leading farmers organization and had served on local government councils in the general area of his constituency. Mrs. Emmet had an outstanding record of local and national governmental service. Captain Litchfield had had a distinguished career in the Royal Navy and also experience in local government. King and Dodds-Parker were former ministers. And Lord Balniel was a scion of the aristocracy with an impeccable education and service in a national party agency. All, in short, had qualities which help explain why they managed to get good seats where most of their contemporaries failed to do so.

The age distribution of all non-incumbents given Conservative candidatures in this period is shown in Table 4.4.

TABLE 4.4

AGES OF CONSERVATIVE NON-INCUMBENT CANDIDATES RELATED TO
WINNABILITY OF CONSTITUENCY

Winnability of Constituency	Age Groups				
	21–29	30–39	40–49	50–59	60 and over
High	4%	10%	14%	9%	†
Medium	19	26	31	35	27%
Low	75	62	50	51	73
Other	2	2	5	5	0
	100%	100%	100%	100%	100%
Index of winnability*	−71	−52	−36	−42	−73
Number of cases	165	522	382	205	37

* Computed by subtracting the per cent in the high-winnability category from the per cent in the low-winnability category. The lower the index number the higher the proportion of the candidates in the category in the most desirable constituencies.

† Less than 0.5 per cent (all percentages rounded to the nearest whole number).

The largest proportion of the candidatures (40 per cent) were by candidates in their thirties, the second largest (28 per cent) by those in their forties, and the third largest (16 per cent) by those in their fifties. Thirteen per cent went to persons under thirty, and only 3 per cent to persons sixty or more. Table 4.4 shows some tendency for the proportion of candidates in the more winnable seats to increase in each successively older group from the twenties to the forties, and to decline for those in their fifties and sixties.

It may appear that this tendency merely reflects the fact that older persons have had more time in which to acquire the electoral experience which, as we noted previously, is highly related to candidatures in the more winnable seats. Certainly the new candidates were younger (58 per cent under forty) than the previous losers (38 per cent under forty). Yet when we hold constant the factor of previous electoral experience, we find that the age-to-winnability relationships shown in Table 4.4 persist among both new candidates and experienced candidates alike. They also persist when we hold constant such other traits of "civic visibility" as having held office on a local government council, and having held local or national party office.

There was, then, a distinct and apparently independent relationship between the candidates' ages and the desirability of the constituencies in which they were adopted—a relationship which was not merely a reflection of other factors.

EDUCATION

In most western countries, reaching the higher levels of formal education is one of the principal stepping-stones for entering at least the lower echelons of political leadership. This may be because the more highly educated acquire more of the learning and intellectual skills leadership requires. Or it may be that attending a particular university or other school gives one a circle of influential friends—an "old boy net"—spread about in strategic positions ready to tip him off where candidatures are available and to press for his adoption.

The British sociologist W. L. Guttsman concludes that this is particularly important in British social and political circles:

The reinforcing of initial material advantages by a restrictive and exclusive educational system and the selective social ties which may be formed in the "old school" or an Oxbridge Junior Common Room is probably more than anything else responsible for the "closed" character of British élite groups. Lord Maugham, a former Lord Chancellor, who had only been to a minor public school, thought that men who had been educated at one of the well known institutions had gained no advantage over him except one, but one which was very important. "Wherever they go they find friends, probably wearing the same 'school tie' to give them a helping hand; and in many cases their kindly words spoken in time, may make all the difference between success and failure."[9]

How, then, was education related to Conservative candidate selection in the post-war era?

1. *Conservative Candidates and the General Public*

The non-incumbents who received Conservative candidatures in this period had a far higher level of formal education than the British general public. For example, only 6 per cent of all British boys between the ages of twelve and seventeen attended the 133 fee-paying public schools; but public school products filled no less than 50 per cent of the Conservative candidatures. For another example, only 4 to 8 per cent (depending on whether teacher-training and technical colleges are classified as universities) of British schoolchildren went to universities, but university products filled 50 per cent of the candidatures.[10]

Similar though smaller disparities between political élites and general publics obtain in other modern democracies,[11] but with British Conservatives the interesting question is whether some kinds of education are more valued than other kinds.

2. *Attendance at Public Schools*

It is said that Conservative local activists are often more concerned that their candidates have the right social background ("come from the right stable" is an expression previously noted) than that they have high academic distinction or highly developed intellectual skills. Attending a public school—especially a high-prestige school such as Eton, Harrow, Winchester, and perhaps fifteen or twenty others—is widely regarded as the best way to acquire

---

[9] W. L. Guttsman, *The British Political Elite* (London: MacGibbon & Kee, 1963), pp. 383–84.

[10] The figures for the general public are given in Anthony Sampson, *Anatomy of Britain* (London: Hodder & Stoughton, 1962), pp. 184, 195.

[11] Cf. Donald R. Matthews, *The Social Background of Political Decision-Makers* (Garden City, L. I.: Doubleday & Co., Inc., 1954), Table 6, p. 29.

this background. The fortunate 6 per cent who attend public schools are believed to acquire a manner of speaking, a circle of friends, and an outlook that gives them a great advantage over their contemporaries who attend the state-supported grammar schools and, even more, those who attend secondary modern, comprehensive, or other secondary schools.

Of the 1,311 Conservative candidatures we are considering, 30 per cent went to persons who had attended state-supported elementary or secondary schools only, 20 per cent to those who had attended secondary schools and universities, 20 per cent to those who had attended public schools only, and 30 per cent to those who had attended public schools and universities. If the foregoing estimate of the role of public school attendance is correct, we would expect candidates who had attended public schools to be better represented in the more winnable seats than those who had not. Table 4.5 shows that this was indeed the case.

TABLE 4.5

ATTENDANCE AT PUBLIC SCHOOLS BY CONSERVATIVE NON-INCUMBENT
CANDIDATES RELATED TO WINNABILITY OF CONSTITUENCY

Winnability of Constituency	Education			
	Elem. or Second. Only	Secondary and University	Public School Only	Public School and University
High	3%	6%	16%	16%
Medium	29	28	30	25
Low	66	61	53	54
Other	2	5	1	5
	100%	100%	100%	100%
Index of winnability	−63	−55	−37	−38
Number of cases	391	264	262	394

Table 4.5 shows that the candidates who had attended public schools were substantially better represented in the more desirable seats than those who attended other secondary schools. It also shows that while the secondary-and-university group fared better than the secondary-only group, the public-school-and-university group fared about the same as the public-school-only group.

3. *Secondary-University Combinations*

Whatever may be the academic justification, most observers would surely agree with Anthony Sampson's statement that in Britain the only distinction among universities that counts socially is that "between Oxford and Cambridge, and the Rest." "Less than one per cent of Britain's population go to Oxbridge," he continues, "but, once there, they are wooed by industry and government. A BA (Oxon) or BA (Cantab.) is quite different from an ordinary BA."[12]

Oxford and Cambridge were once the exclusive domain of public school graduates. The post-war "meritocratic revolution" in British education, however, has extended access to the two ancient universities to the point where, in 1957, it was estimated that 55 per cent of Oxford undergraduates and 45 per cent of Cambridge undergraduates had not attended public schools.[13] Accordingly, if Conservative local activists valued an "Oxbridge" education as much as they do attendance at a public school, we would expect persons with a secondary-school-and-Oxbridge educational combination to get a higher proportion of the winnable constituencies than those with secondary-only or secondary-and-other-university combinations. And we would also expect the public-school-and-Oxbridge group to do better than either the public-school-only group or the public-school-and-other-university group. Table 4.6 shows that this was not the case, however.

Table 4.6 shows that the public-school-only group had nearly as high a proportion in the more winnable seats as those who went on to Oxbridge from public schools. On the other hand, the public-school-and-other-university group did somewhat better than the secondary-and-Oxbridge group. Hence the general impression emerging from the data in Tables 4.5 and 4.6 is that Conservative local selectors viewed formal education more as a badge of social status than as an index of intellectual achievement.

OCCUPATION

An aspirant's occupation can affect his chances of being adopted in several ways. For one, an occupation which permits the adjust-

---

[12] Sampson, *Anatomy of Britain*, p. 198.
[13] *Ibid.*, p. 199.

TABLE 4.6

SECONDARY-UNIVERSITY COMBINATIONS OF CONSERVATIVE NON-INCUMBENT CANDIDATES
RELATED TO WINNABILITY OF CONSTITUENCY

Winnability of Constituency	Secondary-University Combination					
	Secondary Only	Secondary and Univ. Other than Oxbridge	Second-ary and Oxbridge	Public School Only	Pub. Sch. and Univ. Other than Oxbridge	Pub. Sch. and Oxbridge
High	3%	3%	12%	16%	13%	17%
Medium	29	32	21	30	18	26
Low	66	59	66	53	65	51
Other	2	6	1	1	4	6
	100%	100%	100%	100%	100%	100%
Index of winnability	−63	−56	−54	−37	−52	−34
Number of cases	391	181	81	262	71	325

ment of his working hours to political needs is clearly preferable to one which demands his presence for a fixed forty or forty-five hours a week. For another, an occupation which requires and enhances skills useful for politics (e.g., public speaking, ability to get along with people) is preferable to one which requires skills of little relevance to politics (e.g., mathematical aptitude or musical talent). For yet another, some occupations are likely to strike the selectors simply as more "suitable" than others (e.g., barristers more than carnival barkers, manufacturers more than junk dealers); and in Britain as in most western societies a man's occupation, along with his education, is the principal index of his social status.[14] And for still another, an occupation which puts an aspirant in constant contact with politically active and influential people is preferable to one that keeps him confined to his laboratory or lathe or in contact with people uninterested in politics.

In most modern democracies, accordingly, lawyers, businessmen,

---

[14] For the roles of education and occupation as indices of social class in Britain, see Jean Blondel, *Voters, Parties, and Leaders* (London: Penguin Books, Ltd, 1963), pp. 26–42. See also Guttsman, *The British Political Elite*, p. 27.

teachers, and journalists have provided a large share of political candidates and officeholders, while physicians, scientists, and factory workers have provided a much smaller share.[15] Table 4.7 shows how these factors operated in the selection of Conservative candidates in this period.

TABLE 4.7

OCCUPATIONAL DISTRIBUTION OF CONSERVATIVE CANDIDATURES BY NON-INCUMBENTS
COMPARED WITH THAT OF THE BRITISH POPULATION*

Occupational Category	British Population	Conservative Candidatures
Proprietor, managerial	13%	39%
Professional	7	37
White-collar	11	19
Intermediate	5	2
Manual, wage-earning	64	3
	100%	100%
Number of cases	34,200,000	1,311

* The figures for the general population are taken from Robert R. Alford, *Party and Society* (Chicago: Rand, McNally & Company, 1963), Table 6-2, p. 128.

Table 4.7 shows that blue-collar manual workers were greatly underrepresented among British Conservative candidates, as among political leaders in other democratic countries. The proprietor-managerial and professional categories were substantially overrepresented in Conservative candidatures, and the white-collar and intermediate categories were represented approximately as in the general population.

When we distribute the candidatures among more narrowly defined occupational categories and rank-order each category according to its proportion of high-winnability to low-winnability constituencies, as in Table 4.8, several interesting patterns emerge.

[15] Cf. Max Weber, "Politics as a Vocation," in *Essays in Sociology*, translated and edited by Hans H. Gerth and C. Wright Mills (New York: Oxford University Press, 1946), pp. 83 ff; Matthews, *Social Background of Political Decision Makers;* Seymour Martin Lipset, *Political Man* (Garden City, L.I.: Doubleday & Co., Inc., 1960), pp. 198–99; and Lane, *Political Life*, pp. 331–34.

TABLE 4.8

WINNABILITY OF CONSTITUENCY RELATED TO OCCUPATIONS OF
CONSERVATIVE NON-INCUMBENT CANDIDATES

Occupation	Index of Winnability *	Number of Cases	Per Cent of All Cases
Farmer	−12	72	5
Civil servant	−15	20	2
Private means	−27	11	1
Political organizer	−28	11	1
Journalist, publicist, author	−39	54	5
Barrister	−40	174	13
Small business proprietor	−44	102	8
Armed services	−44	43	3
Solicitor	−49	101	8
Company executive or director	−51	328	25
Teacher	−54	86	6
Doctor, dentist, or other professional	−57	32	3
Housewife	−59	18	1
White-collar	−60	124	9
Manual worker	−66	40	3
Chartered accountant	−71	41	3
Civil engineer or surveyor	−73	34	3
Student	−92	13	1
Not ascertained	—	7	—
		1,311	100

* Computed by determining the percentages of each occupation in each category of constituency winnability, and subtracting the per cent in the "high" category from the per cent in the "low" category.

Table 4.8 shows that a quarter of the candidatures went to company executives and directors, another 21 per cent to barristers and solicitors, and another 9 per cent to clerical workers of one kind or another. Is also shows that civil servants and farmers were distributed far more heavily among constituencies of high winnability than were persons with other occupations.

Examples of persons in the "private means" category adopted in constituencies of high winnability include:

Viscount Lambton, adopted for Berwick-upon-Tweed in 1951; heir to the Earl of Durham; educated at Harrow; two previous contests in northeastern constituencies; occupation given as "landowner" in *Times* biography.

Major William Anstruther-Gray, adopted for Berwick and East Lothian in 1951; former M.P. for North Lanark, which he lost in 1945; educated at Eton and Christ Church, Oxford; served in Coldstream Guards; occupation given as "landowner" in *Times.*

Miss Harvie Anderson, adopted for East Renfrewshire in 1959; three previous losing contests in Scottish constituencies; member of the Stirling County Council since 1945; occupation given as "landowner and factor" in *Times.*

The term "farmer" may be a somewhat misleading label for the occupational group with the highest proportion in constituencies of high winnability. Few of the candidates placed in this category were quite in the dirt farmer or yeoman class. For example, eight of the nine new candidates in safe seats whose occupations were given as "farmers" had attended public schools, and two had gone on to Oxford or Cambridge. Three had been members of the executive council of the National Farmers Union, and three had served on rural district councils; only Anthony Bourne-Arton, adopted and elected at Darlington in 1959, was a "farmer" selected by a winnable urban constituency.

Conservative selectors in the vacant winnable rural seats, then, tended to pick men with strong farm connections, while the selectors in the vacant winnable urban seats tended to look with favor on journalists, company executives or directors, and former career officers in the civil or armed services. All of the latter occupations permit the desired flexibility of working hours, all are prestigious, and all are likely to elicit and enhance the personal qualities and skills the selectors look for in their candidates.

EXPERIENCE IN LOCAL GOVERNMENT,
CIVIC ORGANIZATIONS, AND PARTY OFFICES

The biographical information about the contenders on short lists given to most selection conferences by association chairmen (see Chapter 3) almost always includes the local government councils on which they have served, the civic and religious organizations in which they have been active, and the local and national party offices they have held. Such information would seem to be highly relevant to the contenders' qualifications for candidature. Having served on a local council is good evidence that an aspirant has a practical knowledge of governmental matters, and it also proves that he can win an election. Activity in nonpartisan civic and religious organizations shows commendable civic spirit and also endows him with what may be called "civic visibility." Having held a local or national party office not only shows that a contender has served the cause but also that his fellow partisans have thought well of him.

Accordingly, it seems reasonable to expect that a substantial proportion of the non-incumbent candidates would have had one or more of these qualifications, and that those who had them would be better represented in the more winnable seats than those who had not.

The information in Table 4.9, however, shows that no such tendencies were evident in this period.

TABLE 4.9

EXPERIENCE OF CONSERVATIVE NON-INCUMBENT CANDIDATES IN LOCAL GOVERNMENT, CIVIC ORGANIZATIONS, AND PARTY OFFICE RELATED TO WINNABILITY OF CONSTITUENCY

Winnability of Constituency	Prior Service on Local Govt. Council		Prior Activity in Civic or Religious Org.		Prior Local or National Party Office	
	Some	None	Some	None	Some	None
High	10%	10%	16%	10%	13%	9%
Medium	29	27	36	27	24	29
Low	59	59	46	60	60	58
Other	2	4	2	3	3	4
	100%	100%	100%	100%	100%	100%
Index of winnability	−49	−49	−30	−50	−47	−48
Number of cases	477	834	88	1,223	342	969

Almost two-thirds of the candidatures went to persons who had held no local government office, almost three-quarters to persons who had held no party office, and over 90 per cent to persons who had not been prominent in civic or religious organizations. The few candidates active in civic and religious organizations got better seats than the others, but evidently most Conservative selectors did not insist that their candidates have any of these sorts of experience.

PERSONAL CONNECTIONS IN THE CONSTITUENCY

1. *In General*

One of the questions about candidate selection most widely debated by observers of and participants in British politics is to what extent and under what circumstances having personal connections in a constituency helps a nonincumbent win its candidature. A number of Conservative leaders interviewed by the author took a position similar to that put in a letter to the *Times* by a member of the South Hammersmith association:

Conservatives, and the "floating voters" we have to win, are not cattle to be herded to market by any old drover who turns up. To change the metaphor, Central Office, which includes several noted sportsmen, should appreciate the virtue of horses for courses. The man to choose is the man most likely to win. Other things being equal, a man who knows the place and the people, a man with local ties, is a more likely winner than a stranger. The old argument that a member is not a delegate has been overdone. Nothing contributes more to despondency and slackness in local organisation than a succession of "carpet-bagger" candidates; the feeling that this newcomer, foisted on us from goodness-knows-where, is not intended to win but is merely having a trial gallop to fit him for the real race elsewhere. Conservatives work better for a man they know; a man who knows them; not a man they only see in the fleeting hubbub of the election.[16]

Lord Kilmuir has put the contrary position in these words:

One of the great weaknesses of the Labour Party has been its fondness for local members, with the result that a great number of somewhat tedious local worthies or party hacks have been given safe seats while far abler younger men and women have been ignored, to the great detriment of the Parliamentary Labour Party and the House of Commons as a whole. To my dismay, I have seen the Conservative Party commit the same error. Very few of the new Members who entered the Commons in 1955 and 1959 had achieved a reputation outside Westminster in any field, and far too many of them were obscure local citizens with obscure local interests, incapable—and indeed downright reluctant —to think on a national or international scale. . . . What made the situation particularly annoying was that many excellent candidates, who would have made first-class Members and probably Ministers, were left to fight utterly hope-

---

[16] R. F. Johnson, *Times* (London), March 21, 1952, p. 7. For similar views see William Rees-Mogg, "The Selection of Parliamentary Candidates: The Conservative Party," *Political Quarterly*, XXX (July-September, 1959), 215–19, at p. 218; and Ivor Bulmer-Thomas, *The Party System in Great Britain* (London: Phoenix House, Ltd., 1953), p. 209.

less seats not once, but two and even in some cases three times, while the safe seats went to men of far lower calibre. This was to cost the party dear.[17]

Entirely aside from the question of whether local candidates *should* be preferred to outsiders, the fact is that being a local man is by no means invariably an asset. A leading Central Office official put it this way to the author:

> Whatever people may say, the fact is that only outstanding local candidates get selected. There is no mystery about why this is so. After all, if a person is not outstanding, it is a handicap, not an asset, to be well known locally. Most selection committees prefer evils they do not know to evils they know only too well. And if you have two or more local contenders you can create a good deal of ill will locally by choosing one over the others. In a situation like that it is much better to pass over *all* local contenders and adopt an outsider. So we always recommend that all local contenders be interviewed, but we are seldom downcast when an association adopts an outsider.

There is little doubt that many Conservative associations say they want a local man, and it is not uncommon for them to stipulate local residence as one of the prime conditions for their candidatures. It is quite common, moreover, for selection committees and executive councils to ask outsiders if they would be willing to move to the constituency if adopted and elected.

But what did Conservative selectors actually do in this period? Table 4.10 gives part of the answer.

Over two-thirds of the candidatures in this period were given to persons who had no discernible personal connections in the constituencies in which they were adopted. Table 4.10 shows a small but significant difference in the two groups' distributions among the more and less desirable constituencies. Indeed, when we turn the table on its side to see how the constituency connections in each category of winnability were distributed, we find that only 22 per cent of those in the high-winnability category went to candidates with local connections, while 36 per cent of those in the medium-winnability category and 32 per cent of those in the low-winnability category went to locally-connected candidates. In part this no doubt reflects a number of instances in which Conservative associations in hopeless constituencies were unable to persuade attractive outsiders to stand and had to turn to local men. The latter stood, not with

---

[17] *Political Adventure: The Memoirs of the Earl of Kilmuir* (London: Weidenfeld and Nicolson, 1964), pp. 158–59.

TABLE 4.10

PERSONAL CONSTITUENCY CONNECTIONS* OF CONSERVATIVE NON-INCUMBENT
CANDIDATES RELATED TO WINNABILITY OF CONSTITUENCY

Winnability of Constituency	Local Connections	
	Some	None
High	7%	12%
Medium	31	26
Low	59	59
Other	3	3
	100%	100%
Index of winnability	−52	−47
Number of cases	425	886

* This includes having been educated in the constituency, making a living there, holding a trade union or trade association office there, holding a local government office there, or being the child or spouse of the present or former M.P. The information is collected from published sources, which usually do not reveal to the uninformed outsider connections with locally prominent families. Accordingly, the figures in Table 4.10 probably understate rather than exaggerate the incidence of local connections among Conservative candidates.

any hope of winning or even of using their candidatures as stepping-stones to better constituencies later, but simply to "show the flag" at home. It is also consistent with the impression of the Central Office official quoted above that many local associations with wide ranges of choice in winnable constituencies deliberately pass over all local contenders in favor of outsiders.

Do some areas prefer local candidates more than other areas? Several persons the author interviewed agreed with Sir Herbert Williams's view that "in urban areas there is usually a preference for strangers rather than local people," while "rural constituencies, on the other hand, tend to prefer a person who lives in the constituency . . . ."[18] Large cities, they reason, are amorphous social agglomerations that inspire among their residents little feeling of local identity or pride; hence they have no particular interest in adopting local candidates. On the other hand, many rural constituencies have maintained their identities for centuries and have developed strong feelings of local patriotism; hence they are likely to

[18] Sir Herbert Williams, "The Member of Parliament and his constituency," *Parliamentary Affairs*, I (Spring, 1948), 49–55.

choose candidates who know and understand local people and problems because they have lived and worked with them.

This theory certainly seems plausible. Yet when we divide the candidatures by local connections and population types of the constituencies, as in Table 4.11, we find that it is not supported by the facts.

TABLE 4.11

POPULATION TYPE OF CONSTITUENCY RELATED TO PERSONAL CONSTITUENCY
CONNECTIONS OF CONSERVATIVE NON-INCUMBENT CANDIDATES

Local Connections	Population Type of Constituency*									
	London	Other Metropoiltan	Other Urban	Semi-rural	Semi-rural, Mining	Rural	Rural, Mining	Scot. Burghs	Scot. County	Ulster
Some	21%	63%	30%	29%	14%	25%	21%	57%	28%	54%
None	79	37	70	71	86	75	79	43	72	46
	100%	100%	100%	100%	100%	100%	100%	100%	100%	100%
Number of cases	135	116	665	21	22	75	94	87	83	13

* For definitions of these categories, see the Appendix.

Table 4.11 shows that the smallest proportions of candidatures given to locally-connected candidates were in the mining seats, most of which had consistently large Labour majorities during this period; evidently, then, there was little local "flag-showing" in these seats. Only 25 per cent of the candidatures in the rural constituencies went to local men. And strikingly larger proportions went to locally-connected candidates in Ulster, the Scottish Burghs, and the largest English and Welsh cities other than London. The exact figures for each of the latter are shown in Table 4.12.

Table 4.12 shows that in eight of the ten largest English, Welsh, and Scottish cities (Bristol and Swansea were the exceptions) from 56 per cent to 94 per cent of the candidatures by non-incumbents went to persons with local connections. In all other types of constituencies outside Ulster the proportions ranged from 14 per cent to 30 per cent. Accordingly, it is clear that since 1945 the strongholds of

TABLE 4.12

PERSONAL CONSTITUENCY CONNECTIONS OF CONSERVATIVE NON-INCUMBENT CANDIDATES
IN LARGEST CITIES

City	Number of Candidates	Candidates with Constituency Connections	Per Cent with Constituency Connections
England			
Birmingham	30	19	63
Bristol	16	4	25
Leeds	17	10	59
Liverpool	13	10	77
Manchester	22	16	73
Sheffield	17	16	94
Wales			
Cardiff	9	5	56
Swansea	6	2	33
Scotland			
Edinburgh	14	9	64
Glasgow	39	32	82

"localism" in Conservative candidate selection have not been, as some suppose, the rural constituencies but rather the metropolitan constituencies.

2. *"Hereditary Seats"*

A special variation on the local-connections theme is the "hereditary seat"—a safe constituency which has given its candidatures to members of the same eminent family for generation after generation.

Perhaps the best known instance in recent years has been a seat in the Essex resort of Southend-on-Sea, which has been a "fief" of the Guinness brewing family for almost half a century. Rupert E. C. L. Guinness represented Southend from 1918 to 1927, when he became the second Earl of Iveagh. The candidature and the seat were then turned over to the Countess of Iveagh until 1935, when they were passed on to Sir Henry Channon, who had married the second Earl's daughter in 1933. Sir Henry held the seat and, after division, Southend West until his death in January, 1959. For the ensuing by-election the local association adopted Sir Henry's son, Henry Paul Guinness Channon, who, at the age of twenty-three became the youngest member of the House. After Channon had taken his seat, Sir Winston Churchill reportedly said, "When I look around these benches, I cannot resist the conclusion that Guinness is good for you!"

Comparable instances include: Hornsey, which after Sir David Gammans's death in 1957, adopted Lady Gammans—not without some protest[19]—as his successor; North Antrim, which up to 1959 had been held by a member of the O'Neil family for ninety-one of its hundred and one years; Hemel Hempstead, which, when its member, John Davidson, was made a peer in 1937, adopted his wife as his successor; and Thirsk and Malton, held by Sir Edmund Turton from 1914 to 1929, and by his nephew, Robert, ever since.

3. *Controversies over Local Candidates*

Many Conservative constituency associations have a faction which insists that the parliamentary candidate be a local person. In many others local candidates thought to be particularly suitable have been pressed from time to time. In a great many such instances the local contenders have been passed over in favor of outsiders, and on some occasions the decisions have been publicly challenged, sometimes successfully sometimes not.

An example of a successful challenge came in 1953 when the Birmingham Edgbaston association selected a candidate for the by-election necessitated by the elevation of their Member to the peerage. A majority of the executive council reportedly favored Miss (now Dame) Edith Pitt, a prominent member of the Birmingham City Council and a well-regarded leader in the city's Conservative circles. The selection committee, however, passed her over in favor of Colonel Douglas Glover, a member of the party's national executive with a distinguished war record. The executive council reluctantly adopted their recommendation by a narrow margin, but the general meeting of the association reversed the decision and adopted Miss Pitt instead.[20]

An example of an unsuccessful challenge came in the same year when the Crosby association's executive council passed over a prom-

---

[19] See the *Hornsey Journal*, June 7, 1957, p. 7.

[20] *Birmingham Mail*, June 10, 1953, p. 1; June 12, 1953, p. 1. Colonel Glover was adopted and elected Member for Ormskirk at another by-election later in the same year. A similar controversy occurred in Chippenham in 1962, and in Altrincham and Sale in 1964: see the *Sunday Times* (London), August 19, 1962, p. 5, and the *Times* (London), December 18, 1964, p. 5.

inent local aspirant, Councillor J. A. Freeman, in favor of London solicitor R. G. Page. Councillor Freeman challenged the decision on the ground that "a local man is better able to represent the interests of the constituents of the division," but the association meeting accepted Page. Freeman stood in the by-election as an independent Conservative, but Page was elected comfortably and Freeman lost his deposit.[21]

One of the most acerbic disputes took place in Beckenham in 1957.[22] This safe Conservative seat was vacated in January when its incumbent was elevated to the peerage. A faction in the association publicly urged that a local man be selected, and the name most often mentioned was that of David Cobbold, the association chairman. One member of his faction told the local newspaper that while it no doubt had been an honor to have the previous member, P. G. Buchan-Hepburn, in the Cabinet, it had also prevented him from working effectively for Beckenham's interests. The next member, he said, should be a local man and a backbencher.[23] However, another faction publicly declared that if Cobbold were adopted, they would put up another local man as an Independent candidate at the next election.[24]

The split over which local man should be adopted encouraged the selection committee to pass over both and choose an outsider. They finally recommended only one name to the executive council: Philip Goodhart, a London journalist of American antecedents. When the executive proposed Goodhart's name to the association meeting, a member of the Cobbold faction, Councillor G. I. White, objected:

Mr. Goodhart has a very well-off father and was born and educated in America. He is still an American citizen and his wife, born and brought up in America, has strong American connections. A man with such a background cannot be naturalised to English ideals. Let us reject him! I have lived in the United States and I know their way of life. It is not our way and they do not know our way.[25]

---

[21] *Crosby Herald*, October 10, 1953, p. 1; October 16, 1953, p. 1; November 6, 1953, p. 1. A similar episode took place in Tonbridge in 1956: see the *Tonbridge Free Press*, May 11, 1956, p. 1; May 18, 1956, p. 1.

[22] For further discussion of this episode, see p. 59, footnote 3.

[23] *Beckenham Journal*, January 26, 1957, pp. 1, 8.

[24] *Ibid.*, February 2, 1957, p. 1.

[25] *Ibid.*, March 9, 1957, pp. 3–4.

A member of the executive then produced a birth certificate proving that Goodhart had been born on Wigmore Street in St. Marylebone, and thus was a bona fide Englishman. After some further discussion of whether an outsider should be selected, Goodhart was adopted, and the Cobbold faction, not without some ill humor, accepted the verdict.

4. *Localism in Conservative Candidate Selection: A Summary*

Nothing in the foregoing discussion is inconsistent with the common and correct belief that localism plays a far smaller role in Conservative candidate selection than it does in the nominating processes of the United States. Yet the vision of some analysts (see Chapter 1) that each local association looks over a national pool of candidates and, with guidance from Central Office and without reference to local connections, picks the best qualified is far from accurate. After all, Table 4.10 shows that almost a third of all the candidatures by non-incumbents from 1951 to 1964 went to candidates with personal connections in the constituencies for which they were adopted. And there is good reason to believe that in many more instances local contenders were seriously considered and their local connections regarded as assets overborne by even more desirable qualities of outside contenders.

We conclude, accordingly, that there is more localism in Conservative association politics and candidate selection than is commonly supposed, and that, while local connections are not decisive in nearly so many instances as in the United States, they play a role of considerable importance in the selection of Conservative parliamentary candidates.

CHARACTERISTICS OF CANDIDATES: OTHER FACTORS

The evidence used in the preceding discussion has consisted of certain publicly recorded facts about the Conservative candidates adopted for the general elections of 1951–1964. It has permitted a kind of quantitative analysis that raises its conclusions at least one level above opinion, speculation, and guesswork. If we were to stop here, however, we would leave out of account a number of factors emphasized by most of the national and local Conservative leaders the author interviewed. The most prominent factors are as follows.

IDEOLOGY

Most Conservative leaders testify that ideology plays only a minor role in most local choices of candidates. To be sure, many of the questions asked in the selection committees' interviews and raised from the floor during selection conferences are concerned with the contenders' views on the issues of the day. But most selectors seem to be more concerned with how ably the aspirant deals with the questions than with measuring his answers against some checklist of the right ones.

This view is supported by John Biffen's study of the attitudes of Conservative selectors in eight West-Midlands constituency associations. Only a small minority of his respondents said that the policy views of an aspirant would even affect—let alone determine—their votes. Biffen concluded:

> Constituency associations are rarely concerned with the finer points of party policy. Parliamentary candidates are frequently chosen on an almost charmingly non-political basis. Willingness to live in the constituency or to support the activities of the association, is often of much more moment than a "correct" attitude to Schedule A or the Common Market.[26]

RELIGION

Although they deplore it and fight it wherever they can, Conservative Central Office officials freely admit that there is considerable anti-Semitism in some local associations. It is sometimes strong enough, they say, to make impossible the adoption of a Jew, however well qualified he may be on other grounds. Aspirants of Jewish origin who have joined the Established Church are in a somewhat better position than those who have clung to Judaism, but they have by no means shed all their handicaps. At the present writing there are only two Conservative M.P.s of the Jewish faith: Sir Henry d'Avigdor-Goldsmid and Sir Keith Joseph, both of whom are members of old, well-established families and unusually able and attractive men.

---

[26] "The Constituency Leaders," *Crossbow*, IV (Autumn, 1960), 27–32. Mr. Biffen, a young Central Office employee and adherent of the party's progressive wing, was elected Member for Oswestry in the 1961 by-election and re-elected in 1964.

This kind of anti-Semitism, of course, operates so far removed from the public gaze that there have been very few instances in which there was even a public hint that it was at work.[27] Central Office has nevertheless publicly acknowledged its existence by including the following injunction in its official pamphlet on candidate selection:

> The Candidate's religion is not stated on the biography supplied by Central Office. This information can, however, be obtained by application by the Constituency Chairman or Chairman of the Selection Committee, if required. Religious prejudices should in no circumstances be allowed to sway the judgment of the Selection Committee.[28]

SOCIAL POSITION

In 1962, Sir Reginald Manningham-Buller, Conservative Member for South Northamptonshire, was made Lord Chancellor. As the local association began its search for his replacement, a reporter summarized the agent's views about the qualities they sought:

> The person chosen, he says, should be (a) local; (b) knowledgeable about farming and industry and (c) a member of a good old county family. Not surprisingly the Tories expect to spend several weeks looking for someone who meets these specifications and who will be a good candidate as well![29]

This is a balder statement of priorities than one usually encounters, but it lends credence to the widespread belief that many Conservative associations put having the right kind of social position above most other criteria—a belief also supported by our findings on the educational and occupational backgrounds of the candidates (see above). This tendency explains the failure of Central Office,

[27] One such episode evidently took place in the East division of Harrow in the late 1940's. F. Ashe Lincoln, a K.C. and a Jew, had fought the seat in the 1945 general election, but was passed over for readoption in 1948. Several association members publicly charged that Lincoln had been pushed out because he was a Jew, but he made no public comment and accepted his dismissal quietly: *Harrow Observer*, November 11, 1948, p. 1. In 1962, however, it was announced that he had joined the Labour party and was available to stand as a Labour candidate: *Daily Telegraph* (London), June 18, 1962, p. 7.

[28] *Notes on Procedure for the Adoption of Conservative Candidates in England and Wales* (published by the Conservative and Unionist Central Office, 1960), p. 8.

[29] J. W. M. Thompson. *Evening Standard* (London), July 26, 1962, p. 7. It is interesting to note that the candidate actually chosen fulfilled most of these requirements excellently: Mr. Arthur Jones, an estate agent, company director, and farmer in North Bedfordshire, was a former mayor of adjacent Bedford and member of the Bedfordshire County Council; he had stood unsuccessfully for the adjoining constituency of Wellingborough in 1955, and was well known in South Northamptonshire.

noted in Chapter 2, to get more trade unionists adopted in winnable seats. Most association activists have no particular prejudice
against trade unionists as such—indeed, many belong to trade
unions themselves. But they do have in mind a certain picture of
how a Conservative candidate should look and talk; and since few
trade unionists have attended Eton or Christ Church, they simply
do not fit the picture and so are passed over. The local selectors
almost always agree with Central Office's general view that more
trade unionists should be adopted; but evidently most also decide
that this or that particular trade unionist simply is not the right
kind of person for their particular constituency.

In many Conservative associations, as we noted in Chapter 3,
many of the activists are lower-middle-class small merchants and
skilled-worker trade unionists. Yet only rarely do they choose someone like themselves as a candidate. Evidently most believe that it
takes someone *better* than themselves to look and sound as a Conservative candidate should. If this be called snobbery, they do not
seem to mind very much.[30]

CHARACTER

Central and local party workers told the author repeatedly that
what Conservative selectors want most of all is a man of *character*.
By this, they said, they did not mean a man of great brilliance or
eloquence or outstanding success in his business or profession. They
meant, rather, a man who could be depended upon in a tight spot;
a man of good judgment and coolness in time of crisis; a man loyal
to his friends and to his party; a man, in short, who is "solid," not
"flashy."

When asked how the selectors could, on the basis of a few short
speeches at a selection conference, pick out the contender who pos-
sesses these qualities to a higher degree than his competitors, one
association chairman replied, not unjustly:

---

[30] Cf. Guttsman, *The British Political Elite,* pp. 288–89; and Richard Rose, *Politics
in England* (Boston: Little, Brown and Company, 1964), pp. 40–41. One Conservative
constituency agent told the story that in a marginal Midlands constituency the association adopted an able working-class candidate in the early 1950's, and he did well
in his first contest. It became the talk of the association, however, that at an election
meeting he ushered the association's leading peeress to her seat with the invitation,
offered in tones all could hear, "Sit here, luv!" He was not readopted.

Look, Professor, I can tell you what "character" means to us and how we decide who has it and who hasn't, but only up to a point. After that point it can't be put into words. You either recognize it or you don't. What you must realize is that we have to rely on our own judgment. If we are consistently wrong, we suffer and so does the party. But wouldn't you agree that, on the whole, we haven't done badly?

INTER-CONSTITUENCY MOVEMENT
OF CANDIDATES, 1951–59[31]

The last rule requiring an M.P. to reside in the constituency he represents was repealed in 1774.[32] This has made it legally possible for members who have seats, and others who have lost previous contests to be adopted in different constituencies. It has also enabled promising and ambitious young men to stand anywhere they can get adopted without being confined, as in the United States, to their home constituencies.[33]

The period covered by the present analysis, 1951–1959, was one of the most stable in the history of British politics, and so most of the factors usually thought to stimulate inter-constituency movement were more quiescent than they had been for many years. Even so, considerable movement did take place, and we will conclude our description of Conservative candidatures by noting the kinds of candidates who moved and where they moved.

FREQUENCY OF MOVEMENT

Table 4.1 shows that in the general elections of 1951, 1955, 1959, and 1964 a fraction over 11 per cent of all Conservative candidatures went to persons who had previously stood in other constituencies; 48 per cent went to incumbent M.P.s standing again in the constituencies they already held; 32 per cent to new candidates; and 9 per cent to persons fighting again in the constituencies they had

---

[31] The following section is drawn largely from the author's paper, "Inter-Constituency Movement of British Parliamentary Candidates, 1951–1959," *American Political Science Review*, LVIII (March, 1964), 36–45.

[32] J. F. S. Ross, *Elections and Electors* (London: Eyre and Spottiswoode, 1955), p. 229.

[33] The unsuccessful "carpet-bag" candidature of Pierre Salinger in California and the successful one of Robert Kennedy in New York for the U.S. Senate in 1964 have made this contrast somewhat more blurred than before.

previously lost. So the first characteristic of inter-constituency movement is that it affected a relatively small fraction of all candidatures.

MOVEMENT BY INCUMBENT M.P.S.

The Representation of the People Act of 1948 reduced the number of seats in the House from 640 to 625, and left only 80 constituencies entirely unchanged.[34] As a result, in the 1950 general election no less than 126 M.P.s of both parties moved to new constituencies because the seats they had held were either abolished or drastically revised. The redistribution of 1954 increased the number of members from 625 to 630, abolished six existing constituencies, created eleven new ones, and made major boundary revisions in 152 more.[35] This produced most of the movement by incumbent Conservative M.P.s recorded in Table 4.1

Only two M.P.s during this period, both Conservatives, changed constituencies without being impelled to do so by the 1955 redistribution.[36] Sir Harry Hylton-Foster, Conservative Member for York since 1950, was made Solicitor-General in 1954. For his purposes York was both too marginal (a majority of only 1,104 in 1955) and too far from London; so in 1959 he was able to move to the Cities of London and Westminster, which was not only a geographical improvement but also much safer (a Conservative majority of 18,044 in 1955). He subsequently became the Speaker. Sir Fitzroy Maclean, Conservative Member for Lancaster since 1941, wanted to represent a constituency in his native Scotland, and moved to Bute and North Ayrshire in 1959. He thereby not only returned home but exchanged a seat with a majority of 4,549 in 1955 for one with a majority of 9,155 in the same year.

---

[34] David E. Butler, *The Electoral System in Britain Since 1918*, 2nd. ed. (Oxford: at the Clarendon Press, 1963), Ch. V.

[35] *Times House of Commons, 1955* (London: The Times Office, 1955), p. 25.

[36] This does not include Sir David Maxwell Fyfe, a Conservative minister who had held the marginal (majority of 1,707 in 1951) West Derby division of Liverpool since 1935, but became prospective candidate for the safe (majority of 19,749 in 1951) seat of Epsom in 1954. He was made Lord Chancellor before the 1955 general election, however, so his move did not become final as did the two instances discussed in the text.

EFFORTS BY DEFEATED M.P.S.

TO RE-ENTER PARLIAMENT

The Conservative party lost a horrendous total of 172 seats in the debacle of 1945.[37] Only seventeen of the losing M.P.s were adopted as candidates by different constituencies for the 1950 general election, of whom eleven (including such prominent names as Henry Brooke and Duncan Sandys) were elected while six (including Leslie Hore-Belisha and Randolph Churchill) were defeated.

Only eighteen Conservative M.P.s were defeated in the 1950, 1951, 1955, and 1959 general elections. Of these, seven were adopted in new constituencies, four winning and three losing; one stood and lost again in his former constituency; and ten did not stand again. The author cannot say, however, how many of the latter voluntarily withdrew from further electoral competition and how many unsuccessfully sought candidatures in their former constituencies or new ones.

INTER-CONSTITUENCY MOVEMENT

BY OTHER CANDIDATES

Most inter-constituency movement by Conservative candidates in this period, then, was made by persons who had never been M.P.s. They necessarily were men who had lost in one or more previous elections, and who were subsequently adopted in other constituencies.

We shall describe the incidence and circumstances of such movement by considering the later electoral careers of the 350 Conservative candidates who first stood and lost in the general elections of 1951 and 1955. Fifty-four per cent had no second candidature, 17 per cent stood again in the constituencies they had lost in their first tries, and 23 per cent moved on to more favorable constituencies.[38] Only 6 per cent moved to newly-formed or less favorable constituencies.[39] So while slightly over half of the first-time losers

---

[37] R. B. McCallum and Alison Readman, *The British General Election of 1945* (London: Oxford University Press, 1947), p. 248.

[38] Note that in this discussion of inter-constituency movement the basic unit of analysis becomes the individual candidate rather than, as up to now, the candidature.

[39] A second candidature was classified as in a "newly-formed constituency" if it was

had no second candidatures anywhere,[40] most of the remainder either tried again in the same constituencies or moved to more promising ones. In what respects, then, did the "dropouts," "stayers," and "upward movers" differ from each other?

1. *Electoral Performance in First Candidature*

It is often said that how well or badly a candidate performs in his first contest strongly affects his chances of getting a second candidature—and perhaps also his desire to seek a second candidature. We have no way of measuring such aspects of our 350 candidates' performances as their eloquence on the hustings, diligence in canvassing, or cordiality of relations with local party workers. But we can compare each candidate's share of the poll in his first try with what his party had received in the general election preceding his first try and see what kind of candidature, if any, he got thereafter. This information is given in Table 4.13.

Table 4.13 shows fewer dropouts among the candidates whose electoral performance in their first tries bettered the party's national average performance. Among the repeaters, however, there was no significant relationship between the candidates' showings in their first tries and the *kinds* of second candidatures they received. Electoral performance, in short, seems to have counted for something but it clearly was not the sole factor determining a first-time loser's subsequent electoral career.

2. *Age at First Candidature*

We have already seen that candidates' ages were significantly related to the kinds of constituencies in which they were adopted. Table 4.14 shows that age at the time of the first candidature was also related to the second candidature, if any.

---

initially established by the 1955 redistribution. It was classified as "more favorable" or "less favorable" by comparing the Conservative percentage of the vote in the candidate's first constituency in his first contest with that in his second constituency in the same election as that of his first candidature.

[40] It should be emphasized again that we cannot say what proportion of the dropouts sought no second candidature and what proportion tried but failed.

TABLE 4.13

Conservatives' Electoral Performance in First Candidature
Related to Second Candidature, 1951–1959

Second Candidature	Electoral Performance in First Candidature*			
	Decrease	"Normal" Increase	"Extra" Increase	Other
None	52%	55%	42%	61%
In same constituency as the first	21	14	23	18
In constituency more favorable than the first	20	25	23	19
Other	7	6	12	2
	100%	100%	100%	100%
Number of cases	102	138	48	62

* Electoral performance was measured by comparing the candidate's percentage of the poll in his first candidature with the Conservative percentage in the same constituency in the preceding general election. Since in the elections of 1951 and 1955 the national swing to the Conservatives was 1.1 per cent and 1.8 per cent respectively, "normal" increase means an increase of 0.1 per cent to 4.9 per cent, and "extra" increase means an increase of 5.0 per cent or more. "Other" means that no comparison is possible because the first candidature was a newly-formed constituency or one in which no Conservative candidate stood in the preceding general election.

TABLE 4.14

Conservatives' Age at First Candidature Related to
Second Candidature, 1951–1959

Second Candidature	Age Groups				
	21–29	30–39	40–49	50–59	60 and over
None	35%	51%	60%	70%	88%
In same constituency as the first	23	16	18	12	12
In constituency more favorable than the first	36	24	18	12	0
Other	6	9	4	6	0
	100%	100%	100%	100%	100%
Number of cases	61	136	95	50	8

Table 4.14 shows an increasing proportion of dropouts in each successively older age group, although those in their thirties and forties who did make second tries went on to more promising seats

in about the same proportions as those in their twenties. Combining these facts with those presented in Table 4.4 leads to several conclusions. First, a majority of candidates made their first races under the age of forty, and were less likely to get winnable seats than candidates over forty with previous electoral experience. Second, the younger candidates who lost in their first races were less likely to drop out than their older counterparts. And third, the older candidates who did not drop out after their first losses were as likely as their younger colleagues to move on to better seats.

3. *Personal Connections in Constituency of First Candidature*

Of the 350 first-time losers we are considering here, 108 (31 per cent) had some kind of personal connection in the constituencies in which they first stood. Sixty-three per cent of the locally-connected candidates dropped out after their first losses, as compared with only 50 per cent of those with no local connections. We cannot say whether the former were mainly local "flag showers" (see above) who felt that one sacrifice was enough or whether they aspired to better things but lacked sufficient attractive qualities in addition to their local connections to enable them to move to more favorable constituencies.

It is suggestive, however, that when we hold constant age at first candidature we find that the dropout-local connections relationship holds for those under forty but disappears for those over forty. As we shall see in Chapter 7, quite the reverse happens when Labour candidates are ordered in the same fashion. So it appears that Conservatives, unlike Labour, drew their local "flag showers" more from persons under forty than persons over forty.

4. *Education*

We observed earlier the apparent advantages of attendance at public schools for being adopted in the more winnable seats, and noted that the non-incumbents who had attended universities, even Oxford or Cambridge, did not secure any larger proportions of the most desirable constituencies than people with comparable public- or secondary-school backgrounds who had not attended universities. And we concluded that these facts were consistent with the impression that Conservative local selectors value education more as a mark of social status than as an indication of intellectual achievement.

Table 4.15 shows a significantly different relationship between education and movement after first candidature, however.

TABLE 4.15

CONSERVATIVE SECONDARY-UNIVERSITY COMBINATIONS RELATED
TO SECOND CANDIDATURE, 1951–1959

Second Candidature	Secondary-University Combination					
	Secondary Only	Secondary and Univ. Other than Oxbridge	Secondary and Oxbridge	Public School Only	Pub. Sch. and Univ. Other than Oxbridge	Pub. Sch. and Oxbridge
None	60%	58%	33%	54%	74%	40%
In same constituency as the first	16	15	6	16	9	28
In constituency more favorable than the first	19	20	33	24	17	26
Other	5	7	28	6	0	6
	100%	100%	100%	100%	100%	100%
Number of cases	133	40	18	68	23	68

Table 4.15 shows that the secondary-and-Oxbridge and the public-school-and-Oxbridge groups had markedly fewer dropouts than any of the others. And while the public-school-only group had the fewest dropouts of the remainder, clearly an Oxbridge background was more strongly related and a public school background less strongly related to moving on to desirable second candidatures than to securing desirable first candidatures.

CONCLUSION:
CONSERVATIVE PATHWAYS TO PARLIAMENT

In the post-war period there were many Conservative pathways to Parliament, ranging from Henry Paul Guinness Channon's "inheritance" of the safe seat of Southend West at the age of twenty-three to Robert Mathew's adoption for the safe seat of Honiton at the age of forty-four after four previous losses in other constituencies. The pathway most commonly followed, however, took the following course.

To begin with, at each general election most of the safe and near-safe Conservative seats were pre-empted by incumbent M.P.s standing for re-election. Most of the few seats not pre-empted adopted experienced candidates—either former M.P.s or persons who had fought and lost one or more previous contests.

Two-thirds of the candidates secured their first candidatures between the ages of thirty and forty-nine, in most cases after having first established themselves in their businesses or professions. Most new candidates fought hopeless seats, although some managed to get adopted in marginal or even safe seats. Higher proportions of the non-incumbents who had attended public schools than of those who had not got winnable seats. There was no significant difference in the winnability of constituencies secured between those who had held office in a local government council or in a national or local party organization or in a nonpartisan civic or religious organization and those who had not. About a third had some kind of personal connection in their first constituencies, but they were more heavily concentrated in the marginal and hopeless constituencies than in the safe ones, and in the metropolitan areas outside of London than in the rural areas.

Of the 797 new candidates, 83 (10 per cent) won in their first tries, and the remaining 714 (90 per cent) lost. Of these who lost in 1951 and 1955, slightly over half had no second candidatures, some because they did not want them and others because they were unable to get them. Of the remainder, slightly over half were adopted in other, more favorable constituencies, slightly less than half made second efforts in the same constituencies they had previously lost, and only a small fraction moved to less favorable or newly-formed constituencies.

The older first-time losers dropped out at a higher rate than their younger colleagues, although the same proportions of those who made second tries moved on to better seats. Those under forty with local connections in their first constituencies dropped out at a higher rate than those under forty with no local connections, although there was no difference among those over forty in this regard. Fewer of those with Oxbridge backgrounds than of those without dropped out after their first losses. And fewer of those who in their first races received greater increases in their shares of the poll than the party's national average increases dropped out than of those whose share of the vote was "par" or less.

In short, while by no means every Conservative candidate was genuinely trying to get to Parliament, and while by no means everyone who did try followed the pathway outlined above, it nevertheless constitutes the course by which most new Conservative M.P.s since 1945 have entered the House.

| Chapter 5 | *The Role of Labour's Transport House* |

In Smith Square, Westminster, a few doors from the headquarters of the National Union of Conservative and Unionist Associations, stands Transport House, home since 1928 of Britain's largest trade union, the Transport and General Workers' Union. The building also houses the Labour party's National Executive Committee and Head Office staff. Thus British politicians and journalists customarily use the shorthand expression "Transport House" to refer to the NEC and its staff.

As we noted in Chapter 1, Labour parliamentary candidates, like their Conservative opponents, are selected by local party organizations subject to certain controls from the center. In the Labour party these local bodies are known as constituency Labour parties or CLPs. Labour's methods of candidate selection differ in three important respects from the Conservatives'. First, an individual may not formally bring his own name before a CLP; he becomes an official contender only when nominated by a body directly affiliated with the CLP—e.g., a ward committee, a trade union, or local socialist society. Second, a nominee may be sponsored by a trade union or by the Co-operative party, in which case it is understood that the sponsoring organization will contribute substantially to both the candidate's election expenses and the CLP's general funds. Third, the Labour party's national agencies have greater formal power than the Conservatives' over candidate selection. How much, if any, greater is their actual power constitutes the main question discussed in this chapter.

FORMAL NATIONAL SUPERVISION OF LOCAL CANDIDATE SELECTIONS

NATIONAL AGENCIES CONCERNED WITH CANDIDATES

The formal structure of the Labour party's national organization as it affects candidatures is shown graphically in Figure 2.

Matters affecting the selection of Labour parliamentary candidates in England, Wales, and Scotland are handled by the following four agencies.

1. *The National Executive Committee*

The National Executive Committee (NEC) has at present twenty-eight members: the party Leader, Deputy Leader, and Treasurer, all *ex officio;* twelve members elected at each annual conference by the nationally affiliated trade unions; one member elected at each conference by the nationally affiliated socialist, co-operative, and professional organizations; seven members elected at each conference by the CLPs; and five woman members elected annually by all the delegates at the conference.

The party Constitution stipulates that the NEC "shall, subject to the control and directions of the Party Conference, be the Administrative Authority of the Party."[1] Under this heading falls the general supervision of the selection of parliamentary candidates. All decisions are taken by votes of the whole NEC,[2] usually upon recommendations made by the Organisation Sub-committee. The whole NEC can, of course, override the sub-committee's recommenda-

---

[1] Clause VIII, section (1). The Constitution and Standing Orders of the Labour party are reprinted as appendices to each year's report of the annual conference.

[2] As McKenzie notes, since 1954 the NEC has bound itself by a sort of "cabinet solidarity" not to disclose its internal disagreements unless a majority specifically authorizes suspension of the rule: Robert T. McKenzie, *British Political Parties*, 2nd ed. (London: Mercury Books, 1964), p. 523. No such suspension has been granted on a controversy over candidate selection.

FIGURE 2
THE ORGANIZATION OF THE LABOUR PARTY*

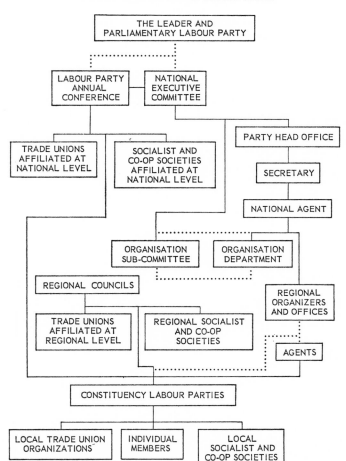

* Adapted from the figure in Robert T. McKenzie, *British Political Parties,* 2nd. ed. (London: Mercury Books, 1964), p. 487.

tions; in practice it almost never does. In effect, the Organisation Sub-committee is the principal national agency dealing with candidatures.[3]

---

[3] Prior to 1959 matters affecting candidatures were handled by a special Elections Sub-committee (see *ibid.,* pp. 527–28) or the Chairmen's Committee, which was composed of the chairmen of the other sub-committees. Since 1959, however, these committees have been dissolved, and the Organisation Sub-committee handles all candidature matters.

2. *The Organisation Sub-committee*

Of the NEC's five sub-committees, the Organisation Sub-committee is easily the most powerful. Its importance is underlined by the fact that the two leading contenders for the post of party Leader in 1963 were its two most recent chairmen: Harold Wilson (1955–60) and George Brown (1960–63). The subcommittee has five *ex officio* members—the Leader, Deputy Leader, party Treasurer, and the Chairman and Vice-Chairman of the NEC—and ten to twelve other members. The latter are chosen by the party Secretary, in consultation with the *ex officio* members, in accordance with expressed preferences for sub-committee assignments.[4]

3. *Head Office: The Secretary, National Agent, and Organisation Department*

The Labour party's paid employees are known corporately as Head Office, and work under the direction of the party Secretary.[5] The National Agent serves as the Secretary's chief deputy for organizational matters, including candidate selection, and by custom acts as secretary of the Organisation Sub-committee. The routine work of supervising candidatures is carried on by the Organisation Department working under the National Agent and Organisation Sub-committee.

4. *The Regional Organizers*

Like the Conservatives, the Labour party maintains both part-time amateur and full-time professional organizations in each of twelve party regions. Labour's regional boundaries differ from the Conservatives'.[6] Each of the twelve regional offices is managed by

---

[4] *Ibid.*, p. 526.

[5] In 1963, according to R. L. Leonard, Labour's Head Office employed a total of 78 administrative and 89 clerical personnel (compared with the Conservatives' 132 and 186 respectively): *Guide to the General Election* (London: Pan Books, Ltd., 1964), Table 6, p. 47.

[6] The specific constituencies included in each region are given in the appendices of the reports of the annual party conferences in the years in which general elections are held. As of 1959 the regions and the number of constituencies in each were as follows: (1) Northern (Cumberland, Durham, Northumberland, and the North Riding of Yorkshire), 37 constituencies; (2) North-Western (Cheshire, parts of Derbyshire, Lancashire, and Westmorland), 80 constituencies; (3) North-Eastern (remainder of

a regional organizer, who is appointed and paid by the NEC to enforce its rules, administer its policies, and supervise and assist the CLPs in his region. As we shall see, Labour regional organizers play, if anything, an even more active role in candidate selection than do the Conservative area agents (see Chapter 2).

DIRECT CENTRAL SUPERVISION OF CANDIDATE SELECTION

In Chapter 2 we observed that the Conservative party's national agencies are authorized only to recommend that the constituency associations follow certain procedures in selecting their parliamentary candidates. For the most part the local bodies follow the recommendations closely enough to satisfy Central Office, but on occasion they choose to ignore them. In such cases Central Office's only formal sanction is to refuse endorsement of the candidate. In fact, however, this sanction has never been used for this reason.

The Labour party's national agencies have considerably greater formal power to prescribe and supervise local adoption practices. Some procedures are specified by the party Constitution, others are contained in the CLPs' constitutions and standing orders. Moreover, since 1930 the Constitution has required every CLP to adopt certain rules (the so-called Model Rules) laid down by annual party conferences. These rules are codified, printed in pamphlet form, and circulated by Head Office.[7] They may be modified only with the express permission of the NEC.

The NEC's principal supervisory powers over local candidate selections are as follows:

Yorkshire), 51 constituencies; (4) Southern (Hampshire, Kent, Surrey, East Sussex, West Sussex, and the Isle of Wight), 66 constituencies; (5) London, 42 constituencies; (6) South-Western (Cornwall, Devonshire, Dorset, Gloucestershire, Somerset, and Wiltshire), 43 constituencies; (7) Eastern (Cambridgeshire, Isle of Ely, Essex, Huntingdonshire, Norfolk, and Suffolk), 43 constituencies; (8) Wales, 36 constituencies; (9) Scotland, 71 constituencies; (10) Northern Home Counties (Bedfordshire, Berkshire, Buckinghamshire, Hertfordshire, Middlesex, and Oxfordshire), 54 constituencies; (11) East Midlands (parts of Derbyshire, Leicestershire, Lincolnshire, Northamptonshire, and Nottinghamshire), 41 constituencies; and (12) West Midlands (Herefordshire, Shropshire, Staffordshire, Warwickshire, and Worcestershire), 54 constituencies.

[7] Under the title of *Constitution and Rules for Constituency Labour Parties and Local Labour Parties in Single and Undivided Boroughs*, (Set A). There are also slightly modified sets for county constituency parties (Set B), local parties in county constituencies (Set C), central Labour parties in divided boroughs (Set D), and constituency Labour parties in divided boroughs (Set E).

1. *Authorizing the CLP to Select a Candidate*

The Model Rules begin the section on candidate selection by stipulating:

(1) The desirability of contesting the Constituency for Parliament shall be considered by the Executive Committee of [the constituency] Party in consultation with the National Executive Committee or its officers prior to the procedure laid down in this Clause being set in motion.

(2) If it is thought expedient to contest the constituency the General Committee shall be asked to give authority to the Executive Committee of [the constituency] Party in co-operation with the National Executive Committee to secure nominations for the candidature.[8]

In other words, a CLP may not officially begin selecting a candidate until the NEC has given permission; that permission, in turn, depends upon agreement between the NEC and the CLP that the constituency should be contested. Since 1945 the NEC has always granted permission, usually immediately and without discussion; but it has been known to withhold it. From 1940 to 1945, for example, Labour entered into an electoral truce with the Conservatives, the terms of which prohibited each party from contesting a seat previously held by the other in a by-election caused by the death or resignation of the incumbent. On more than one occasion a CLP eager to fight a seat they felt they could capture from the Conservatives was denied permission by the NEC.

2. *Prescribing the CLP's Selection Procedures*

The Model Rules prescribe the nature and sequence of the steps a CLP must take in selecting a candidate. They also stipulate the terms of the official documents to be used, including the circular in which the CLP's executive announces its intention to select a candidate and invites nominations, the form on which nominations are submitted to the executive, and the form for the executive's notification to the members of the management committee of the time and place of the selection conference.[9]

---

[8] Model Rules, Set A, Clause XII, sections (1) and (2).

[9] These forms are given as appendices to the Model Rules, under the general title, "Prescribed Circulars and Form referred to in the Rule governing the selection of Parliamentary Candidates."

3. *Setting the Qualifications for Candidature*

The party Constitution specifies that:

No person may be selected as a Parliamentary Labour Candidate by a Constituency Labour Party, and no Candidate may be endorsed by the National Executive Committee, if the person concerned:—

(a) is not an Individual Member of the Party and, if eligible, is not a member of a Trade Union affiliated to the Trades Union Congress or recognised by the General Council of the Trades Union Congress as a *bona fide* Trade Union; or

(b) is a member of a Political Party or organisation ancillary or subsidiary thereto declared by the Annual Party Conference or by the National Executive Committee in pursuance of Conference decisions to be ineligible for affiliation to the Labour Party: or

(c) does not accept and conform to the Constitution, Programme, Principles, and Policy of the Party; or

(d) does not undertake to accept and act in harmony with the Standing Orders of the Parliamentary Labour Party.[10]

Paragraph (c), as we shall see, gives the NEC broad constitutional power—which it has sometimes used—to veto local adoptions on ideological grounds.

4. *Regulating Local Financial Arrangements*

The NEC regulates the financial arrangements among CLPs, candidates, and sponsoring organizations in three ways. First, endorsement of any candidate is withheld until the NEC has "received an undertaking by one of its affiliated organisations (or is otherwise satisfied) that the election expenses of the Candidate are guaranteed."[11] In pursuance of this regulation, Transport House requires the completion of a form, entitled "Financial Agreement Respecting the Candidature of ———," which specifies the amounts the candidate and his sponsoring organization, if any, have agreed to contribute to campaign expenses and to the CLP's general funds. It must be signed by the candidate and by the CLP's chairman and secretary.

Second, the NEC enforces certain limits upon contributions by candidates and sponsors first adopted by the annual conference at

---

[10] Party Constitution, Clause IX, section (7).

[11] *Ibid.*, Clause IX, section (4).

Hastings in 1933 (and thus called the Hastings Agreements) and revised in 1948 and 1957. The present limits are as follows:

(1) The sponsoring organization, if any, may not contribute more than 80 per cent of the maximum election expenses the law allows the candidate (see Chapter 1).

(2) The CLP must undertake to provide at least 20 per cent of the candidate's allowable election expenses.

(3) The sponsoring organization's annual contribution to the CLP's general funds may not exceed £350 in a borough constituency or £420 in a county constituency, or 50 per cent of a full-time agent's salary in a borough constituency or 60 per cent of his salary in a county constituency—whichever amount is the largest.

(4) Any person interested in a parliamentary candidature, whether a prospective candidate or not, may not contribute to election expenses more than the candidate's personal expenses nor make annual contributions of over £50 to the CLP's general funds.[12]

The limits on sponsors' contributions, it should be emphasized, are maxima; they do not mean that the sponsoring organization or the candidate must contribute the full amounts, and not infrequently their contributions fall well short of the maxima.[13]

Third, the NEC prohibits any CLP from making an inquiry about or reference to the financing of a candidature until after the candidate has been selected—although the mere presence of a contender's name on list A (see below) informs everyone that adopting him will bring financial support from his sponsoring organization.

5. *Endorsement*

The Constitution stipulates:

The selection of Labour Candidates for Parliamentary Elections shall not be regarded as completed until the name of the person selected has been placed before a meeting of the National Executive Committee, and his or her selection has been duly endorsed.[14]

---

[12] Before 1957 a candidate could make personal contributions on the same scale as a sponsoring organization, but this was changed in accordance with the recommendation of a report of the Organisation Sub-committee, under the chairmanship of Harold Wilson.

[13] Cf. Martin Harrison, *Trade Unions and the Labour Party since 1945* (London: George Allen & Unwin, Ltd., 1960), pp. 80–85.

[14] Party Constitution, Clause IX, section (3).

This is the counterpart of the Conservative Standing Advisory Committee's veto power (see Chapter 2) and constitutes one of the NEC's main formal weapons for enforcing the rules described above. Later we shall examine the frequency and conditions of its actual use.

6. *Suspension of the Normal Procedure*

All the foregoing rules apply to the so-called normal procedure for candidate selection. Lest anything be overlooked, the Model Rules also provide:

Where no valid nominations are received, or when an emergency arises, or when the Executive Committee of [the constituency] Party or the National Executive Committee are of [the] opinion that the interests of the Labour Party demand the suspension of the procedure laid down in Section 3 of this Clause, normal procedure may be dispensed with after consultation and agreement between the Executive Committee of [the constituency] Party and the National Executive Committee.[15]

This section has seldom been invoked, but it provides the NEC with all the residual formal authority it needs to deal with any unusual situation in any way it wishes. It goes far beyond any authority formally given the Conservatives' national agencies.

7. *Special Procedure for By-Elections*

In Chapter 2 we noted that Conservative Central Office plays a more active role in the selection of candidates for by-elections than for general elections. The same may be said of Transport House, whose authority to intervene at by-elections is formally set forth in the Model Rules:

If a Parliamentary by-election occurs in the Constituency the procedure laid down in Section 3 of this Clause shall be suspended and the National Executive Committee shall co-operate with the Executive Committee of [the constituency] Party in the nomination of a candidate. The National Executive Committee may, if it deems it necessary in the interests of the Labour Party, advise the Executive Committee of [the constituency] Party to select a nomination it may submit to it. The National Executive Committee may also give advice and guidance on any special issue to be raised or in the conduct of the campaign during the by-election.[16]

---

[15] Model Rules, Set A, Clause XII, section (4)

[16] *Ibid.*, Clause XII, section (5)

Clearly, then, Labour's Constitution and Model Rules give its national agencies much greater formal central power over candidate selection than their Conservative opposite numbers enjoy. Whether this has resulted in substantially greater *actual* central control in the Labour party is our next concern.

THE CENTRAL PLACEMENT POWER

THE TWO LISTS OF APPROVED CANDIDATES

Transport House, like Conservative Central Office, assembles the names and other particulars of persons regarded as suitable parliamentary candidates and makes them available to all CLPs. Unlike the Conservatives, however, the Labour party maintains two separate lists of approved candidates.

1. *List A of Union-Sponsored Candidates*

List A includes persons nominated by trade unions and approved by the NEC. The national unions assemble their own "panels"—i.e., lists of union members they feel would make suitable parliamentary candidates. They submit the names to the National Agent, who requires each nominee to complete the Candidate's Form of Particulars (see below). The Organisation Sub-committee interviews the nominees and recommends to the NEC that certain names be put on the list. The list is made available to any CLP that requests it, and it is understood (though no formal rule requires it) that if a CLP adopts a person on the list, his sponsoring union will make financial contributions within the limits outlined above. No one on List A can be validly adopted by a CLP as its prospective candidate until the executive committee of his sponsoring union has given its written consent.[17]

2. *List B of Unsponsored Candidates*

Since 1960 List B has consisted of persons not sponsored by trade unions or by the Co-operative party whom the NEC considers suitable for parliamentary candidature. It is understood that if a CLP adopts a person from List B, he will at most contribute only his own personal election expenses and an annual contribution to the CLP's general funds of no more than £50, and the CLP will have to find the remainder of its funds elsewhere.

---

[17] *Ibid.*, Clause XII, section (3), paragraph (c).

Before 1960 List B was simply a collection of the names, addresses, and other particulars of all party members who notified the NEC they wished to be put on the list. The NEC did not interview or screen them in any way, and acted solely as a clearing house. In the late 1950's, however, a growing number of party leaders came to feel there should be stronger central control over the personal quality and political reliability of candidates and that converting List B into a list of recommended candidates comparable to the Conservative Standing Advisory Committee's list would help achieve this end.

Prior to the 1960 annual conference, an assembly of party agents in the Midlands proposed that the names on both List B and List A be carefully screened by the NEC and that the CLPs be required to pick their candidates exclusively from the two lists.[18] The NEC did not feel it could go quite that far, but its report to the conference declared:

A great deal of attention has been paid to improving the quality of the Lists of Available and Possible Parliamentary Candidates . . . . Previously, List B, Possible Parliamentary Candidates, included the names and addresses of nominated members who were willing to consider invitations to become Parliamentary candidates. It was not a recommended list.

The National Executive Committee has now decided that the List shall consist of members who have been approved by the National Executive Committee as suitable for consideration by constituency parties seeking a candidate, and who have been nominated by constituency parties and other nationally affiliated organisations.

List A, Available Parliamentary Candidates, is a list of members who are on their union's official Parliamentary panels and who will be sponsored financially by their organisations if selected as candidates.

A panel of National Executive Committee members is to interview nominees for the lists where this is thought to be necessary.[19]

List B is still not a recommended list in the Conservatives' sense of the term, for there is no express or implied guarantee that the NEC will endorse the candidature of any person on the list.[20] But it is more nearly a recommended list than it was before 1960, inclusion on it is by no means automatic for every applicant, and it

---

[18] *Labour Organiser*, XXXIX (May, 1960), 94–95.

[19] *Report of the Fifty-Ninth Annual Conference of the Labour Party, 1960*, p. 24.

[20] For example, in 1962 the NEC refused to endorse the candidature of Illtyd Harrington even though his name was on List B (see below).

unquestionably creates a presumption in favor of the persons on it in the eyes of most CLPs.

Anyone who seeks inclusion on List B must first be formally nominated to the NEC by his CLP or by some other organization nationally affiliated with the party. The Organisation Department then asks him to complete a "Candidate's Form of Particulars," which resembles the form for Conservative applicants in some respects but differs in others. The Labour form, for example, asks for certain items not mentioned in the Conservative: length of party service, "languages and similar qualifications," publications, and experience abroad. For another, the Labour form omits some items requested by the Conservative: marital status, place of birth, "rank, title, and decorations," and nationality.

The Labour applicant completes his form by giving the names and addresses of two referees "who must be well known members of the Labour Party" and by confirming that "the completion of this form indicates acceptance of the conditions applying to Parliamentary Candidates and Labour Members of Parliament laid down in the National Constitution of the Party and its Constituency Rules."

The applicant is then interviewed by members of a panel established by the Organisation Sub-committee. The interviews ordinarily last from fifteen to thirty minutes. As with the Conservatives, the questions are usually designed more to probe the applicant's personal qualities than to explore his political ideology. But in recent years, applicants known to be opponents of the party leaders' views on public policy have been questioned closely about their political opinions. Some, as we shall see, have been denied admission to the list on political rather than personal grounds.

After the interview and its review of the applicant's form and the opinions of his referees, the interviewers recommend to the Organisation Sub-committee that he be included or not. The sub-committee periodically recommends to the NEC that certain approved names be added to the list, and the NEC invariably accepts the recommendations.

TRANSPORT HOUSE'S PLACEMENT OBJECTIVES

1. *Placing Particular Individuals*

Transport House's general object in supervising the selection of parliamentary candidates is precisely the same as Conservative Central Office's: to build a roster that will make the maximum possible contribution to the party's efforts to win a parliamentary majority, and to provide the parliamentary party with the talents and backgrounds it needs to conduct its business in the House with the greatest effectiveness. Like their opposite numbers in Central Office, Transport House officials always have in mind a number of particular individuals they would like to see "placed" in winnable seats: e.g., valued M.P.s defeated in general elections, and young men regarded as "good front-bench material" who are seeking their first entry into the House.

2. Making the List Representative

Transport House is also concerned that the CLPs generally adopt the right kinds of candidates. Like the Conservatives, they claim to place high value on achieving a "truly representative" national list —that is, one in which each major segment of the population is adequately represented. They want to see the CLPs adopt dons as well as day laborers, women as well as men, Jews as well as Gentiles, Catholics as well as Protestants. The problem of building such a list appears less formidable in Transport House than it does in Central Office, for anti-Semitism and misogyny are thought to be rarer in the CLPs than in Conservative associations. But Transport House has its own peculiar problems. In many CLPs there runs a strong undercurrent of feeling that only a man in a "cloth cap" with many years of devoted service to "the Movement" deserves the honor of a Labour candidature.[21] Transport House occasionally tries to exert gentle pressure for the idea that the ablest contender should be chosen regardless of his social origins, manner of speech, or occupation.

3. Strengthening the Parliamentary Party's Leadership

The often-bitter struggle between Left and Right which has characterized the Labour party's internal politics since 1945 is too long

---

[21] For example, the Amalgamated Society of Woodworkers at their annual conference in 1954 expressed great concern over the tendency of CLPs to pass over union candidates. To great applause, one speaker said: "I want to remind this conference that the Labour Party is our party, and I want to see more members of Parliament who have come up the hard way from factories, building sites, and so on": *Times* (London), June 8, 1954, p. 2.

and familiar a story to be recounted here. It is important for our purposes to note that during most of this period the party's national machinery affecting candidatures has been firmly controlled by the right-wing leadership of the parliamentary party. Some CLPs, on the other hand, have been dominated by the left-wing anti-leadership group, while others have been more or less evenly split between the two factions.

For both Left and Right, the selection of parliamentary candidates has been a battleground of the highest importance, for the policy preferences and factional loyalties of the candidates selected determine the kinds of Labour M.P.s elected, and they in turn select the parliamentary party's leaders. The author has the distinct impression that the Right have understood this fact of life better than the Left. The Left have made little organized national effort to get their adherents adopted, and on a number of occasions CLPs with Left majorities have adopted candidates from the Right because they seemed abler than their Left opponents or because no contenders from the Left appeared on the short lists (see below). On the other hand, the right-wing Campaign for Democratic Socialism group continued to work for the adoption of Gaitskellite candidates even after Hugh Gaitskell's victory over the unilateral disarmers in the annual conference of 1961.

The leadership has on occasion used its control of the party's national machinery to encourage CLPs to adopt right-wing candidates and pass over left-wing potential rebels. The circumstances, methods, and success or failure of these efforts, summarized below, reveal a good deal about the actual "placement" and "veto" power of the party's national agencies.

THE PLACEMENT POWER IN PRACTICE

1. *Powers and Problems*

At first glance Transport House appears considerably better equipped than Central Office to accomplish its objectives. Not only does it have far more extensive formal powers, but it is even authorized to make its own nominations directly whenever it thinks "the interests of the Labour Party demand."

Yet Transport House has used its nominating powers infrequently and with circumspection—and for essentially the same reasons that have restrained Central Office. In the Labour party, as in the Conservative, the final selection of the candidate constitutionally belongs to the local party, and there is no direct procedure by which Transport House can impose a candidate on any constituency.

Moreover, CLPs are every bit as jealous as Conservative associations of their prerogative of adopting candidates, and are just as likely to pass over any contender they feel the national agencies are trying to push off on them. Consequently Transport House has to be as circumspect as Central Office in putting a particular name before a particular local party. Even when a CLP asks for suggestions, Transport House as a matter of policy almost invariably puts forth two or more names. Thus, no particular contender need bear the onus of being "Transport House's Man."[22]

One leading party "civil servant" told the author that Transport House is in fact considerably less active in placing desirable candidates than it could and should be. This, he said, is because it takes the narrow view that its proper function is merely to carry out the NEC's orders rather than the broader view that it should take the initiative in pursuing the NEC's general objectives.

The NEC itself, as one of its members told the author, does not even try to keep a close check on candidate selections in all CLPs. There are too many of them, the NEC has too many other matters to deal with, and in any case the dangers of pushing particular candidates are usually too great to warrant the risk.

Most party officials agree that certain regional organizers rather than the NEC or the Organisation Department have played key roles in the relatively few instances in which the party Leader's wish to have a particular person adopted has been gratified. One regional organizer put it thus:

Every now and again Hugh Gaitskell, who knows me and trusts me, tells me privately, "Look, young X is a very able chap and we could use him to good purpose in the House. Would you see what you can do for him?" When he does, I review the situation in all the parties in my region carefully. If I see one that is winnable, that is looking for a candidate, and that has officers who are good friends of mine, I drive over and have a quiet chat with them. Usually they can at least guarantee that my man will get on the short list, and sometimes they can also see to it that he is the only able man on the list. After that, of course,

---

[22] Cf. McKenzie, *British Political Parties*, pp. 552–53; T. E. M. McKitterick, "The Selection of Parliamentary Candidates: The Labour Party," *Political Quarterly*, XXX (July–September, 1959), 219–23, at pp. 219–21; and Ivor Bulmer-Thomas, *The Party System in Great Britain* (London: Phoenix House, Ltd., 1953), pp. 208–9.

it's up to the man himself to convince the selection conference that he's what they want. But they usually do rather well.

This particular organizer has scored several triumphs, but by no means all of his eleven colleagues have been equally successful.

2. *Successful Efforts at Placement*

In the general elections of 1950, 1951, 1955, and 1959 eighteen Labour M.P.s of ministerial rank were defeated. Of these, eleven were subsequently adopted in other constituencies, and ten returned to the House.[23] Seven did not stand again. We have no evidence, however, as to how many of the nine were "taken care of" by Transport House and how many were selected simply because the CLPs preferred them to their rivals.

Edith Summerskill and Warrington, 1955. Perhaps the best known instance of a successful attempt by Transport House to place a particular candidate was its backing of Dr. Edith Summerskill (now Lady Summerskill) in 1955. Dr. Summerskill was elected Member for West Fulham in 1938, becoming Minister of National Insurance in 1950 and Chairman of the party in 1955. The redistribution of 1954 merged the two Fulham seats, and Michael Stewart, the Member for East Fulham since 1945 and himself of ministerial rank, was adopted by the new Fulham party as its prospective candidate. Dr. Summerskill accordingly needed a new seat, and, with help from Transport House, was put on the short list at Warrington, a safe Labour constituency in southern Lancashire. She faced stiff competition, however, from W. T. Williams, then Labour and Co-operative Member for Hammersmith South, whose seat was also abolished by redistribution. Williams also appeared on the short list at Barons Court, a new seat adjacent to Fulham, which was expected to be marginal. The NEC tried and failed to persuade the Barons Court executive to hold its selection conference before Warrington's so that Williams, if adopted there, could withdraw at Warrington and leave the field free for Dr. Summerskill. The Warrington selection conference, however, adopted Dr. Summerskill by a vote of 79 to 59, and the following day Williams was adopted by Barons Court. The result was splendid news in Trans-

---

[23] These figures include two defeated Labour M.P.s, Aiden Crawley and E. M. King, who later stood as Conservatives and were elected: Crawley at West Derbyshire in a 1962 by-election, and King at South Dorset in the 1964 general election.

port House, although they could hardly claim to have been its sole authors.[24]

3. Unsuccessful Efforts at Placement

Transport House has openly supported particular candidates on only a few other occasions. Their efforts have not always succeeded.

Sir Frank Soskice, Konni Zilliacus, and Manchester Gorton, 1955. Sir Frank Soskice, Attorney-General in the Labour government of 1951 and one of the party Leader's most valued lieutenants, was singularly unfortunate in his choice of seats. He was first elected for Birkenhead East in 1945, but the seat was abolished in the redistribution of 1948. In 1950 he fought Bebington but lost. Shortly thereafter, with help from Transport House (see below), he was adopted for the by-election in the Neepsend division of Sheffield. This seat he won, but it in turn was abolished by the 1954 redistribution, and Sir Frank and Transport House began looking for another seat. He was put on the short list for the Gorton division of Manchester, formerly a safe Labour seat, which had undergone a major boundary revision and was expected to be marginal. His chief opponent was Konni Zilliacus, a highly vocal spokesman of the Left who had been expelled from the party in 1949 for opposing the Attlee government's foreign policy (see below). Although he had been readmitted in 1952, the leadership still did not regard him quite as a Gibraltar of loyal support. Transport House made no secret of their strong preference for Sir Frank, but the selection conference selected Zilliacus, by the narrow margin of 39 votes to 36.[25] One such defeat, some felt in Transport House, outweighs several victories.

Morgan Phillips and North-East Derbyshire, 1959. Morgan Phillips served as Secretary of the Labour party from 1944 to 1962, and was one of its most respected elders as well as its most eminent "civil servant." Toward the end of his long career he decided, for the first time, to let himself be nominated for a parliamentary candidature, in the safe Labour seat of North-East Derbyshire. He made the decision strictly on his own, without consulting other national leaders. But the Derbyshire Area Council of the National

---

[24] *Warrington Guardian*, April 30, 1955, p. 9. See also Peter G. Richards, *Honourable Members* (London: Faber & Faber, Ltd., 1959), p. 20.

[25] *Times* (London), April 26, 1955, p. 12; May 2, 1955, p. 8.

Union of Mineworkers regarded the constituency as a miners' seat
—i.e., one in which Labour's votes come mainly from miners and
which should therefore be represented by a miner. Openly resentful
of what they viewed as Transport House's attempt to "grab" the
seat for a "carpet-bagger," however eminent and respected, the
miners nominated Thomas Swain, an NUM official. Both Phillips
and Swain were put on the short list with three others, and the selection conference—heavily attended by NUM delegates—chose
Swain on the third ballot by 108 votes to 81.[26]

THE PLACEMENT POWER IN BY-ELECTIONS

1. *The Special Procedures*

Transport House cannot by itself adopt a candidate, but the special procedures stipulated by the Model Rules for by-elections (see
above) appear to give the NEC the power virtually to compel a
CLP to select a particular candidate. And Transport House, like
Central Office, is undoubtedly more concerned and active at by-
elections than general elections. As a member of the NEC told
the author, there are several good reasons why this is so. For one,
at by-elections it is much easier to keep a close watch on how things
are going. For another, the national publicity a by-election attracts
makes its candidates' personal qualities more visible and therefore
more important than at a general election. And for yet another, the
likelihood that the result will be regarded as evidence of a national
trend makes it imperative that the party present the most attractive candidate it can.

In many by-elections, particularly those in seats vacated by a Labour member, the NEC and the regional organizers carefully scrutinize the short lists before they go to selection conferences and
sometimes alter them. When, for example, the Middlesbrough East
party were selecting their candidate for the 1962 by-election the
executive left off the short list the nominee of the British Iron,
Steel & Kindred Trades' Association (BISAKTA). Believing
BISAKTA's enthusiastic co-operation to be necessary for the party's

---

[26] The *Times* reporter estimated that the NUM controlled at least 100 votes out of
a total management committee membership of 220, and their members almost all
turned out while a number of the other delegates did not attend: *Times* (London)
September 21, 1959, p. 15.

success in this constituency, the NEC ordered the CLP executive to restore the BISAKTA nominee to the short list. This they did.[27]

Yet the NEC's placement powers in by-elections are far from absolute. If, for instance, the by-election takes place in a constituency vacated by a Conservative or Liberal Member, the CLP may already have adopted its prospective candidate for the next general election. Nothing in the Constitution or Model Rules clearly prohibits the NEC from replacing him with another candidate, but it is extremely unlikely that they would even attempt such a replacement—let alone succeed if they tried.

Even where no prospective candidate has been selected the NEC is empowered only to advise the CLP to select a particular candidate. It cannot formally compel his selection, for in by-elections as in general elections the final selection rests with the CLPs. And, as in selections for general elections, there is always a danger of local resentment against "Transport House dictation," so the NEC and its agents must proceed with caution and due regard for local sensibilities. And in by-elections as in general elections, their success in placing candidates depends mainly upon the quality of their nominees, the skill of the regional organizers, and the relations they maintain with the influential members of the CLPs.[28]

2. *Successful Placements in By-Elections*

We noted above how well the Labour party took care of its defeated M.P.s of ministerial rank after 1950. We should add here that of the sixteen who remained in the party after their initial defeats (two subsequently joined the Conservatives), no fewer than ten moved to safer constituencies, five within a year of their defeats.

Patrick Gordon Walker and Frank Cousins, 1964–65. The NEC's quickest and safest placement method is to persuade an incumbent M.P. in a safe seat to accept a life peerage, and then persuade his CLP to adopt the NEC's choice for his replacement in the ensuing by-election. For example, after Labour's victory in the 1964 general election, Prime Minister Wilson named two men for leading cabinet posts who were not M.P.s: Patrick Gordon Walker, who had lost his Smethwick

---

[27] He was not adopted, but the NEC's action mollified BISAKTA sufficiently to prevent a split in the local party.

[28] Cf. McKitterick, *Political Quart.,* Vol. XXX, at p. 221.

seat in the 1964 election; and Frank Cousins, who had never been in Parliament. The NEC sounded out a number of M.P.s in safe seats about their willingness to accept life peerages, and, after several refusals, found two: Reginald Sorensen, 73, in Leyton; and Frank Bowles, 62, in Nuneaton. (Bowles told reporters, "My first reaction was to say to myself, 'I can't and I won't.' " But after twenty-four hours' reflection he decided he would, adding, "It is the biggest sacrifice I can make and I make it now.") The Leyton CLP accepted Gordon Walker and the Nuneaton CLP accepted Cousins.[29] In January, 1965, Cousins won, but Gordon Walker lost again.

3. Unsuccessful Efforts
at Placement in By-Elections

In the Gordon Walker and Cousins cases apparently all the circumstances were highly favorable for the NEC: eminent and respected candidates, detachable M.P.s in "safe" seats, able regional organizers enjoying good relations with the officers of the CLPs, and CLPs with low proportions of rebels. As a result they were able to place their men as swiftly and surely as any model "responsible party" (see Chapter 1) possibly could.

When the circumstances have been less favorable, however, all the NEC's formal placement powers have not been enough, as the following instances demonstrate.

Arthur Creech Jones and Bristol South-East, 1950. Arthur Creech Jones, who had served in the Cabinet as Colonial Secretary since 1946, was defeated at Shipley in the 1950 general election, and immediately began to seek another seat. In October, 1950, Sir Stafford Cripps announced that he would resign his safe seat in Bristol South-East, and Creech Jones, who was a native of Bristol, became the "hot favourite" to succeed.[30] He was placed on the short list along with Mrs. Muriel Nichol and Anthony Wedgwood Benn, the son of a Labour peer and minister. The selection conference surprised the nation and gave Transport House a rude shock by selecting Wedgwood Benn. The word later got around that the man-

---

[29] *Times* (London), November 6, 1964, p. 12; November 11, 1964, p. 8; November 20, 1964, p. 12; November 21, 1964, p. 6.
[30] *Bristol Evening World*, November 1, 1950, p. 5.

agement committee had been unhappy with Sir Stafford's inactivity in CLP and constituency affairs, and had ascribed his lassitude mainly to his age (then sixty-one). When they were faced with the choice between Creech Jones (age fifty-nine) and Wedgwood Benn (age twenty-five), Transport House's known desire to return the former minister to the front bench was outweighed by the CLP's desire to be represented by an energetic and attractive young man who would be active in local as well as parliamentary affairs. (In this they certainly have not been disappointed—see Chapter 1.)

Tom Driberg and St. Helens, 1958. Tom Driberg, a journalist, sometime Bevanite rebel, and favorite of the Left, represented the marginal seat of Maldon from 1942 to 1955. Shortly before the 1955 general election, he stood down "for professional reasons" (he later explained that the constituency was so spread out that he could not service it adequately and still do justice to his journalistic assignments). The candidate who replaced him lost, and some felt Driberg had thrown away the seat by depriving the party of the advantage of having an incumbent candidate. Despite this, Driberg remained active in the party, and became party Chairman for 1957–58.

In March, 1958, Sir Hartley Shawcross announced that he would resign his seat at St. Helens, a Labour stronghold in Lancashire. Driberg made a quick trip to St. Helens to confer with some of the CLP's members (though not its officers), and was assured of their support.[31] Thereupon the "chairmen's committee" of the NEC (an informal committee composed of the chairmen of the regular subcommittees), acting under Clause XII, section (5) of the Model Rules (see above,) nominated Driberg for the St. Helens candidature.

On learning the news, Edwin Hall, the Lancashire area secretary of the National Union of Mineworkers, told a reporter:

> I hope the selection committee at St. Helens will have sufficient wisdom to realize that Driberg had the opportunity of fighting a marginal seat at the last election. He did not take that opportunity. Now he has the cheek to come along to try to take a safe Socialist seat. When the selection committee are making their choice I can't see them adopting a man of that description to a safe seat

---

[31] *St. Helens and District Reporter,* April 15, 1958, p. 1.

which trade unionists have built up and which is composed of industrial constituents.[32]

A few days later the whole NEC met, and the trade union members protested the chairmen's committee's assumption of the right to make a nomination without reference to the whole NEC. A resolution was adopted prohibiting any such nomination in the future.[33] Shortly before the St. Helens executive were due to meet to draw up the short list, Driberg asked that his name be withdrawn. This was widely regarded as a humiliating setback not only for Driberg but for Transport House as well.[34]

4. *Differences in Candidates*

These scattered episodes suggest that, however generous may be Transport House's formal placement powers in by-elections, it can in fact place a particular candidate in a particular constituency only when it has the right man for the right CLP at the right time and when it presses his cause with due regard for local sensibilities. But it may be that on many more occasions, which did not become public, Transport House was able to use its powers effectively. Or it may be that without direct pressure from Smith Square the CLPs were more inclined than usual to select persons of the general sort the national leaders recommend. Either would represent a type of Transport House influence: the former direct, the latter indirect. And if either or both operated, the characteristics of persons given candidatures at by-elections should have differed significantly from those adopted at general elections.

In order to see whether this was true, we have compared the characteristics of the persons given the 113 Labour by-election candidatures between the general election of 1951 and the end of 1961 with those of persons given the 1,035 candidatures by non-incumbents in the general elections of 1951, 1955, and 1959.[35]

---

[32] *Ibid.*, April 22, 1958, p. 1.

[33] *Times* (London), April 24, 1958, p. 6.

[34] *Ibid.*, April 28, 1958, p. 5. Driberg was adopted and elected for Barking in 1959, and re-elected in 1964.

[35] Note that, as in the similar comparison of Conservative candidates in Chapter 2, the basic unit of analysis here is the *candidature*, not the individual candidate. Any person who stood more than once in either by-elections or general elections appears

Local Connections. In the Labour party as in the Conservative, whatever pressures there are for adopting local men come from the local parties, not from the national leaders. Accordingly, if Transport House's placement power has been significantly stronger in by-elections than in general elections, we would expect a smaller proportion of locally-connected persons in candidatures for by-elections than for general elections, especially in the safe seats. In Chapter 2 we saw that this was not the case with the Conservatives. Table 5.1 shows that it was with Labour.

TABLE 5.1

LABOUR GENERAL ELECTION AND BY-ELECTION CANDIDATURES BY NON-INCUMBENTS RELATED TO PERSONAL CONNECTIONS IN CONSTITUENCY, BY WINNABILITY OF CONSTITUENCY*

Local Connections	Winnability of Constituency					
	High		Medium		Low	
	Gen. Elect.	By-Elect.	Gen. Elect.	By-Elect.	Gen. Elect.	By-Elect.
Some	44%	30%	24%	29%	27%	20%
None	56	70	76	71	73	80
	100%	100%	100%	100%	100%	100%
Number of cases	41	30	194	17	768	65

* For definitions of "personal connections" and the categories of constituency winnability, see Chapter 2, the first footnote to Table 2.1, and the Appendix.

Table 5.1 shows significantly lower proportions of locally-connected persons in by-election than in general election candidatures, a difference especially marked in the constituencies of high winnability. This supports the belief that Transport House, unlike Conservative Central Office, has greater influence over by-election candidatures than over general election candidatures. It does not, of course, tell us whether this is the direct influence from pressure on

more than once in the tables. We have omitted from the tables the thirty-two general election candidatures and the one by-election candidature in constituencies in the "other" category of winnability.

the CLPs or the indirect influence from the CLPs' voluntary acceptance of the general sort of candidates recommended by Transport
House.

Previous Electoral Experience. It is often said that the national
agencies of both parties like to see promising novices make their
first races in hopeless seats where they can prove their electoral
mettle, and more experienced candidates adopted in the winnable
seats. In Chapter 2 we saw no evidence that Conservative Central

TABLE 5.2

LABOUR GENERAL ELECTION AND BY-ELECTION CANDIDATURES BY NON-INCUMBENTS
RELATED TO PREVIOUS ELECTORAL EXPERIENCE, BY WINNABILITY OF CONSTITUENCY

| Previous Electoral Experience | Winnability of Constituency | | | | | |
| | High | | Medium | | Low | |
	Gen. Elect.	By-Elect.	Gen. Elect.	By-Elect.	Gen. Elect.	By-Elect.
First contest	71%	53%	42%	23%	57%	46%
One previous loss	10	17	26	18	26	37
Two or more previous losses	12	7	15	18	14	17
Former M.P.s	7	23	17	41	3	0
	100%	100%	100%	100%	100%	100%
Number of cases	41	30	194	17	768	65

Office has been able to achieve this allocation in by-elections any
more than in general elections. Table 5.2 shows, again, a different
pattern for the Labour party.

Not only did a significantly smaller proportion of all by-election
than general election Labour candidatures go to new candidates,
but the difference persists in each of the three categories of constituency winnability. This, too, supports the belief that Transport
House's influence is greater over by-election than general election
candidatures, and greater than Conservative Central Office's influence.

Sponsorship. In Chapters 7 and 8 we shall see that almost half of
the most desirable Labour candidatures by non-incumbents in general elections were given to persons sponsored by trade unions and

by the Co-operative party. Table 5.3 shows that this tendency was even more pronounced in by-elections.

Table 5.3 shows that in the constituencies of high and medium winnability higher proportions of the candidatures went to sponsored candidates in by-elections than in general elections; but in the low-winnability constituencies the reverse was true, though by only a narrow margin. Since Transport House neither urges nor opposes the adoption of union-sponsored candidates, this tells us noth-

TABLE 5.3

LABOUR GENERAL ELECTION AND BY-ELECTION CANDIDATURES BY NON-INCUMBENTS RELATED TO SPONSORSHIP, BY WINNABILITY OF CONSTITUENCY

Sponsorship	Winnability of Constituency					
	High		Medium		Low	
	Gen. Elect.	By-Elect.	Gen. Elect.	By-Elect.	Gen. Elect.	By-Elect.
By constituency Labour parties	51%	40%	74%	59%	89%	92%
By the Co-operative party	12	17	7	18	4	3
By trade unions	37	43	19	23	7	5
	100%	100%	100%	100%	100%	100%
Number of cases	41	30	194	17	768	65

ing about its placement power. It does indicate that the unions have had even greater success in by-elections than in general elections in placing their nominees in winnable seats.

Other Characteristics. There were no significant differences between by-election and general election candidatures in the distributions of the candidates' ages, experience in local government, experience in civic or party organizations, education, or occupations.

In summary, then, this comparison of Labour candidatures in the two types of elections supports the belief that Transport House's actual influence as well as its formal power to intervene is greater in by-elections than in general elections. It also supports the conclusion that Transport House's advantages in this regard are substantially greater than Conservative Central Office's.

THE NEC'S VETO POWER

The Labour party's Constitution, Standing Orders, and Model Rules provide four principal devices by which the NEC can prevent persons it deems unacceptable from becoming official Labour parliamentary candidates. The following review of each device and of the circumstances in which it has been used provides a basis for estimating the impact of the veto power on the selection process.

EXCLUSION FROM LIST B

We observed previously that since 1960 the NEC's List B of possible parliamentary candidates has become almost—but not quite—a recommended list. To be sure, inclusion in it does not guarantee nor absence preclude NEC endorsement. Yet inclusion is generally regarded as a good sign that the NEC will approve, and the list's wide circulation among CLPs makes it the principal vehicle by which outside aspirants let local selectors know they are available. Thus, even if List B is not, strictly speaking, a recommended list, inclusion in it is a distinct advantage and exclusion a real handicap in getting adopted.

No outsider knows exactly how many applicants the NEC has excluded since 1960, but some have undoubtedly been turned down. On one recent occasion controversy over an NEC exclusion became public. In late 1961 two members of the Brighton party applied for the list. One, Derek Lesley-Jones, had been a follower of Sir Oswald Mosley as late as 1951, and after he had joined the Labour party the NEC had twice denied his application for inclusion on List B because of his former Fascist associations. The other, Councillor Dennis Hobden, was an outspoken left-wing critic of the party leadership. On the recommendation of the Organisation Subcommittee, the NEC voted to include Lesley-Jones but exclude Hobden. The Brighton party protested Hobden's exclusion, but the NEC refused to reconsider. The Left's principal organ commented bitterly that having been a Fascist was apparently no bar to getting on List B, but that having criticized the party leadership evidently was.[36]

---

[36] *Tribune* (London), January 5, 1962, p. 4.

EXPLUSION FROM THE PARTY

The party Constitution authorizes the NEC

to enforce the Constitution, Standing Orders, and Rules of the Party and to take any action it deems necessary for such purpose, whether by way of disaffiliation of an organisation or expulsion of an individual, or otherwise. Any such action shall be reported to the next Annual Conference of the Party.[37]

The best-known instances in which the NEC has used its power since 1945 occurred in 1947–1949 when it expelled four far-Left Labour M.P.s (J.F.F. Platts-Mills, L. J. Solley, Konni Zilliacus, and H. L. Hutchinson) and one far-Right M.P. (Alfred Edwards). We shall review the Solley, Zilliacus, and Hutchinson cases here and the Platts-Mills and Edwards cases in Chapter 6.

L. J. Solley and Thurrock, 1949–50. L. J. Solley was elected for the safe Labour seat of Thurrock in Essex in 1945, and soon became one of the Left's most vocal opponents of the Labour government's anti-Communist foreign policy. In March, 1949, the Thurrock party readopted him as their prospective candidate and sent his name to the NEC for endorsement. The NEC, however, decided to consider not merely his suitability as a candidate but his membership in the party as well. They summoned Solley for an interview, and asked him to give an undertaking that he would henceforth refrain from open attacks on the party's leaders and official policies. When he refused, they voted to expel him from the party altogether (which made him ineligible for readoption under Clause IX, section 7 (a) of the Constitution).[38] Informed of his expulsion, Solley said, "It may be that Transport House thinks it can do what it likes to the local Party and that Thurrock has not got the guts to object. We shall see."[39]

---

[37] Clause VIII, section (b). In 1963 the NEC considered a proposal by Clive Jenkins to allow any person expelled to appeal to a new appeals tribunal rather than, as at present, be forced to persuade a majority of the annual conference to approve a motion suspending the rules to let him speak in his defense—a motion carried only on the occasion in 1939 when Sir Stafford Cripps was allowed to speak after his expulsion. The NEC, however, decided against the Jenkins proposal, and the rule remains that expulsions need only be reported to the annual conference: *Times* (London), September 19, 1963, p. 6.

[38] "No person may be selected as a Parliamentary Labour Candidate . . . if the person concerned (a) is not an Individual Member of the Party . . . ."

[39] *Essex and Thurrock Gazette,* May 28, 1949, pp. 1, 5.

The Thurrock party executive voted by 55 to 17 to protest Solley's expulsion and seek his reinstatement. At the party conference in Blackpool in June they moved that the standing orders be suspended and Solley and Zilliacus permitted to address the conference in their own defense. They were defeated by a card vote of 3,023,000 to 1,993,000. Then a motion to refer back that part of the NEC's report expelling the two from the party was defeated by a card vote of 4,721,000 to 714,000.[40]

Their constitutional remedies exhausted, some of Solley's supporters in the Thurrock party formed the "Leslie Solley Campaign Committee" to fight for his reinstatement and, if necessary, to support his candidature as an Independent. Two weeks later the Thurrock executive voted to expel the Solley Committee's members from the CLP, and the NEC upheld their right to do so.[41] In October the Thurrock party adopted a new candidate, H. J. Delargy, then Member for the Platting division of Manchester, which was to be abolished in the redistribution. Solley stood in the 1950 general election as Independent Labour candidate, and finished a distant third of four in the poll. The local Labour agent later reported, "At Transport House they went wild with joy when I told them over the 'phone of the result in Thurrock."[42]

Konni Zilliacus and Gateshead East, 1949–50. Konni Zilliacus, elected for Gateshead in 1945, was the best known and ablest of the left-wing critics of the Attlee-Bevin foreign policy. Redistribution divided his seat in two, and the CLP of the new East division in December, 1948, unanimously adopted him as their prospective candidate for the next general election. When the NEC received the request for endorsement, they decided to consider Zilliacus's membership in the party along with Solley's.

Zilliacus later wrote a seventy-two-page pamphlet describing in detail the subsequent events and quoting at some length exchanges between himself and the NEC.[43] While its interpretations fall somewhat short of strict judicial impartiality, it does provide an

---

[40] *Times* (London), June 7, 1949, p. 2.

[41] *Essex and Thurrock Gazette*, September 10, 1949, p. 1.

[42] *Ibid.*, March 4, 1950, p. 1.

[43] *Why I Was Expelled*, published and distributed by Collet's Holdings (Bookshops) Ltd., 1949.

illuminating step-by-step account of the expulsion proceedings. As Zilliacus tells the story, matters began with a letter from the party Secretary, Morgan Phillips, asking him to meet with the Elections Sub-committee[44] on January 16, 1949, to answer charges specified in an attached "charge sheet." These consisted mainly of quotations from Zilliacus's speeches attacking the government's "unsocialist" foreign policy. He immediately wrote a lengthy reply and sent it to Transport House in advance of his interview.

At his hearing Zilliacus was questioned by various committee members, with Attlee himself taking an active part, and defended rather than apologized for his criticisms. He later learned, he wrote, that after Attlee had left the meeting the sub-committee voted by nine votes to none to recommend that his candidature be endorsed. When the whole NEC met to consider the recommendation, however, Attlee and Herbert Morrison, with strong support from the trade union members, argued that the candidature be disapproved. Their motion was carried, but, for the moment at least, Zilliacus was still a party member.

Shortly after his interview he was invited to attend the Communist-organized "world peace congress" in Paris, and some of his Gateshead supporters urged him to decline in the hope that if he remained quiet the NEC would eventually reverse themselves and endorse his candidature. Zilliacus, as he wrote, "was pretty sure my attendance at the World Peace Congress would be thankfully seized on as a pretext for turning me out of the Party, but I went there because it was part of the fight for peace."[45] On his return from Paris, the Elections Sub-committee summoned him for another interview to justify his attendance at a Communist convocation. Zilliacus again refused to apologize or mend his ways, and two days later the NEC announced that both he and Solley had been expelled from the party.

After their failure to get the NEC's decision reversed by the annual conference (see above), the East Gateshead CLP split over the question of whether to stand by Zilliacus or accept his expulsion and select another candidate. The NEC warned them through the

---

[44] This, as we noted above, was the NEC body that handled matters of candidature before 1959.

[45] *Why I Was Expelled,* p. 48.

Northern regional organizer that anyone who supported Zilliacus's candidature would be expelled from the party. A majority of the executive bowed to the inevitable and started the procedure to select a new candidate. Several members, including Councillor G. C. Esther, the CLP chairman, resigned their party offices and formed a Zilliacus committee. The CLP adopted as its official candidate A. S. Moody, then Member for the Fairfield division of Hull, which was to be abolished by redistribution. The NEC speedily endorsed him. In the 1950 general election Zilliacus stood as an Independent Labour candidate, and although he displayed a letter of support from George Bernard Shaw, he finished a distant third in the poll.[46]

Lester Hutchinson, Manchester Ardwick, and Middleton and Prestwich, 1949. Lester Hutchinson was elected Member for the Rusholme division of Manchester in 1945, and joined the left-wing critics of the Labour government's foreign policy. His seat was abolished in the redistribution, and he was nominated for adoption in the Ardwick division of Manchester, a marginal Labour seat. In February, 1949, the NEC wrote to the Ardwick party's executive committee noting that Hutchinson was being considered and reminding them of its power to withhold endorsement. The Ardwick executive took the hint and did not put Hutchinson on the short list.[47]

Hutchinson looked about for another constituency, and finally was adopted at Middleton and Prestwich, a safe Conservative seat. The Middleton party secretary told a reporter after the selection conference that the NEC's letter to the Ardwick party had not influenced them in Middleton and Prestwich. After all, he said, any candidate *may* be denied endorsement and most of the delegates at the selection conference had believed Hutchinson when he had said that he was sure the NEC would in the end endorse his candidature.[48]

The NEC, however, deferred action on the endorsement, summoned Hutchinson to Transport House for an interview in July,

---

[46] For other accounts of the Zilliacus-Gateshead case, see the *Newcastle Journal,* May 19, 1949, p. 1; February 24, 1949, p. 1; May 25, 1949, p. 1; October 6, 1949, p. 1; *Manchester Guardian,* May 19, 1949, p. 5.

[47] *Manchester Guardian,* February 26, 1949, p. 5.

[48] *Middleton Guardian,* April 9, 1949, p. 5.

and then voted to expel him from the party. Some members of the Middleton party protested, but the management committee immediately began a search for a new candidate.[49] Hutchinson registered his protest by standing as Independent Labour candidate in Attlee's own seat of Walthamstow West, in the 1950 general election. He finished a poor fourth and lost his deposit.

KEEPING NAMES OFF THE SHORT LIST

The Model Rules provide:

> Prior to a meeting of the General Committee being called to consider the nominations [for the short list to be put before the selection conference] the Executive Committee of [the constituency] Party shall consult with the National Executive Committee or its officers to determine the validity of the nominations received.[50]

Head Office officials are careful to point out that this procedure is purely technical and routine, intended only to ensure that all the nominees on the short list meet all the formal qualifications for candidature.[51]

To the author's knowledge no nominee has been struck off a short list at this stage simply because Transport House regarded him as politically undesirable, but several party officials told him that on a number of occasions undesirable nominees have been kept off short lists by informal pressures from Transport House. As in many other matters, the regional organizer plays a key role here. As a matter of course he often sits with the executive committees of the parties in his region when they are drawing up short lists. When his relations with an executive committee are good and when they are considering a candidate regarded by Transport House as particularly objectionable, a statement from him that harmony within the CLP and cordial relations with Transport House would be well served by quietly dropping the objectionable contender will often be heeded. One particularly able and successful regional organizer told the author that the main reason why so few anti-leadership candidates were adopted by the CLPs in his region was that he

---

[49] *Ibid.*, July 30, 1949, p. 5.
[50] Model Rules, Set A, Clause XII, section (d).
[51] Cf. Sara E. Barker, "Selecting the Candidate," *Labour Organiser*, XXXV (January, 1956), 13–14.

made it his business to see they were kept off short lists wherever he could prevent it. Any regional organizer who does not do the same, he felt, is not doing his job properly.

WITHHOLDING ENDORSEMENT

1. *The Formal Power*

The Labour party's Constitution as we have seen, stipulates that "the selection of Labour Candidates for Parliamentary Elections shall not be regarded as completed until the name of the person selected has been placed before a meeting of the National Executive Committee, and his or her selection has been duly endorsed."[52] This formal power closely resembles that given the Conservatives' Standing Advisory Committee (see Chapter 2), and certainly gives the NEC all the authority it needs to keep undesirables out of the parliamentary party.

Harold Lawrence and Bristol West, 1951. If the NEC endorses a candidate, he remains the official Labour candidate whether or not the party Leader personally approves. This was made clear in 1951 in a by-election for the safe Tory seat of Bristol West. The CLP adopted Harold Lawrence, and the NEC endorsed him. At an election meeting soon afterward Lawrence was asked if he supported the Labour government's rearmament policy. He replied that, being a pacifist, he could not. This so incensed Prime Minister Attlee that he refused to send Lawrence the letter of best wishes and support that the party Leader customarily sends each Labour candidate. Transport House was careful to point out, however, that Lawrence was nevertheless the official Labour candidate, because the NEC had endorsed him.[53]

2. *The Veto in Practice.*

We observed in Chapter 2 that the Conservative SACC's power of veto over candidates has been used only once since 1945, and concluded that when a candidate has been adopted by a Conservative constituency association he almost certainly will be accepted by the national party agencies.

---

[52] Clause IX, section 3.
[53] *Times* (London), February 10, 1951, p. 4.

A similar but not identical presumption obtains in the Labour party. It stems partly from the strong tradition of local control of candidate selection noted previsouly and the danger of local resentment and demoralization if central control is laid on with too heavy a hand. It stems also from the handicaps under which the NEC operates. As one of its members told the author, the NEC does not and cannot carefully scrutinize each and every candidate it is asked to endorse. If he happens to be a prominent national figure or if the regional organizer sends in a detailed report about his virtues and failings, the NEC has something to go on. But in most instances its members know no more about the candidate than what appears on his "Form of Particulars," and the regional organizer confines his report to warranting that the selection conference employed proper procedures. The NEC is simply not in a position to investigate each candidate carefully, and in the great majority of cases it does the only thing it can: endorse the choice of the constituency party.

3. The Power Exercised

Whatever may be its strength measured against an idealized notion of a highly centralized and "responsible" party, the central veto of candidates has played a distinctly greater role in the Labour party than the Conservative in recent years. By contrast with the single direct veto imposed by the SACC since 1945, Transport House has vetoed at least five candidates in addition to the five M.P.s it expelled from the party. The five cases were the following:

W. G. Fisher and Bridgwater, 1949–50. In August, 1949, the CLP in Bridgwater, a marginal seat then held by an Independent, adopted as its prospective candidate W. G. "Bud" Fisher, a prominent local trade union official and town councillor. In November, the NEC refused to endorse Fisher, reportedly[54] on the ground that he had supported the Independent against the official Labour candidate in the 1945 general election.[55] The Bridgwater party pro-

---

[54] The NEC has invariably refused to state publicly the reasons for withholding endorsements of candidates or denying admission to List B. This policy stems in part from the feeling that whatever political wounds its actions have caused will heal more rapidly if public controversy can be avoided. The principal reason, however, is the ever-present danger of libel action.

[55] *Bridgwater Mercury*, November 29, 1949, p. 1.

tested and tried to persuade the NEC to reverse its decision, but the NEC was adamant. In January, 1950, the local management committee adopted a resolution declaring that they would not contest the 1950 election at all! Two weeks later an ad hoc meeting of local Labour party and Co-operative party members, called with the encouragement of the NEC under the emergency provisions of the Model Rules (see above), adopted as prospective candidate Norman Carr, a London audit clerk. The NEC immediately endorsed him, and the Bridgwater party accepted him as their candidate.[56] Carr failed to win the seat in either the 1950 or 1951 elections, however.

Tom Braddock and Wimbledon, 1955. Tom Braddock was elected Member for Mitcham in 1945, and before his defeat in 1950 became one of the better-known members of the left-wing opposition to the leadership—though he did not defy the whip so often or so vocally as the five M.P.s who were expelled from the party. After unsuccessfully searching for another seat for several years, he was adopted in early 1954 by his own CLP in Wimbledon, a safe Conservative seat. The NEC, however, refused to endorse him. The Wimbledon party asked them to reconsider, and arranged for Braddock to go to Transport House for an interview with the Elections Sub-committee. The interview took place in March, 1955, and Braddock later reported that the questions put to him had been "formidable" and that he had "got on very badly." The sub-committee recommended that there be no reversal of the decision to withhold endorsement.[57] The Wimbledon executive then voted to "stand by" Braddock, without making clear what they meant by this. The Southern regional organizer met with them and was reported to have warned they were courting expulsion from the party. The executive accepted defeat, and a month later Wimbledon adopted a new candidate.[58] In March, 1958, Braddock was adopted in another safe Conservative seat, Kingston-upon-Thames, and this time he evidently got on better in his interview with the NEC, for it endorsed his candidature. He stood in 1959 and again in 1964, but lost both times.

---

[56] *Ibid.,* January 24, 1950, p. 1; February 28, 1950, p. 1.
[57] *Wimbledon Boro' News,* March 25, 1955, p. 16.
[58] *Ibid.,* May 6, 1955, p. 1; May 13, 1955, p. 1.

Sam Goldberg and Nottingham South, 1957. In early 1957 the CLP in Nottingham South, another safe Conservative seat, adopted Sam Goldberg as its candidate. He was a well-known Labour councillor in Birmingham, a leading member of the Electrical Trades Union, and a man widely believed to merit the label "crypto-Communist" even more than the four expelled in 1949. The NEC invited him to appear before it to answer queries about his affiliations with Communist-front organizations, but Goldberg wrote a letter instead. The NEC was not impressed, and refused endorsement. The CLP protested, but recognized the hopelessness of a fight and adopted another candidate.[59]

E. A. Roberts and Horsham, 1961. E. A. "Ernie" Roberts, the assistant general secretary of the Amalgamated Engineering Union and another well-known member of the far-left opposition to the party's leaders, fought and lost Stockport South in 1955. He did not stand in the 1959 general election, but in November, 1961, he was adopted by the CLP in Horsham, a marginal Conservative constituency. The Organisation Sub-committee recommended that endorsement be refused, and the NEC agreed.[60] A writer for the left-wing organ *Tribune* complained:

> What in effect [the NEC] are doing is saying that constituency parties have no longer got the right to select their own candidates. Transport House will continue to veto them until they get someone who is suitable to their purpose. I cannot say that I know of one constituency party in the Labour Party which would accept such a situation. That is why I'm sure that the Horsham Party will have massive support in its struggle in 1962.[61]

This may well have been a correct diagnosis of what the NEC was doing, but it was bad prophecy about the consequences. The 1962 annual conference not only produced no "massive support" for the Horsham party but, indeed, no fight at all. The Horsham party gave up on Roberts and set about selecting another candidate.

Illtyd Harrington and Dover, 1962. The most recent instance of an NEC veto is in several respects the most unusual. In March, 1962, the CLP in Dover, a marginal Conservative seat which Trans-

---

[59] *Nottingham Guardian Journal*, March 15, 1957, p. 2; *Nottingham Evening Post*, March 15, 1957, p. 9; *Manchester Guardian*, March 15, 1957, p. 2.
[60] *Times* (London), December 14, 1961, p. 18; *ibid.*, December 21, 1961, p. 6.
[61] Frances Flavius, *Tribune* (London), December 29, 1961, p. 4.

port House had high hopes of recapturing in 1964, adopted Illtyd Harrington, a thirty-year-old London schoolteacher, chairman of the Paddington party, and a member in good standing on List B. He was also an active member of the Campaign for Nuclear Disarmament, and prominently displayed his CND badge in many appearances in the constituency. The right-wing minority in the Dover party wrote the NEC a long report alleging that Harrington was involved with Communist-front organizations. The NEC interviewed Harrington and sent two members of the Organisation Sub-committee down to Dover to investigate further. Finally, it decided not to endorse him.[62] According to one member of the NEC, Harrington was regarded as "marginal, not clearly unacceptable like Sam Goldberg or Ernie Roberts." They would probably have endorsed him if they had not been tipped off by the Dover party minority. And if Dover had been a hopeless seat instead of a winnable one, they would probably have accepted Harrington despite his involvement with these organizations. But Dover, they felt, was winnable—but not by a strong CND man. Everything considered, they decided not to endorse him for this particular seat. However, he remained on List B and was later adopted, with NEC approval, for the safe Tory seat of Wembley North, where he lost in 1964. The Dover party adopted a new candidate, David Ennals, a former Liberal, who won the seat in the 1964 election.

THE IMPACT OF THE NEC'S VETO POWER

One way or another, then, since 1945 Transport House has denied at least ten locally adopted candidates the right to stand as official Labour candidates on the ground that they were politically too far Left. Several other candidatures have been voided on technical procedural grounds,[63] but for our purposes the significant cases are the ten vetoes on political grounds.

---

[62] Cf. Anthony Howard, "The Dover Road," *The New Statesman and Nation,* June 1, 1962, p. 782.

[63] In June, 1959, for example the NEC ordered the reconvening of the selection conference in Nottingham North, because the local NUM branch had complained that many of its delegates had not received their credentials to vote. The second selection conference, however, chose the same man again, and this time he was endorsed without protest: *Nottingham Guardian Journal,* July 3, 1959, p. 2; July 6, 1959, p. 1; August 17, 1959, p. 3.

Five of the ten involved incumbent M.P.s in good Labour seats. The device used for these five was not merely to refuse endorsement of their readoptions but to expel them from the party altogether and to threaten to expel also any local party member who supported their candidatures under other labels. But two aspects of the situation should be emphasized: first, all five episodes occurred in the late 1940's when the party in the country and the leadership in the party were each at the zenith of their power and security; and second, four of the five were believed to be Communists or near-Communists infiltrating the party to serve not Labour but an alien cause.

When neither the party nor its leaders were so powerful or secure in the 1950's and early 1960's, and when no question of Communist affiliations or loyalties entered in, other rebellious M.P.s were dealt with considerably less harshly. In 1954, for instance, the whip was withdrawn from eight Bevanite rebels, including Aneurin Bevan himself. None, however, was expelled from the party, and the whip was restored to all before the 1955 general election. The same pattern was followed in all respects in the cases of the five left-wing M.P.s who were deprived of the whip in 1961 and returned to grace in 1963.

It appears, then, that the party's national leaders have used the extreme weapon of expulsion against rebel M.P.s only when they believed they were dealing with Communists or near-Communists and when they were confident the expulsions could be made to stick both locally and in the annual conferences. When the rebellions were ideologically less offensive and when Transport House was less sure of its power, it prudently avoided uncompromisable challenges to popular M.P.s in safe Labour seats.

The other five candidates vetoed since 1945 had all been adopted in Conservative-held seats, four of which appeared unwinnable. In these cases the less drastic sanction of denying endorsement without expulsion from the party was deemed sufficient, and although each CLP complained it eventually accepted the NEC's verdict and adopted another candidate acceptable to Transport House.

At the same time, however, a considerable number of left-wing, anti-leadership candidates have been adopted in safe, marginal, and hopeless seats, and the NEC has endorsed them all. Enough have been adopted in good seats, indeed, to give some reason to believe that there is a higher proportion of left-wing M.P.s in the parliamentary party in the early 1960's than there was a decade earlier.[64]

The central veto power in the Labour party, then, has undoubtedly been used far more often than in the Conservative party. This, more than the sporadic and hesitant use of the central placement power, justifies the widespread impression that the Labour party's national organs have more power over candidate selection than their Conservative counterparts. So they do. But even in the Labour party the final word in the selection of most parliamentary candidates rests, in party law and political fact, in the constituency Labour parties, not in Transport House.

---

[64] This is the thesis of Leon D. Epstein, "New M.P.s and the Politics of the PLP," *Political Studies*, X (June, 1952), 121–29.

Chapter 6	*The Role of the*
	Constituency Labour Parties

The Constitution of the Labour party stipulates:

> Each Constituency Labour Party, Central Labour Party, and Federation must, . . . adopt the Rules laid down by the Party Conference."[1]

In accordance with this provision, a series of Model Rules were laid down by the annual conferences of 1929 and 1930.[2] The National Executive Committee is empowered to allow modifications if local circumstances warrant, but for the most part the Model Rules are closely followed by all constituency Labour parties.[3] The main features of the CLPs' organization affecting the selection of parliamentary candidates are as follows.

ORGANIZATION

MEMBERSHIP

Constituency Labour parties, unlike Conservative local associations, have two classes of membership: (1) *affiliated organizations,*

---

[1] Constitution of the Labour party, Clause III, section 2.

[2] See Chapter 5. Unless otherwise indicated, we shall refer to Model Rules, Set A.

[3] See Robert T. McKenzie, *British Political Parties,* 2nd ed. (London: Mercury Books, 1964), pp. 538–49, for an excellent concise summary of the organization of constituency Labour parties.

such as trade union branches, co-operative societies, branches of the Co-operative party, branches of socialist societies, youth sections, and the like; and (2) *individual members,* i.e., all persons over the age of sixteen years "who subscribe to the conditions of membership"[4] and pay an annual subscription of six shillings. Individual members participate in CLP affairs through the polling district committees (usually ward committees) where they live or in which they are registered voters. Consequently, a Labour activist can participate in his CLP only through an organization intermediate between him and the CLP's governing bodies. The CLPs have nothing comparable to the annual or special general meetings of Conservative constituency associations.

GENERAL MANAGEMENT COMMITTEE (GMC)

The CLP's basic authority is vested in a general management committee (GMC) composed of representatives (usually called "delegates") selected by the affiliated organizations and ward committees. The basis of representation for the various constituent bodies varies, but in most CLPs delegates are chosen in proportion to the membership of the affiliated organizations.[5] Since the CLP's prospective parliamentary candidate is selected by a special meeting of the GMC called a selection conference, its part in candidate selection is comparable to that of the executive council in local Conservative associations.

EXECUTIVE COMMITTEE

The executive committee is composed of the CLP's officers—the president, two vice-presidents, treasurer, financial secretary, and secretary—and a number of GMC members selected by the GMC to represent the various constituent organizations.[6] The CLP exec-

---

[4] That is, they must accept the program, principles, and policy of the Labour party; if eligible, be a member of a trade union affiliated with the Trades Union Congress; either reside in the constituency or be registered therein as a parliamentary or local government elector; etc.: Party Constitution, Clause III, section (3).

[5] The Southampton Labour party, for example, awards one GMC delegate per 100 members to each affiliated organization and ward committee up to a maximum of 6 delegates per organization or committee. The total size of the GMC is 280 delegates: "The Southampton Labour Party," a mimeographed description circulated by its Secretary in 1961.

[6] The executive committee of the Southampton Labour party, for example, consists

utive occupies a position comparable to that of the finance and general purposes committees of most Conservative associations; in candidate selection it draws up the short list from which the GMC makes the final choice.

THE SPECIAL CASE OF CENTRAL PARTIES IN DIVIDED BOROUGHS

The Model Rules also provide for the establishment of central (i.e., borough-wide) party organizations in divided boroughs (i.e., those containing two or more parliamentary constituencies). A central Labour party's GMC is composed of delegates from organizations affiliated at the borough level, from individual members, and from each of the CLPs in the borough's parliamentary constituencies. In this case each CLP selects its parliamentary candidate by the usual procedures, with three exceptions: the central party's executive joins with the NEC and the CLP's executive in deciding whether the constituency should be contested; the circular inviting nominations for the CLP's candidature is sent to all the organizations affiliated with the central party as well as to all those affiliated only with the constituency party, and all these organizations may make nominations; and the normal selection procedures may be suspended in emergencies or in by-elections after consultation by the NEC with the central party's executive as well as with the CLP's executive.[7]

In the interests of simplicity, however, we shall confine our discussion to CLPs in undivided boroughs except in a few cases in which central parties in divided boroughs have played prominent parts.

THE STAGES OF CANDIDATE SELECTION

NOMINATIONS

We have noted before that no person may be officially considered for a CLP's candidature until he has been formally nominated by one or more of its affiliated organizations, or ward committees, or

---

of the 5 officers, 4 GMC members representing the ward committees, 4 representing the affiliated trade unions, 2 representing the affiliated co-operative societies, and one each representing the affiliated socialist societies, the women's section, and the youth section: *ibid.*

[7] Model Rules, Set D, Clause XIII, sections (1), (3), (4), and (5).

—although this is very rare—by the NEC itself. This rule has the effect, particularly in winnable seats, of making these bodies the main agencies for preliminary screening of the contenders. Thus in winnable seats it is common for local aspirants and hopeful outsiders to sound out acquaintances in ward committees or affiliated trade union branches about the possibilities of being nominated. It is not unusual for as many as ten or fifteen nominations to be made.

In the less desirable seats, of course, far fewer aspirants come forward, and the ward committees and affiliated organizations are less active in screening potential candidates. Under these circumstances the executive often takes the initiative by writing to likely persons on List B, asking them if they would like to be considered, and requesting the constituent organizations to nominate those who express interest.[8] CLP executives, in short, often play more active roles in the preliminary screening stage than the formal requirement of nomination by constituent bodies contemplates, but usually less active roles than those played by selection committees in Conservative associations (see Chapter 3).

THE SHORT LIST

1. *Drawn Up by the Executive Committee*

When the announced deadline for receiving nominations has passed, the executive draws up the short list. The nomination requirement often means that it has a smaller number of choices than its Conservative counterparts usually face,[9] but the range of choice

---

[8] The following illustrations, taken from interviews with local party officials, give some notion of the range of nominations. For a safe Labour seat in Derbyshire, approximately fifty persons sounded out affiliated organizations and ward committees about possible nominations. Fourteen nominations were made, from which the executive chose a short list of four. For a safe Labour seat in Lincolnshire, an estimated thirty-five persons tried for nominations, eleven were nominated, and the executive drew up a short list of five. For a safe Conservative seat in West Sussex, the executive wrote twenty-three persons on List B, none of whom wished to be considered. Eighteen more were approached, three consented and were nominated, but two dropped out. One more was added, and a short list of two went before the selection conference. For a safe Conservative seat in North-West London, the executive wrote to sixty-eight persons on List B, six responded favorably, four were nominated, and all were put on the short list.

[9] Labour short lists, on the other hand, tend to be longer than Conservative. The latter, as we saw in Chapter 3, usually have three or four names, while Labour lists

may often be as great or greater. A CLP executive may consider only six or seven nominees, but one may be a devout believer in unilateral nuclear disarmament, another may be a faithful supporter of NATO, and yet another may be a trade unionist concerned with little beyond his union's welfare. The typical CLP executive, accordingly, plays every bit as critical a role as the Conservative screening committees. We noted in Chapter 5 that the exclusion of left-wing nominees from short lists by right-wing executives working with the regional organizers has been perhaps the most effective device in recent years for minimizing the number of left-wing candidates and M.P.s.[10]

2. *Validated by the National Executive Committee*

When the executive has agreed upon a tentative short list, it must then be submitted to Transport House for validation. We observed in Chapter 5 that this is usually a routine review dealing with purely technical questions, but on a few occasions the NEC has struck off politically unacceptable persons.

3. *Approved by the General Management Committee*

After the NEC has validated the list, it is submitted to the GMC for approval and for fixing the date of the selection conference. This, too, is usually routine, but sometimes GMCs have ordered substantial revisions.

Michael Foot and Ebbw Vale, 1960. Perhaps the best known example of the latter came in 1960 in the selection of a Labour candidate for Ebbw Vale after the death of Aneurin Bevan. When the nominations for his successor had closed, ten persons had been nominated, including Councillor Don Evans (the local agent), Alderman Frank Whatley (the nominee of the National Union of Mineworkers, which had sponsored Bevan), and three former M.P.s

---

often have four to six names. Professor John Turner of the University of Minnesota told the author of attending a selection conference in Faversham in 1961 which boasted a short list of no less than ten! Nine actually appeared at the selection conference, and the speech-making alone took over five hours. The tea break after the fourth speaker, according to Professor Turner, was the most enjoyable and enjoyed he had ever known.

[10] Cf. John Cole, "Choice of Labour Candidates," *Manchester Guardian,* November 12, 1959, p. 10.

looking for new seats. The best known of the latter was Michael Foot, Member for the Devonport division of Plymouth from 1945 to his defeat in 1955, Bevan's biographer-to-be, and his heir-apparent as the leading spokesman of the Left. The executive drew up a short list of five which omitted both Foot and Whatley—in an effort, some said, to "stack the cards" for Evans.[11] The omissions outraged, respectively, the Left and the Mineworkers. Both asked Transport House if the short list could be changed before the selection conference, and were told that it could. Accordingly, the GMC meeting called to approve the list added both men despite the executive's objections.[12] A week later the selection conference chose Foot on the second ballot.[13]

THE SELECTION CONFERENCE

1. *Similarities with the Conservatives*

In several respects Labour selection conferences are conducted like Conservative selection conferences (see Chapter 3). Each contender is given ten to fifteen minutes to speak and another five to ten minutes to answer questions from the floor. The order of speaking is determined by lot, and no contender hears any of the others. When all have finished, the GMC delegates vote on a formal motion that they do now proceed to ballot. If this motion fails, the executive must adjourn the conference and produce a new short list. If, as usually happens, the motion carries, the delegates vote, usually by secret ballot, until one contender receives an absolute majority of the votes cast.[14]

---

[11] *Times* (London), September 9, 1960, p. 12.
[12] *Ibid.*, September 19, 1960, p. 7.
[13] *Ibid.*, September 26, 1960, p. 8.
[14] The author attended one of the few selection conferences in memory which had to be adjourned because it resulted in a tie. The CLP in a marginal Conservative seat in South-East London met in January, 1962, to consider a short list of six, of whom only five appeared. The results of the first ballot were: A, 6 votes; B, 0 votes; C, 6 votes; D, 6 votes, and E, 3 votes. In the customary manner, B and E were dropped, and a second ballot was held, in which A, C, and D each received 7 votes. The London regional organizer, who was present representing Transport House, explained that another ballot would be taken and that if the results were again a tie, the conference would have to be adjourned and reconvened at a later date. On the third ballot each man again received 7 votes. Some delegates suggested that each contender be brought back for five more minutes of speaking, but the regional organizer said this would be

The attendance at Labour selection conferences varies widely, usually depending upon the desirability of the seat. As few as fifteen or twenty delegates may attend in hopeless seats, and as many as two hundred or more may be present in winnable seats. Whatever the number of delegates present, however, Labour selection conferences have a certain atmosphere well rememberd by anyone who has ever attended one. In Chapter 3 we quoted testimony on how a Conservative conference seems to a contender. The following description of a Labour conference by a contender provides some interesting similiarities and contrasts:

When the first contestant is led into the meeting hall a shock awaits him. Instead of the kindly, compassionate faces he has come to know so well from years of work inside the Labour Party, there sitting before him are several score members of the family portrayed in the *New Yorker* by Mr. Charles Addams. In a halting voice (made more nervous by immediate complaints that no one at the back can hear) he then launches into the subtle blend of egotism and idealism which, with the aid of the Labour Party Speakers' Handbook, leading articles from *The Guardian* and the aphorisms of Mr. Adlai Stevenson, he has been busy preparing for weeks. Questions follow, each more bewilderingly irrelevant than the one before. The nominee has painstakingly worked out advance replies to possible queries on nuclear disarmament, German rearmament (yes, still), capital punishment and Clause Four. Now one delegate after another rises to seek his views on street lighting, the aldermanic system and Moral Rearmament.

At last the ordeal is over and, in the dead silence that has prevailed from the moment he entered the hall, he plods dully back to the waiting-room where the others gaze at him with undisguised loathing. There, while each of his fellow contenders (on a strictly regulated equal-time basis) goes through the same procedure, he sits, wincing at the repeated bursts of appreciative laughter which punctuate his rivals' performance.[15]

---

unconstitutional, since the formal motion to ballot had already been adopted. Another suggested that only the top three "finalists" be invited back to the second selection conference, but the chair ruled that this would be an illegal form of short listing. So the selection conference was adjourned and all five contestants were asked to come back a month later. Before the second meeting C and E withdrew. Just after the second meeting opened, B telephoned his withdrawal as well. At the meeting D spoke and answered questions in the usual manner. He was followed by A, who announced that the whole affair had become ridiculous and he would not accept the candidature even if he were selected! Then the formal motion to ballot was made, but lost! The GMC decided to start the whole selection process over again from the beginning.

[15] Gerald Kaufman, "Labour Takes Its Pick," *Time & Tide*, December 28, 1961, p. 2182. Kaufman wrote on the basis of having stood as Labour candidate in two safe Conservative seats: Bromley in 1955 and Gillingham in 1959.

2. *Differences from the Conservatives*

Pre-conference Politicking. We observed in Chapter 3 that in Conservative associations any organized lobbying by or on behalf of a contender prior to the selection conference is much disapproved and, if detected, will probably cost him any chance of adoption. No such taboo prevails in the Labour party, however. Although the degree and forms of pre-conference politicking vary from one CLP to the next and even from one party region to the next (depending to a large degree upon how much the regional organizer tries to prevent it), it is not unusual for campaigns to be conducted on behalf of some aspirants, particularly in the more desirable seats. The candidates and their supporters often try to persuade the executive to put them on the short list, and solicit votes at the selection conference from ward committees, other affiliated organizations, and individual delegates. Any such politicking has to be conducted with due regard for the sensibilities of the delegates and their constituents,[16] but where an aspirant's rivals are already at work he cannot afford to remain inactive.

The Role of Finance: Rules and Reality. Since the Wilson Report reforms of 1957 (see Chapter 5), selection conferences have been prohibited from discussing the financial benefits, if any, the adoption of any contender might bring the CLP. But every GMC delegate knows who is sponsored and who is not and how each alternative will affect the CLP's funds. So in reality financial considerations continue to play a markedly greater role in Labour than in Conservative selections.[17] We shall have more to say about this in Chapter 8.

No Public Discussion of the Nominees' Merits. Labour, unlike the Conservatives, prohibits GMC delegates or officers from publicly discussing the nominees' merits at a selection conference. The rationale for this rule was explained by the present National Agent thus:

---

[16] One regional organizer told the author that advance canvassing often determines the adoption, but where it is too open and/or too crude it can backfire and perhaps even lose the adoption for a contender who might otherwise have won. Cf. T. E. M. McKitterick "The Selection of Parliamentary Candidates: The Labour Party," *Political Quarterly*, XXX (July-September, 1959), 219–23 at pp. 222–23.

[17] Cf. McKenzie, *British Political Parties*, pp. 553–55; McKitterick, *Political Quart.*, XXX, 219–23; and McKitterick's letter to the *Times* (London), August 18, 1959, p. 9.

Each nominee may be questioned, but it is very important to note that when the speeches have been made, and questions answered, no delegate or officer must be allowed to speak on the merits of the nominees. The delegates will vote on the performance of the nominees, and not on opinions expressed by others, or attempts to sum up the merits. A chairman who permits any contribution to be made after the nominees have spoken, is failing in his duties.[18]

No Mandating of Delegates. Transport House stipulates that no delegate may be mandated by his organization to vote for a particular contender, but the rule is generally unenforced and probably unenforceable. Delegates from affiliated organizations, especially in the safe seats, often vote *en bloc* with a unanimity that strongly suggests mandating or at least prior discussion and agreement. Transport House rarely even inquires whether the rule has been violated, let alone invalidates adoptions because it has detected mandating.

No Final Adoption by the Whole CLP. When the National Executive Committee has endorsed the candidate selected by the GMC, he thereby becomes the official prospective Labour candidate. There is no counterpart of the Conservatives' formal adoption by a general meeting of the whole constituency association.

Activists and Influence

In Chapter 3 we sketched the sorts of people who are especially active in Conservative constituency associations and offered some impressions of the distribution of influence among them. Their similarities and differences with local Labour activists explain much about the similarities and differences in the two parties' selecting of candidates.

DIFFERENCES FROM CONSERVATIVE ASSOCIATIONS

1. *Movement* v. *Association*

A. H. Birch describes a significant contrast between Labour and Conservative local activists:

The Labour Party still clings to the idea that the party should be something like a band of comrades, a crusading movement, but the Conservatives have never adopted this attitude. They tend to look upon party associations simply

---

[18] Sara E. Barker, "Choosing Parliamentary Candidates," *Labour Organiser*, XXXI (May, 1952), 89.

as a means of bringing like-, and right-, minded people together, and prominent Conservatives not infrequently have the slenderest connexions with local organizations.[19]

In other words, many local Labour activists feel strongly that they are not merely members of a vote-catching association but rather comrades in a great people's movement against special privilege and social injustice—a crusade in which parliamentary politics plays only one part, and not necessarily the most important part.[20] The strength of this mood varies from one CLP to another, but to some degree it affects candidate selection everywhere. For one thing, it tends to place a higher value on length of party service than is found among Conservatives. For another, it encourages the attitude that it is better to lose with a true believer than win with an agnostic. For yet another, it requires contenders at selection conferences to display devotion to the articles of the true faith in a manner largely unknown to Conservative selection conferences. One anonymous Labour M.P. wrote an all-purpose introduction for any contender's speech to any selection conference guaranteed to assure any GMC that he is truly Labour. Part of it goes like this:

> I support fully the home policies of the Party, although I could wish for a little more enthusiasm among certain of our comrades for the fundamentals of our Socialist faith. (Hear, hear—fervently.) I make no apology for saying it, I mean public ownership. (Applause.) In foreign affairs, I support Labour's initiative for peace, although I would go farther than the present—I repeat the present—policy of the movement to get rid of the appalling weapon which . . . (cheers drown out the end of the sentence).[21]

2. *Devotion to Democracy*

One often encounters among local Labour activists the view that the Labour party, unlike the Tory, is and must be a *democratic* party. Of course they have no very precise or generally accepted pic-

---

[19] *Small Town Politics* (London: Oxford University Press, 1959), p. 50. See also Jean Blondel, "The Conservative Association and the Labour Party in Reading," *Political Studies*, VI (June, 1958), 101–19.

[20] One Labour idealogue, Ralph Miliband, has recently argued that the Labour party has failed to achieve its objectives (or rather what he regards as truly socialist objectives) mainly because it has abandoned working-class militance for the bourgeois conventions of parliamentary politics: *Parliamentary Socialism: A Study in the Politics of Labour* (London: George Allen & Unwin, 1961).

[21] Quoted in Cole, "Choice of Labour Candidates," *Manchester Guardian*, November 12, 1959, p. 10.

ture of just what a democratic party should be. But perhaps the most widespread notion is that the party should make its decisions not by secret deals among a few bosses in the trade unions and Transport House but by free and open public discussion and majority voting by the party's rank-and-file. This devotion to democracy makes many local activists hypersensitive to anything that smacks of "undue influence" or "special favors." It accounts for a number of Labour's unique adoption procedures—e.g., the prohibition against mandating and the rule that there may be no public discussion of the nominees' merits.

3. Suspicion of Leaders

Closely related to the foregoing is another attitude frequently encountered among Labour activists: a suspicion of all forms of party authority from the Leader and the NEC down to the local executive. The more one talks to Labour activists the stronger becomes his impression that many of them assume that the local leaders and the "Transport House establishment" are perennially trying to rig affairs in their own interests rather than to advance the cause of true socialism. The burden of proof, they feel, is on the leaders to prove their innocence, not upon the rank-and-file to prove the leaders' guilt.

This mood, of course, stands in sharp contrast to the article of faith held by so many Conservative activists that the loyal party man must back his leaders to the hilt—or, if he cannot, replace them with leaders he can back. It explains a good deal about why the Labour party's Constitution, Standing Orders, and Model Rules contain so many provisions intended to keep the party's members in line behind the leaders' decisions. Conservative leaders have traditionally acted on the well-justified assumption that so long as they are leaders at all their chaps will loyally close ranks behind them and present a united front to the socialist enemy. The Labour party's leaders, on the other hand, act on the equally justified assumption that they will have to face the capitalist enemy with continual complaints and occasional brickbats sent their way by their own rear ranks. They are only too well aware that their very right to command may be challenged at any moment. Thus it is not surprising that they, far more than their Conservative opposite numbers, feel the need of elaborate constitutional safeguards for their authority.

SIMILARITIES WITH
CONSERVATIVE ASSOCIATIONS

The attitudinal differences between Labour and Conservative activists mean that the two parties' parliamentary candidates are selected in different atmospheres. Yet in at least one respect the two parties are alike: despite Labour's proclaimed devotion to intraparty democracy, most critical decisions in both sets of local parties are made by a few activists holding key positions.

Who are they? To begin with, the nominal memberships of the CLPs, like those of the Conservative associations, are only small fractions—usually 5 to 10 per cent—of the party's vote in the constituencies.[22] The individual memberships range from as few as two hundred to as many as six thousand, and the average is in the neighborhood of twelve hundred.[23]

We noted previously that, unlike Conservative associations, CLPs have no provision for any official assembly of their entire memberships. Candidates are formally adopted by the GMCs, the members of which comprise a small part—perhaps 10 to 15 per cent —of a typical CLP's members. Moreover, in only a few selection conferences—usually those in safe Labour seats in which a trade union tries to control the adoption against powerful opposition—do more than a minority of the delegates appear and vote.[24] McKenzie estimates that the number of activists per CLP who regularly attend GMC meetings and are otherwise active in party work ranges between 20 and 150, which is roughly the same number and proportion as in Conservative associations.[25]

Labour activists differ from Conservative in several respects. They include substantially higher proportions of unskilled and

---

[22] Cf. McKenzie, *British Political Parties*, Table 14, p. 544.

[23] The NEC reported that in 1961 the party's total individual membership was 750,565. The largest membership was 6,660 at Woolwich West, and the average was 1,213: *Report of the Sixty-First Annual Conference of the Labour Party, 1962*, p. 11.

[24] Some representative "turnout" figures at selection conferences: for a safe Labour seat in Wales in 1960, 156 out of 206 attended the selection conference; for a marginal Conservative seat in South London in 1961, 21 out of 51; for a marginal Labour seat in Birmingham in 1954, 75 out of 180; for a safe Labour seat in the Midlands in 1956, 150 out of 320.

[25] Robert T. McKenzie, "The Political 'Activists' and Some Problems of 'Inner Party Democracy' in Britain," mimeo., a paper delivered at the Fifth World Congress of the International Political Science Association, Paris, September, 1961.

semiskilled workers and schoolteachers, and fewer small merchants, scions of the aristocracy, and middle-class housewives. But they are far from being an exact cross-section of Labour's rank-and-file supporters and members: as Blondel points out, while most of the latter come from the working class, more than half of the CLPs' leaders come from the middle class.[26] Whether or not the local leaders are ideologically more extreme than the national leaders or the bulk of Labour voters is a subject of scholarly debate. At least two things are clear, however: the CLPs have provided the main organizational and voting strength for the Left in its post-war struggles with the national leadership, but a smaller proportion than is commonly supposed have been dominated by the Left.[27]

In any case, we are not concerned here with whether the CLP "oligarchies" are more often Left than Right. Our point is that the devotion of Labour's rank-and-file to the dogma of intraparty democracy evidently does not force the CLPs to be less dominated than Conservative associations by small groups of activists. If anything, Labour's constitutional denial of any direct corporate role to all CLP members formalizes the concentration of power in candidate selection and makes all but impossible rebellions by the rank-and-file comparable to those in Conservative associations described in Chapter 3.

In summary, then, the selection of parliamentary candidates in constituency Labour parties is controlled to some degree by the affiliated organizations and ward committees which grant or withhold nominations, to a greater degree by the trade unions and other groups which can mobilize voting majorities in the GMCs, and to the greatest degree by the executive committees who in all but a few instances (see the Ebbw Vale case above) dominate the critical process of short-listing. In this regard, at least, the British Labour party of the 1960's exemplifies the "iron law of oligarchy"

---

[26] Jean Blondel, *Voters, Parties, and Leaders* (London: Penguin Books, Ltd., 1963), pp. 100–101.

[27] See *ibid.*, pp. 150–8; and the works by McKenzie and Rose cited in Chapter 3, footnotes 24 and 28. A careful analysis by Keith Hindell and Philip Williams of the votes in the 1960 and 1961 annual conferences on the unilateral nuclear disarmament issue showed that in both conferences a majority of the CLPs supported the party leadership rather than, as the Left had claimed, opposed it: "Scarborough and Blackpool: An Analysis of Some Votes at the Labour Party Conferences of 1960 and 1961," *Political Quarterly*, XXXIII (July–September, 1962), 306–20.

quite as much as the continental social democratic parties of the early 1900's.[28]

We now repeat the question asked at the end of Chapter 3: Granted that parliamentary candidates are selected by small groups of local activists, what ranges of choice do they have in the Labour party? Again the first factor to be taken into account is the presence or absence of a sitting M.P. who wishes to be readopted.

THE LABOUR MEMBER AND HIS CLP

THE MEMBER'S CLAIM TO READOPTION

Technically speaking, Labour M.P.s, like Conservative, do not automatically become candidates at each general election. They must be formally readopted and CLPs have formal power to refuse readoption. But while Conservative associations operate only under an informal presumption that M.P.s should be readopted, CLPs operate under formal rules that make it quite difficult to do anything else:

> If at any time this Party is represented in Parliament by a Member of the Parliamentary Labour Party procedure for the selection of a prospective Parliamentary candidate shall not be set in motion until an election is imminent when [the section authorizing suspension of the normal procedures] shall apply, unless:
> (a) Such representative intimates his or her intention to retire, or
> (b) The General Committee on securing a mandate from its affiliated and Party organisations intimates by resolution its desire that he or she must retire.[29]

This rule clearly puts—and is intended to put—the burden on those who wish to sack the member. They cannot merely put up a more attractive rival to outpoll him in the selection conference; they must round up enough mandated notes from the ward committees and affiliated organizations to form a GMC majority for a

---

[28] Cf. Robert Michels, *Political Parties*, trans. Eden and Cedar Paul (Glencoe, Ill.: The Free Press, 1949). It should be noted that Michels, at various places in his famous book, used the term "oligarchy" in three quite different senses: (1) the location of policy initiative in a few especially involved and active members of a party rather than its equal distribution among all the members; (2) the exercise of their initiative by the few unchecked by the many; (3) the exploitation of the many by the few in their own selfish interests: cf. C. W. Cassinelli, "The Law of Oligarchy," *American Political Science Review*, XLVII (September, 1953), 773–84. Only sense (1) is intended here.

[29] Model Rules, Set A, Clause XII, section (7).

resolution specifically asking the Member to retire. In a sense, they are required to transcend the old political law that "you can't beat somebody with nobody."

It is not surprising, therefore, that most Labour M.P.s have been readopted, as the figures in Table 6.1 show.

TABLE 6.1

READOPTION OF LABOUR INCUMBENTS, 1950–1964

Election	Number of Incumbents at Dissolution	Number of Incumbents Readopted	Number of Retirements	Known Instances of Attempts to Force Retirements	Known Instances of Forced Retirements
1950	384	353	31	6	6
1951	313	302	11	2	1
1955	293	276	17	5	2
1959	258	234	24	2	2
1964	256	232	24	1	1

Table 6.1 not only shows that most Labour M.P.s, like most Conservative (see Table 3.1), were readopted; it also suggests that most of the few who retired did so voluntarily.

A comparison of Table 6.1 with Table 3.1 shows that a smaller proportion of Labour M.P.s than Conservative have retired in recent years. Part of the explanation for this lies in the fact that some Conservative M.P.s find being a member an unwarranted drain on the time they can spend on their lucrative business and professions and therefore an economic burden. A number of Labour M.P.s, on the other hand, find being a member economically advantageous. As W. L. Guttsman rightly points out:

M.P.s are in demand as journalists, lecturers, broadcasters and as Public Relations men. In addition, a vastly greater number of perquisites and privileges are falling to the lot of even the unknown back-bencher than ever before. Governments and business dispense a much greater degree of hospitality than before the war . . . . Places on foreign missions and delegations are within the reach of M.P.s who will bestir themselves; these in turn widen the opportunities for extra parliamentary activity and earnings. Being an M.P. has become a marketable commodity—even without such dubious forms of activity as guinea-pig directorships.[30]

[30] W. L. Guttsman, *The British Political Elite* (London: MacGibbon & Kee, 1963), p. 246.

The smaller proportion of Labour retirements may also be due in part to the fact that Labour makes it more difficult than the Conservatives to sack an M.P. An inspection of recent instances in which efforts have been made to refuse readoption to Labour M.P.s should help us see to what extent this has been the case.

CONFLICTS OVER THE READOPTION OF M.P.S

In Chapter 3 we noted eighteen instances since 1945 in which serious challenges to the readoption of Conservative M.P.s have become public, and we observed that in each case the challenge came entirely from the local associations, with Central Office almost invariably playing an entirely neutral role. No such consistent pattern has, however, characterized the sixteen comparable challenges to Labour M.P.s the author has investigated. They may be categorized as follows:

1. *Central Challenge and Local Resistance*

In four instances Transport House has taken the initiative in sacking rebel M.P.s by the device of expelling them from the party and thereby automatically disqualifying them for readoption. In Chapter 5 we described the three instances (those involving Konni Zilliacus, L. J. Solley, and Lester Hutchinson) in which the CLPs tried to resist the expulsions but were finally forced to capitulate. There were no comparable cases in the Conservative party during this period.

2. *Central Challenge and Local Acquiescence*

J. F. F. Platts-Mills and Finsbury, 1948. In the other case in which the NEC initiated the expulsion of a rebel M.P., his CLP made no effort to resist. John Faithful Fortescue Platts-Mills was elected Member for Finsbury in 1945, and soon became a prominent far-Left critic of the Attlee-Bevin anti-Communist foreign policy. He was the reputed author of the Nenni telegram in 1948,[31] and the first of the thirty-seven Labour M.P.s who signed it to be summoned by the NEC to explain and defend his defiance of the party leaders. After his interview he was expelled from the party. The

---

[31] This was a telegram of good wishes for the Italian general election sent in April, 1948, to Pietro Nenni, leader of the faction of the Italian Socialist Party which advocated co-operation with the Communists.

following evening the Finsbury GMC held an emergency meeting, and voted, by 45 votes to none, with 7 abstentions, to expel Platts-Mills from the Finsbury party as well—an action of questionable constitutional necessity which the GMC evidently regarded as politically desirable.[32] Platts-Mills stood as Independent Labour candidate in the revised constituency of Shoreditch and Finsbury in the 1950 general election, and finished a poor third.

3. *Local Challenge and Central Acquiescence: Parliamentary Deviations*

The instances most resembling the sackings of Conservative M.P.s were those in which CLPs denied readoption to their M.P.s and Transport House made no effort to interfere. Some of these stemmed mainly from the CLPs' objections to their Members' defiance of the party whip.

Alfred Edwards and Middlesbrough East, 1948. Alfred Edwards, a director of a Middlesbrough ironworks, was elected Member for Middlesbrough East in 1935 and re-elected in 1945. He became the most prominent right-wing rebel M.P., actually voting against the government's 1948 bill to nationalize the iron and steel industries. Shortly after this vote his GMC held a special meeting, to which Edwards was not invited. With only one dissenting vote, it adopted a resolution that the CLP "having lost all confidence in this Member, considers it desirable that Mr. Edwards should retire from his representation in Parliament for the East division of Middlesbrough."[33] A month later the NEC interviewed Edwards, and when he refused to give an undertaking to refrain from future attacks on the party's leaders and policies, they expelled him from the party.[34] The CLP was delighted by this confirmation of their judgment, and adopted as their new prospective candidate Hilary Marquand, then Minister of Pensions, who was due to lose his seat because of redistribution. A year later Edwards joined the Middlesbrough Conservative association (the CLP president commented, "He has at last found his true home"), which then adopted him as

---

[32] *Times* (London), April 22, 1948, p. 4; April 29, 1948, p. 4; April 30, 1948, p. 4; May 1, 1948, p. 2.

[33] *Evening Gazette* (Middlesbrough), April 17, 1948, pp. 1, 8.

[34] *Ibid.*, May 17, 1948, p. 1.

its prospective candidate.[35] He stood as a Conservative in the 1950 general election in his old constituency and lost to Marquand by 29,185 to 12,402 (he had won as Labour candidate in 1945 by 17,427 to 9,352).

Stanley Evans and Wednesbury, 1956. Stanley Evans was elected Member for Wednesbury in 1945 and re-elected in the ensuing three general elections. In 1950 he lost his post as Parliamentary Secretary to the Ministry of Food after arousing a furor by publicly denouncing farm subsidies as "featherbedding" (he was known thereafter as "Featherbed Evans"). A strongly right-wing M.P. with a small-business rather than working-class background, Evans was never popular with the predominantly left-wing Wednesbury party, but they made no move to unseat him. Then in the Suez crisis of 1956 he became the only Labour M.P. to abstain from Labour's motion of censure against the Eden government. The parliamentary party and Transport House took no action against him, stating that his vote had been a matter of conscience and therefore not subject to normal party discipline[36]—and perhaps also because they saw advantages in being seen to tolerate at least one right-wing rebel on an issue in which many voters saw the party's stand as unpatriotic if not downright treasonable.[37] But the Wednesbury party was not so forgiving. In a manner reminiscent of the way the Conservative constituency associations treated their left-wing rebel M.P.s (see Chapter 3), the GMC ordered Evans to appear before them and defend his action. After he had done so, they demanded, by 48 notes to none that he resign his seat immediately.[38] No basis for such a demand existed in either the party's or the nation's constitution, and the NEC intimated that they were prepared, if asked, to consider its propriety. Evans, however, announced his intention to resign. The GMC called on him to resign from the party as well, but he refused. The NEC vounteered the opinion that his party membership was not in question, and the Wednesbury party, which had achieved its main objective without interference from Transport House, was content to let matters rest. It was rumored that the

---

[35] *Manchester Guardian*, August 20, 1949, p. 5.

[36] *Times* (London), November 3, 1956, p. 6.

[37] Cf. Leon D. Epstein, *British Politics in the Suez Crisis* (Urbana: University of Illinois Press, 1964), pp. 128–32.

[38] *Wednesbury and Darlaston Times*, November 24, 1956, p. 1.

Leader and other NEC members had privately urged Evans not to resign his seat and had promised that they would ask the Wednesbury party to reconsider, but he resigned nevertheless. As he explained, "A general without an army, and what is worse living on borrowed time, seldom wields much influence and lacks all dignity."[39]

4. *Local Challenge and Central Acquiescence: Personal Failings*

In other instances CLPs have sought to drop their M.P.s for personal reasons. In all such cases Transport House has not intervened.

Neil Maclean and Glasgow Govan, 1949. Neil Maclean was first elected Labour Member for the Govan division of Glasgow in 1918 and re-elected in the following general elections. In 1929 he stood as an Independent and was re-elected, but by 1945 he had returned to the party and was re-elected as Labour candidate. By 1949 he had reached the age of seventy-five, and many in the Govan party felt he was too old to be an effective M.P. The executive neither proposed him for readoption nor solicited a mandate that he retire according to the procedure stipulated in the Model Rules (see above). Instead they placed him on a short list along with three other contenders. Maclean acquiesced in this procedure despite its apparent unconstitutionality, and spoke at the selection conference. The GMC, however, passed him over in favor of a new prospective candidate, Tom Taylor, an Independent Labour party member of the Glasgow corporation who had joined the Labour party only in 1946.[40] Taylor's name was then forwarded to the NEC for endorsement, but was followed shortly by a letter from Maclean somewhat belatedly protesting the illegality of the procedures by which he had been dropped and asking them to reverse the decision.[41]

The NEC was in a dilemma. On the one hand, most members were less than enthusiastic about Maclean, and not at all eager to start another fight with a strong constituency party (the fights with the Gateshead and Thurrock parties over Zilliacus and Solley had

---

[39] *Midland Advertiser and Wednesbury Borough News*, November 4, 1956, p. 5. See also the speculative story by John Dickinson, *Birmingham Mail*, November 23, 1956, p. 1.

[40] *Govan Press* (Glasgow), September 9, 1949, p. 1; *Glasgow Herald*, September 7, 1949, p. 5.

[41] *Govan Press* (Glasgow), October 14, 1949, p. 1.

only recently been won). On the other hand, Maclean had unquestionably been sacked by unconstitutional procedures, and there was considerable doubt as to how desirable a replacement a left-winger like Taylor would make. So they dealt with the dilemma by means of statesmanlike inactivity. Months passed with neither an endorsement of Taylor nor a ruling against Maclean's sacking. During his period in limbo, Taylor was offered a good job in a town some distance from Glasgow. After waiting as long as he could for some action from the NEC, he finally gave up, accepted the job, and resigned his candidature.[42] The Govan party then adopted a new candidate, Councillor B. J. Davis. The NEC continued to delay action on the endorsement, and for a time Maclean considered standing as an Independent (as he had done in 1929). Finally, however, he wearied of the long wait and was prevailed upon to announce his support for Davis.[43] The NEC shortly thereafter endorsed Davis, who was defeated by a margin of 373 votes in the 1950 general election. Most observers, however, attributed his loss more to boundary revisions than to disaffections arising from the Maclean affair. Labour recaptured the seat in the 1955 general election after another major boundary revision.

J. D. Mack and Newcastle-under-Lyme, 1950. J. D. Mack was elected Member for Newcastle-under-Lyme in 1942 and re-elected in 1945. On the eve of the poll in 1950, D. A. V. Rist, the managing director of Rist's Wires and Cables, Ltd., publicly stated that Mack had asked him for a position with the firm as director or consultant at an annual salary of £1,000, in return for which Mack would use his position in Parliament to "work things" in the firm's interest. Mack denied having made any such proposition, and was re-elected.[44] Shortly after the election, however, he announced that he would not stand again because of "ill health." The GMC formally accepted his decision with an expression of polite regrets, and Mack told the press:

There is no subtle or underground move at all. There is nothing behind it. If people want to distort—I know that all sorts of things have been said—you can take it this has been genuine.[45]

---

[42] *Ibid.*, December 16, 1949, p. 1.

[43] *Ibid.*, February 17, 1950, p. 1.

[44] *Newcastle Times*, February 24, 1950, p. 1.

[45] *Ibid.*, July 21, 1950, pp. 4–5.

Perhaps so, but to a man the Labour "insiders" interviewed by the author were sure that the Newcastle executive had forced Mack to resign because they believed there was substance in Rist's charges, and Mack had not fought back because he did not want any public controversy.

J. E. Glanville and Consett, 1953. J. E. ("Jimmy") Glanville, a longtime member of the Durham Miners Association, was elected Member for Consett, a solid miners' seat, in 1943. He was soon reputed to be one of the House's more accomplished tipplers, a fact which greatly offended the strong nonconformist teetotalling element in the Consett party. His seat, however, was not in serious danger until May 19, 1953, when he caused a minor national sensation with a tongue-in-cheek Commons speech advocating the provision of free beer for all at the coronation ceremonies. He challenged "anyone to dispute my right to say I am a good judge of beer," and added, "I am not concerned about the laughter of my teetotal fanatical friends. So far as I am concerned they can go to hell!"[46] This was too much for his nonconformist opponents in the Consett party. One W. J. Brew[47] wrote to the party Leader:

> The time is long overdue for such people as Mr. Glanville to be publicly dropped from the Party. Feelings run high in his constituency, and many envision the time when the "fanatical teetotallers" in the Labour Party will put up their own candidate in opposition to Mr. Glanville, with a resultant gain to our opponents of the Consett seat.[48]

Another told the press that Glanville "has become the best advertising agent the capitalist brewers have ever had. He is a greater gift to them than Judas Iscariot was to the high priests!"[49] The Consett party issued a statement dissociating themselves from Glanville's views, and Glanville issued another apologizing for his "unfortunate choice of words" which, he said, had evidently concealed the fact that he was really attacking the capitalist brewers for charging for this staff of life rather than making it freely available to all.[50] Four months later Glanville announced that he would

---

[46] *Consett Chronicle,* May 21, 1953, p. 4.
[47] His real name.
[48] *Consett Chronicle,* May 28, 1953, p. 4.
[49] *Ibid.,* p. 6.
[50] *Consett Guardian,* June 11, 1953, p. 3.

not stand again, on the ground that it was "time for a younger man to take over" (he was then 62).[51]

John Baird and Wolverhampton North-East, 1963. The most recent instance of a CLP rejecting its member without interference from Transport House came in February, 1963, when the GMC of the Wolverhampton North-East Labour party voted, by 38 to 21, to advise John Baird, their member since 1945, to retire at the next general election, and to ask the NEC for permission to select a new prospective candidate.[52] The GMC did not make public their reasons for dropping Baird, but he told the press that they were out to get him because of his vigorous espousal of the party's policy against racial discrimination and because of his poor record of attendance in the House during 1960 and 1961 when he was recovering from a serious operation. He said he was appealing to the NEC, but was not optimistic about the outcome: "I have had very little support from Transport House in this critical period. Indeed they have remained completely neutral."[53] He was a good analyst: the NEC two weeks later authorized the CLP to select a new prospective candidate, and the party's General Secretary, A. L. Williams, commented to the press only that Transport House was satisfied that proper procedures had been followed throughout.[54] His successor, Mrs. Renée Short, held the seat in the 1964 election.

5. *Local Challenge and Central Resistance*

In two well-publicized episodes at the height of the Bevanite rebellion of the mid-1950's, left-wing CLPs tried to drop right-wing M.P.s but were prevented from doing so by Transport House.

"Bessie" Braddock and Liverpool Exchange, 1955. Mrs. Elizabeth ("Bessie") Braddock was elected Member for the Exchange division of Liverpool in 1945 by a majority of 665, which increased to 5,000 in 1950 and 7,000 in 1951. She became one of the stoutest supporters of the party leadership, but her CLP came under the domination of Bevanites. Relations between Mrs. Braddock and her party grew steadily worse, and the split flared into the open in 1952. She attended the annual conference of that year as the Exchange

---

[51] *Consett Chronicle*, October 15, 1953, p. 6.
[52] *Times* (London), February 7, 1963, p. 10.
[53] *Ibid.*, February 8, 1963, p. 11.
[54] *Ibid.*, February 28, 1963, p. 10.

party's official delegate, but her speeeches and votes promoted her own right-wing, pro-leadership position rather than her CLP's Bevanite views. After the conference the Exchange GMC summoned her to explain and defend her failure to represent their views, and she denied that they had any right to instruct her how to vote. Thenceforth the GMC refused to name her delegate to the conferences, and she was even denied access to the CLP's committee rooms and had to hold her local "surgeries" in quarters she herself hired. She, for her part, kept the NEC well advised of as many of the Bevanites' plans as she could discover.

Finally, in June, 1954, the GMC decided to dismiss her. They asked their ward committees to indicate their views on the following resolution to be acted upon at the next GMC meeting:

> That the sitting M.P. for this constituency be advised that it is the wish of this Party that she retire as our representative at the next Parliamentary election and that machinery be set in motion in accordance with the Constitution to select a new prospective Parliamentary candidate to contest the next election on our behalf.[55]

Two days later the North-West regional organizer, Reginald Wallis, informed the GMC that this procedure was unconstitutional—presumably on the ground that only the ward committees' views had been solicited—and the resolution did not appear on the agenda at the next GMC meeting.[56] Mrs. Braddock formally requested the National Agent to conduct an official inquiry into conditions in the Exchange party. The NEC sent a committee of inquiry to Liverpool in July, but since the GMC was for the moment making no further effort to unseat Mrs. Braddock, no action was taken on their report.

The situation remained relatively quiet until early in 1955, when the imminence of the general election and rising tension in the national controversy over the Bevanites made the local anti-Braddock forces determine to settle things. In late March the GMC voted by 40 to 39 not to readopt Mrs. Braddock. She immediately appealed to the NEC, which sent out another committee of inquiry, consist-

---

[55] *Liverpool Daily Post,* June 2, 1954, p. 1.

[56] Of the four ward committees, two (Central and Abercromby) voted to ask her to retire and one (St. James) passed a counter-resolution calling on the NEC to conduct an inquiry into the affairs of the Exchange Party. The fourth (Granby) did not meet until after Wallis had declared the proceedings unconstitutional.

ing of the National Agent and James Haworth, an NEC member representing the Transport Salaried Staffs' Association. The committee held hearings in Liverpool for six hours on April 22, interviewing Mrs. Braddock and her leading supporters and opponents. That evening they attended a three-hour meeting of the GMC at which the whole matter was discussed at length. On April 27, the NEC considered the committee's report and notified the Exchange party that their rejection of Mrs. Braddock was invalid and that they would endorse no other candidate for the division.[57]

The Exchange GMC met to consider this ultimatum, and Wallis told them that if they refused to readopt Mrs. Braddock the NEC might be forced to disaffiliate the existing Exchange party and form a new one (a statement greeted with cries of "Heil Hitler!" from the floor). The GMC then voted, by 31 to 7 with 26 abstentions, to withdraw their earlier resolution and to readopt Mrs. Braddock. Councillor Brian Crookes, the CLP secretary and one of the leading Bevanites, told the press afterward:

> We have accepted Mrs. Braddock with a gun at our heads. We have attempted in spite of great provocation to keep the Constituency Party together for the purpose of this election. We believe we should take up the position that the electors will be voting not for Mrs. Braddock but for the candidate of the Labour Party.[58]

Another GMC member, Councillor Lawrence Murphy, resigned in protest and stood as an Independent in the general election. He polled 2,928 votes, but Mrs. Braddock was re-elected with a majority of 7,186. Transport House's intervention had been decisive.

Elaine Burton and Coventry South, 1955. Elaine Burton was elected for Coventry South, a marginal Labour seat, in 1950 and re-elected in 1951. Like Mrs. Braddock, she was a staunch supporter of the party leaders. In March, 1955, the Bevanite revolt came to its climax when the parliamentary party considered a motion by the Leader himself that the whip be withdrawn from Bevan and seven of his most intransigent followers. Protests from Bevanite CLPs came pouring into Transport House. The GMC of the Coventry Borough Central Labour party sent a delegation to Westminster to urge all three Labour M.P.s from Coventry to vote against Attlee's

---

[57] *Liverpool Daily Post,* April 28, 1955, p. 1.
[58] *Ibid.,* April 29, 1955, p. 7.

motion. Two, R. H. S. Crossman (East division) and Maurice Edel-man (North division), voted accordingly. Miss Burton, however, voted with the PLP majority (141 to 112) in favor of the motion. She immediately thereafter wrote a letter to the GMC of the South divisional party—not to the Central party—explaining:

> This has not been a matter of policy, of being Right-wing or Left-wing, but an issue of loyalty. I felt that I had no option but to give Mr. Attlee a vote of confidence.[59]

But appeals to loyalty evidently do not produce the same results among Coventry Labour activists as among their Conservative coun-terparts. The day after the PLP's vote, the Coventry Central party's GMC adopted, by 52 votes to 19, a motion of no confidence in Miss Burton. Three days later she met with the GMC of the South di-visional party, with Sara Barker, the assistant national agent, and Reginald Underhill, the West Midlands regional organizer, also present. Reportedly the two Transport House representatives de-clared that if the CLP tried to sack Miss Burton because she sup-ported the party Leader, the NEC would refuse to permit it and might well disaffiliate the whole divisional party. At the conclusion of the meeting the GMC issued a statement to the press supporting the Central party's views about the withdrawal of the whip from Bevan, expressing "regret that [Miss Burton] did not vote as ad-vised," but making no reference to any lack of confidence or refusal of readoption.[60] The Central party made no further move. Miss Burton was readopted and re-elected in 1955, but was defeated in the 1959 election.

CONCLUSION

The foregoing instances of efforts to refuse readoptions to Labour M.P.s, added to those already discussed in Chapter 5, suggest a dis-tinct pattern. In the instances in which CLPs tried to drop M.P.s for personal failings, Transport House acquiesced—sometimes even when the procedures stipulated by the Model Rules were obviously not followed to the letter. In the two instances in which CLPs tried to drop right-wing rebel M.P.s who had defied the whip Transport House made no effort to protect them. But in the two instances in

---

[59] *Coventry Evening Telegraph*, March 17, 1955, pp. 1, 11.
[60] *Ibid.*, March 26, 1955, p. 1.

which left-wing CLPs tried to sack right-wing M.P.s *for following
the national party leaders,* Transport House intervened decisively
to ensure their readoption. And in the situations in which left-wing
CLPs wished to readopt left-wing M.P.s who had defied the whip
and refused to give undertakings that they would not do so in the
future, the NEC prevented their readoptions by expelling the rebel
M.P.s from the party and by threatening to do the same to any of
their local backers who continued to support them.

In short, when the party's national leaders have become convinced that a CLP's readoption or refusal to readopt a particular
M.P. has constituted a direct challenge to their authority, they have
not hesitated to use their plentiful constitutional power—but only
if they were also convinced that they could make their interventions
stick. The NEC's weapon of last resort for enforcing its will on re-
calcitrant M.P.s has been its constitutional power

> . . . to enforce the Constitution, Standing Orders, and Rules of the Party and
> to take any action it deems necessary for such purpose, whether by way of dis-
> affiliation of an organisation, or expulsion of an individual, or otherwise.[61]

In all these respects, then, Transport House has controlled the
selection of parliamentary candidates more closely than Conservative Central Office. There appear to be several reasons for these differences between the parties. The factional divisions within the
Labour party since 1945 have been much sharper and more stable
than in the Conservative party. As a result, there have been many
more opportunities in the Labour party for clear tests of strength
between Transport House and the CLPs over the selection of candidates. Moreover, whereas loyalty to the party's national leaders
has been the typical attitude of Conservative activists—carried even
to the point of disciplining deviant M.P.s more stringently than
the leaders would have preferred—the local activists in a number of
CLPs have believed it their right and duty to support rebels against
Labour's national leaders.

Yet the relatively large number of cases in which Labour's national agencies have intervened in candidate selection should not
draw our attention away from the much greater number in which
they have not. Since 1945, after all, a great many CLPs have

---

[61] Party Constitution, Clause VIII, section 2, paragraph (b).

adopted left-wing candidates whom the NEC has endorsed without a murmur—in some instances because they were selected for hopeless seats where it did not matter, in many simply because the NEC did not know and did not have the resources to investigate the candidates' ideological reliability, and in some—e.g., Ebbw Vale—because there was real doubt about whether they could win a direct contest of strength with the local party and its popular rebel M.P.

In short, although the Labour party's national agencies are more active in candidate selection than the Conservative party's, the vast majority of Labour candidates are selected according to the desires and standards of their constituency Labour parties, not of Transport House.

Chapter 7 | *Labour Candidatures and Constituencies, 1951–1964*

This chapter considers some characteristics of Labour candidates and the constituencies in which they stood in the general elections of 1951, 1955, 1959, and 1964. It is based on materials and analytical techniques similar to those used for Conservative candidatures in Chapter 4, and its findings are subject to similar limitations.[1]

CHARACTERISTICS OF CANDIDATES: THE PUBLIC RECORD

INCUMBENCY

In Chapter 6 we observed that Labour's Model Rules make it even more difficult to refuse readoption to a Labour M.P. than a Conservative. This is reflected in Table 7.1, which shows an even higher proportion of Labour candidatures going to sitting M.P.s than Table 4.1 showed for the Conservatives.

The table shows that 92 per cent of the Labour candidatures in constituencies of high winnability were given to incumbents, compared with 88 per cent of the comparable Conservative candidatures. This small but significant difference no doubt results in part from the greater protection afforded Labour M.P.s by the Model

---

[1] See pp. 91–92 and the Appendix.

TABLE 7.1

WINNABILITY OF CONSTITUENCY RELATED TO INCUMBENCY OF LABOUR CANDIDATURES*

Incumbency	Winnability of Constituency				All Candidates
	High	Medium	Low	Other	
Held seat being contested	92%	61%	†	0%	42%
Held another seat	†	1	†	26	†
Lost seat being contested in previous election	0	9	17%	4	10
Lost another seat in previous election	2	14	21	25	14
First contest	6	15	62	45	34
	100%	100%	100%	100%	100%
Number of cases	716	607	1,107	53	2,483

* For definitions of these categories, see the Appendix.

† Less than 0.5 per cent (all percentages rounded to the nearest whole number).

Rules and by Transport House.[2] Other factors are also relevant. For example, some Conservative M.P.s have retired because they found they could not afford financially to take the time away from their businesses that Parliament demanded. On the other hand, a number of Labour M.P.s have clung to their seats as long as possible in part because they could not afford to lose their parliamentary salaries.[3] But, whatever the reasons, incumbency was even more powerful a determinant of Labour adoptions than Conservative. Accordingly, we shall control it, as in Chapter 4, by henceforth considering only the 1,431 Labour candidatures by non-incumbents.[4]

PREVIOUS CONTESTS

More non-incumbent Labour candidatures than Conservative went to aspirants with some previous electoral experience. Candidates

---

[2] As, for example, in the Bessie Braddock and Elaine Burton cases: see pp. 188–91.

[3] P. W. Buck's study of parliamentary careers from 1918 to 1959 shows that 33 per cent of Labour M.P.s retired for reasons other than death, elevation to the peerage, or defeat in elections—compared with 41 per cent of the Conservative M.P.s: *Amateurs and Professionals in British Politics, 1918–59* (Chicago: The University of Chicago Press, 1963), Table 16, p. 111.

[4] Note that, as in most of Chapter 4, the basic unit of analysis is the candidature, not the individual candidate. Any person who stood more than once in this period appears more than once in the tables.

fighting for the first time got 58 per cent of Labour's nominations, compared with 61 per cent of the Conservatives'. Those who had lost one or more previous parliamentary contests got 37 per cent of the Labour nominations, compared with the Conservatives' 37 per cent, and former M.P.s got 5 per cent of Labour's adoptions, compared with the Conservatives' 2 per cent.

These differences may merely reflect the fact that Labour, having lost more often in 1951–1959, had a larger pool of experienced candidates to draw on. Or it may also indicate that CLPs valued electoral experience more than Conservative associations. But Table 7.2, which shows the distribution of the candidates' experience among the various categories of constituency winnability, shows no evidence for the latter proposition.

TABLE 7.2

WINNABILITY OF CONSTITUENCY RELATED TO PREVIOUS ELECTORAL
EXPERIENCE OF LABOUR NON-INCUMBENT CANDIDATURES

Previous Electoral Experience	Winnability of Constituency			
	High	Medium	Low	Other
First contest	68%	40%	61%	61%
One previous loss	9	26	23	26
Two or more previous losses	14	18	13	10
Former M.P.s	9	16	3	3
	100%	100%	100%	100%
Number of cases	57	232	1,103	39

The CLPs, as noted above, were able to draw on a larger pool of experienced candidates than the Conservative associations. If they had valued electoral experience as much as or more than their opponents, the Labour candidatures in constituencies of high winnability should have had a lower proportion of newcomers. But a comparison of the figures in Table 7.2 with those given earlier for the Conservatives[5] reveals a striking discrepancy in the opposite direction: 68 per cent of Labour's most desirable candidatures went to newcomers, compared with only 42 per cent of the Conservatives'. Clearly, then, many of the most favorably situated CLPs did not rate electoral experience as highly as did their Conservative coun-

---

[5] Table 4.2, p. 94.

terparts. Quite a few, as we shall see in Chapter 8, rated union sponsorship more highly.

EXPERIENCE IN LOCAL GOVERNMENT, CIVIC ORGANIZATIONS, AND PARTY OFFICE

It may be that the higher proportion of newcomers in the most desirable Labour candidatures is also due in part to a factor mentioned in Chapter 6: Labour activists value a wider variety of experience than Conservative—e.g., service to "the Movement" and in local government. This hypothesis, however, is only partly supported by our data: while 47 per cent of the Labour candidatures were won by persons who had held office in a local government council, as compared with 36 per cent of the Conservative,[6] there was almost no difference between the parties in the proportions holding office in civic and religious organizations (Labour 9 per cent, Conservatives 6 per cent); and only 17 per cent of Labour's candidatures went to persons who had held local or national party office, compared with 28 per cent of the Conservatives'.

We observed in Chapter 4 that the few Conservatives with experience in nonpartisan civic or religious organizations were better represented in the more winnable seats than those who were not, but other sorts of experience made little difference.[7] Table 7.3 shows a somewhat different pattern for Labour.

According to Table 7.3, the Labour candidatures in the most desirable constituencies, like their Conservative counterparts, included no more candidates with local government experience than without, but higher proportions who had held office in civic or religious organizations. Unlike the Conservatives, however, the Labour candidates who had held no party office were significantly better represented in the winnable seats than those who had.[8] This results in large part from the disproportionate number of union-sponsored candidates in the best constituencies and the fact that unions mostly sponsor veteran trade unionists rather than party officeholders (see Chapter 8).

---

[6] Cf. Table 4.9, p. 108.

[7] Cf. pp. 107–8.

[8] A 4×2 table relating activity in civic and religious organizations to winnability of constituency yields a chi-square of 13.7516; with 3 degrees of freedom, this is significant at the .01 level of confidence. A 4×2 table relating holding of party office to winnability of constituency yields a chi-square of 56.8624, which is significant at the .001 level.

TABLE 7.3

EXPERIENCE OF LABOUR NON-INCUMBENT CANDIDATES IN LOCAL GOVERNMENT,
CIVIC AND RELIGIOUS ORGANIZATIONS, AND PARTY OFFICE,
RELATED TO WINNABILITY OF CONSTITUENCY

Winnability of Constituency	Prior Service on Local Govt. Councils		Prior Office in Civic or Relig. Organization		Prior Local or National Party Office	
	Some	None	Some	None	Some	None
High	5%	3%	7%	4%	6%	4%
Medium	16	17	13	16	12	17
Low	77	77	76	77	81	76
Other	2	3	4	3	1	3
	100%	100%	100%	100%	100%	100%
Index of winnability*	−72	−74	−69	−73	−75	−72
Number of cases	677	754	136	1,295	247	1,184

* Computed by subtracting the per cent in the high-winnability category from the per cent in the low-winnability category. The lower the index number the higher the proportion of the candidates in the category in the most desirable constituencies.

SEX

It is commonly supposed that the Socialists harbor less prejudice against women candidates than the Conservatives. This supposition is evidently shared by Transport House and Central Office, for the author found much more concern in the latter than the former with persuading local associations to adopt women. Yet our data show that women are about as poorly represented in one party's candidatures as the other's: 7 per cent of Labour candidatures went to women, compared with 5 per cent of Conservative. Moreover, women in both parties were given less desirable constituencies than men.

AGE

One of the most discussed of all the differences between the major parties is the older mean and median ages of Labour's candidates and M.P.s.[9] Our data confirm this: 44 per cent of Labour's

---

[9] This discrepancy appears to have widened since 1945. McCallum and Readman found the mean age for both parties' candidates in 1945 to be 46: *The British General Election of 1945* (London: Oxford University Press, 1947), p. 77. In 1959 Butler

candidatures went to persons under forty years of age, compared with 52 per cent of the Conservatives'; and 23 per cent of Labour's went to persons over fifty, compared with 18 per cent of the Conservatives'.

Two Labour non-incumbents under thirty (compared with five Conservatives) were adopted for safe seats in general elections.[10] Donald Chapman, adopted for the Northfield division of Birmingham in 1951 at the age of twenty-eight, was educated at Barnsley Grammar School and Emmanuel College, Cambridge; he served as secretary of the Cambridge City Trades Council and Labour party, 1944–1947, and as a member of the City Council, 1945–1947; at the time of his adoption he was general secretary of the Fabian Society. John Morris, adopted for Aberavon in 1959 at the age of twenty-nine, was educated at the University College of Wales, Aberystwyth, and at Gonville and Caius College, Cambridge; he was a member of the council of the British Socialist Agricultural Society, and had been deputy general secretary and legal adviser to the Farmers' Union of Wales. Both, in short, were well educated and had given substantial civic and party service.

On the other hand, while the Conservatives adopted no non-incumbents over the age of seventy, Labour adopted three:

Wilfred Vernon, who was elected for Camberwell Dulwich in 1945 and defeated in 1951; he stood again in 1955 at the age of seventy-three, and lost.

J. Paterson Bryant stood for the safe Conservative constituency of Hastings in 1959 at the age of seventy; he was a retired civil servant, educated at Hastings Grammar School, secretary of the Hastings Labour party, and member of the Hastings Borough Council since 1952—a clear case of a local "flag shower" (see below).

Tom Braddock was elected Member for Mitcham in 1945 and defeated in 1950; he was adopted for his home constituency of Wim-

---

and Rose found that the median age for Labour was 4 to 7 years older than the Conservatives, and noted that the gap was widening: *The British General Election of 1959* (London: Macmillan & Co., Ltd., 1960), pp. 124–25; see also Buck, *Amateurs and Professionals*, pp. 27–29.

[10] Two others were adopted for safe seats at by-elections: Anthony Wedgwood Benn was adopted for Bristol South-East in 1950 at the age of 25 (see pp. 148–49); and Roy Mason was adopted for Barnsley in 1953 at the age of 29.

bledon in 1954, but the NEC, as we saw in Chapter 5, refused to endorse him; in 1959, at the age of seventy-two, he was adopted for the safe Tory constituency of Kingston-upon-Thames, and stood unsuccessfully again in 1964 at the age of seventy-seven.

All three Labour candidates over seventy were adopted in Conservative-held constituencies, two were former M.P.s, and one was a prominent local party leader. All, in short, had special claims to adoption which outweighed their age handicaps.

When we distribute the Labour candidatures in the various age groups according to the winnability of the constituencies, as in Table 7.4, we find a pattern quite different from that shown for the Conservatives in Chapter 4.[11]

TABLE 7.4

AGES OF LABOUR NON-INCUMBENT CANDIDATES RELATED TO
WINNABILITY OF CONSTITUENCY

Winnability of Constituency	Age Groups				
	21–29	30–39	40–49	50–59	60 and over
High	1%	2%	5%	7%	5%
Medium	8	15	21	15	22
Low	88	81	71	75	71
Other	3	2	3	3	2
	100%	100%	100%	100%	100%
Index of winnability	−87	−79	−66	−68	−66
Number of cases	157	479	463	274	58

Table 7.4 shows that, in Labour candidatures as in Conservative, the proportions in the more winnable seats increase in each older age group from the twenties to the forties. But, unlike the Conservatives, Labour candidates in their fifties and sixties did as well as those in their forties. This difference between the two parties stems mainly from the union-sponsored candidates' disproportionate share of the most winnable constituencies and the fact that the trade unions tend to put older men on their parliamentary candidate panels (see Chapter 8).

---

[11] See Table 4.4, p. 99.

EDUCATION

1. *Labour* v. *Conservative Candidates*

We earlier found education to be significantly related to the allocation of Conservative candidatures among the more and less desirable constituencies. Moreover, we concluded that to many Conservative local activists education has been a badge of social status more than a certificate of academic knowledge or intellectual skill, as evidenced by the far greater incidence of persons with public school backgrounds in the most desirable seats.[12]

We would expect Labour candidatures to be very different: the party claims to represent the working class; it opposes special privilege for the rich and well-born; trade unions supply much of its money, many of its local activists, and a fair proportion of its candidates. Table 7.5 shows that education indeed had a different relationship to Labour candidatures than to Conservative.

The data in Table 7.5 suggest that in one respect the pre-war educational gap between the parties has narrowed, while in another it has remained as wide as ever. Before 1945 far fewer Labour than Conservative candidates had attended universities, which were largely reserved for the offspring of the well-to-do. The post-war extension of educational opportunities for the intellectually meritorious from all ranks of society evidently has changed this: the table shows that 43 per cent of Labour's candidatures since 1951 have gone to persons who had attended universities, a figure respectably close to the Conservatives' 50 per cent.

But this expansion of educational opportunities has not altered the fact that in Britain one's station in society is fixed more by *where* he goes to school than by how long. In this regard there are two divisions that count: attending a public school or not, and attending Oxbridge or not.[13] In both respects the two parties were as far apart after 1945 as before: 50 per cent of the Conservatives' candidatures went to persons who had attended public schools, compared with only 14 per cent of Labour's; and the figures for attendance at Oxford or Cambridge were, respectively, 31 per cent and 17 per cent.

---

[12] See pp. 101–2.

[13] See p. 103.

TABLE 7.5

EDUCATION OF NON-INCUMBENTS RECEIVING LABOUR AND
CONSERVATIVE CANDIDATURES

Education	Candidatures	
	Conservative	Labour
Elementary only	3%	9%
Elementary plus †	*	10
Secondary only	20	21
Secondary plus †	7	14
Secondary and university other than Oxford or Cambridge	14	24
Secondary and Oxford or Cambridge	6	8
Public school only	20	3
Public school and university other than Oxford or Cambridge	5	2
Public school and Oxford or Cambridge	25	9
	100%	100%
Number of cases	1,311	1,431

* Less than 0.5 per cent.

† These categories are the same as those used in the Nuffield general election studies. The elementary-plus and secondary-plus categories include those "whose formal educations ended at these stages, but who subsequently attended part-time classes or went to adult education classes": Butler and Rose, *The British General Election of 1959*, p. 128.

2. *Labour Candidates* v. *the General Public*

Most Labour candidatures, like most Conservative, went to persons who had much higher levels of formal education than the general public. For example, while only 8 per cent of the British population attend universities, 43 per cent of Labour's candidatures went to persons with some university training. For another, 6 per cent of the general public attend public schools, while 14 per cent of Labour's candidatures went to public school products. In short, while Labour candidates had somewhat less formal education than Conservative, they had far more than the general public. By one of Britain's main indicators of social class, the candidates of the workingman's party were not representative of the whole society and still less of the working class.

3. *Education and Winnability of Constituencies*

Did Labour's most desirable candidatures go to persons with the most schooling? Table 7.6 shows that the answer is something of a paradox.

TABLE 7.6

EDUCATIONAL DISTRIBUTION OF CANDIDATURES BY LABOUR NON-INCUMBENTS
RELATED TO WINNABILITY OF CONSTITUENCY

Winnability of Constituency	Elem. and Elem. Plus	Second. and Second. Plus	Second. and Univ. Other than Oxbridge	Second. and Oxbridge	Public School Only	Pub. Sch. and Univ. Other than Oxbridge	Pub. Sch. and Oxbridge
High	9%	4%	3%	3%	0%	3%	2%
Medium	13	14	18	16	20	20	23
Low	74	79	76	80	77	74	75
Other	4	3	3	1	3	3	0
	100%	100%	100%	100%	100%	100%	100%
Index of winnability	−65	−75	−73	−77	−77	−71	−73
Number of cases	267	506	347	117	40	35	119

The table shows that persons with elementary-only or elementary-plus educations did distinctly the best, while there was relatively little difference among the distributions of the other educational groups among winnable and hopeless constituencies. This, as we shall see in Chapter 8, is due largely to the trade unions' domination of the more desirable constituencies, with sponsored candidates having relatively little schooling.

OCCUPATION

In British society, as we have seen, occupation rivals education as a sign of social status. Consequently the occupations of aspirants for Labour candidatures pose a dilemma quite unknown to the Conservatives. On the one hand, the Labour party has always claimed to be the workingman's party—the political arm of the broader labor movement. Most of the party's votes and funds come from manual workers in the affiliated trade unions. Accordingly, some trade unionists have argued that Labour candidatures—especially in the most winnable constituencies—should go mainly to manual workers, partly as a reward for their service to the movement and partly because they know better than donnish intellectuals the needs and aspirations of the party's rank and file.[14]

On the other hand, for reasons we reviewed in Chapter 4, the

[14] Cf. p. 141.

occupations most likely to attract and enhance the skills and demeanor most suitable for attractive candidates and effective M.P.s
are those of lawyer, teacher, journalist, businessman, and the like.

How the CLPs have resolved this dilemma is suggested in Table
7.7, which compares the occupational distribution of the general
public with that of persons receiving Labour and Conservative candidatures.

TABLE 7.7

Occupations of Non-Incumbents Receiving Labour Candidatures
Compared with Conservatives and with the General Public

Occupational Class	General Public, 1951*	Conservatives	Labour
Proprietor, managerial	13%	39%	11%
Professional	7	37	24
White-collar	11	19	45
Intermediate	5	2	3
Manual, wage-earning	64	3	17
	100%	100%	100%
Number of cases	34,200,000	1,311	1,431

* Taken from R. R. Alford, *Party and Society* (Chicago: Rand McNally & Company,
1963), Table 6-2, p. 128. For the specific occupations included in each category, see Appendix I.

Labour drew its candidates from the various occupational classes
in quite different proportions from the Conservatives: there were
many more manual workers (17 per cent to 3 per cent) and white-
collar workers (45 per cent to 19 per cent), and far fewer candidates from the high-status business and professional groups (35 per
cent to 76 per cent. On the other hand, Labour candidates were
no more representative of the general public or the working class
occupationally than they were educationally: they included many
more professionals (24 per cent to 7 per cent) and white-collar workers
(45 per cent to 11 per cent), and fewer manual workers (17 per cent
to 64 per cent).

Arranging the candidates' occupations according to their distribution among the more and less winnable constituencies, as in
Table 7.8, reveals a pattern quite different from that shown earlier
for the Conservatives.[15]

---

[15] Cf. Table 4.8, p. 106.

TABLE 7.8

WINNABILITY OF CONSTITUENCY RELATED TO OCCUPATIONS OF
NON-INCUMBENTS GIVEN LABOUR CANDIDATURES

Occupation	Index of Winnability *	Number of Cases	Per Cent of All Cases
Political organizer	−18	17	1
Trade union official	−46	69	5
Chartered accountant	−57	14	1
Manual worker	−67	182	13
Journalist, author, publicist	−67	101	7
Civil engineer or surveyor	−68	28	2
Barrister	−70	85	6
Civil servant	−72	47	3
Farmer	−73	37	3
Small business	−75	52	4
Solicitor	−76	55	4
Teacher	−77	322	22
White-collar	−80	257	18
Company executive or director	−83	71	5
Doctor, dentist, clergy, other professional	−83	45	3
Housewife	−85	20	1
Student	−89	18	1
Armed services	−89	9	1
Not ascertained	—	2	—
		1,431	100

* Computed by determining the percentages of each occupation in the high- and low-winnability constituencies, and subtracting the former from the latter.

Table 7.8 shows that the two occupational groups which enjoyed the highest ratio of desirable-to-undesirable Labour candidatures were those employed to render direct service to the movement. Trade union officials fared very well. And party organizers fared even better. The latter included men like Wilfred Fienburgh, an employee of Transport House's Research Department, who was adopted for the safe seat of Islington North in 1951 at the age of thirty-two; John Taylor, for twenty-five years a Labour party organizer and for eleven years Scottish secretary of the party, adopted in 1951 for the safe seat of West Lothian; David Ginsburg, secretary of the research department from 1952 to 1955, adopted for the safe seat of Dewsbury in 1959; and Peter Shore, head of the research department, adopted for the safe seat of Stepney in 1964.

In sharp contrast stand two of the three occupational groups most favored by the Conservatives, both of which belong to what was once called the landed gentry: persons of private means like Viscount Lambton and Major Anstruther-Gray; and nine "farmers," eight of whom had attended public schools.[16]

Occupationally as well as educationally, then, Labour and Conservative candidates came from very different segments of British society, which served to perpetuate and accent their class differences. But despite its posture as the party of the workers, Labour drew its candidates far more from the "petty bourgeoisie" than from the "proletariat."[17]

PERSONAL CONNECTIONS IN THE CONSTITUENCY

1. *In General*

In Chapter 4 we observed that 32 per cent of Conservative candidatures were given to persons with personal connections in the constituencies in which they were adopted. The corresponding figure for Labour was 30 per cent. But whereas the Conservative outsiders had a small but significant advantage over the locals in the allocation of the desirable constituencies, Table 7.9 shows that the reverse was true for Labour.

The table makes clear that while somewhat fewer Labour candidatures than Conservative went to persons with local connections, the most desirable Labour candidatures had a slightly higher proportion of local men. As we shall see in Chapter 8, this stems mainly from the concentration of union-sponsored candidates in the most desirable constituencies.

2. *In Constituencies of Different Population Types*

We observed earlier that local aspirants got especially high proportions of the Conservative candidatures in metropolitan areas outside London, in the Scottish burghs, and in Ulster. Table 7.10 shows a similar pattern for Labour, with one addition.

---

[16] See pp. 106–7.

[17] W. L. Guttsman shows that this is nothing new. His careful study of the *embourgeoisement* of the Labour party shows that up to 1918 most Labour candidates and M.P.s were of the working class, but from the early 1920's on they included increasingly large proportions of middle-class intellectuals: *The British Political Elite* (London: MacGibbon & Kee, 1963), pp. 236–39.

TABLE 7.9

WINNABILITY OF CONSTITUENCY RELATED TO PERSONAL CONSTITUENCY CONNECTIONS
OF NON-INCUMBENTS RECEIVING LABOUR CANDIDATURES

Winnability of Constituency	Local Connections	
	Some	None
High	6%	3%
Medium	14	17
Low	77	77
Other	3	3
	100%	100%
Index of winnability	−71	−74
Number of cases	428	1,003

Table 7.10 shows that not only were more local men especially favored in both parties in the three types of constituencies mentioned above, but more Labour candidatures than Conservative went to local aspirants in the rural constituencies in which mining is the predominant industry. Some recent examples are: Hemsworth, a safe Labour constituency, which in 1959 adopted Alan Beaney, a member of the Hemsworth Labour party with no previous electoral experience who was sponsored by the National Union of Mineworkers; North-East Derbyshire, also safe for Labour, which in 1959 adopted Thomas Swain, an NUM-sponsored local miner with no

TABLE 7.10

POPULATION TYPE OF CONSTITUENCY RELATED TO PERSONAL CONSTITUENCY
CONNECTIONS OF NON-INCUMBENTS GIVEN LABOUR CANDIDATURES

Local Connections	Population Type of Constituency									
	London	Other Metropolitan	Other Urban	Semi-rural	Semi-rural, Mining	Rural	Rural, Mining	Scot. Burghs	Scot. Counties	Ulster
Some	27%	82%	30%	37%	27%	29%	50%	72%	29%	88%
None	73	18	70	63	73	71	50	28	71	12
	100%	100%	100%	100%	100%	100%	100%	100%	100%	100%
Number of cases	60	89	660	119	11	305	18	53	99	17

previous contests, over party Secretary Morgan Phillips,[18] and North Somerset, a marginal Conservative constituency which, in 1955, adopted D. R. Llewellyn, an NUM-sponsored miners' agent and member of the Somerset County Council, with no previous parliamentary contests.

Table 7.11 shows the number and proportions of local men given

TABLE 7.11

PERSONAL CONSTITUENCY CONNECTIONS OF PERSONS GIVEN LABOUR
NON-INCUMBENT CANDIDATURES IN LARGEST CITIES

City	Number of Candidatures	Number Given Persons with Local Connections	Per cent to Persons with Local Connections
England			
Birmingham	23	15	65
Bristol	9	5	56
Leeds	8	7	88
Liverpool	22	15	68
Manchester	16	13	81
Sheffield	6	4	67
Wales			
Cardiff	4	3	75
Swansea	1	0	0
Scotland			
Edinburgh	16	11	69
Glasgow	27	22	81

candidatures in the largest cities in England (excluding London), Wales, and Scotland.

Taken together, Tables 4.12 and 7.11 show that in Bristol, Leeds, and Cardiff substantially more Labour candidatures than Conservative went to local men, while in Liverpool, Sheffield, and Swansea the contrast was reversed.[19] With only two exceptions (Bristol and Swansea), both parties in each of the ten largest cities gave over half of their candidatures by non-incumbents to local aspirants. So for Labour as for the Conservatives, the main strongholds of localism were the big cities other than London and, for Labour only, also the

---

[18] After some controversy: see pp. 145–46.
[19] See Table 4.12, p. 113.

rural-mining areas where, as we shall see in Chapter 8, the National Union of Mineworkers dominates the selection of candidates.

CHARACTERISTICS OF CANDIDATES: OTHER FACTORS[20]

IDEOLOGY

Ideology plays a more prominent role in the Labour party's affairs than the Conservatives'. The party Constitution's famous Clause IV[21] commits Labour to goals ideologically more precise than any known to its rivals.[22] And the quarrel between Labour's left and right wings over whether the parliamentary party is actually pursuing these goals has been more sharply defined and persistent than any post-war disagreement within the Conservative party.

Accordingly, ideological considerations have played a much greater role in Labour candidate selections than Conservative (where, as we have seen, they have played hardly any role at all). A number of Labour selection conferences have become tests of strength between Left and Right.[23] In other situations, as we saw in Chapter 5, regional organizers and CLP executives have blocked the adoption of left-wing candidates by keeping them off short

---

[20] For one view of the criteria that *should* guide Labour adoptions, see the views of the former national agent and chief whip in the House of Lords: Lord Shepherd, "How to Select a Candidate," *Labour Organiser*, XXXII (February, 1953), 34–35. Lord Shepherd emphasized speaking ability, political and general knowledge, personality, irreproachable personal character and habits, and "the right age, sex, and background for the particular constituency."

[21] Clause IV declares that the party's objectives are "To secure for the workers by hand or by brain the full fruits of their industry and the most equitable distribution thereof that may be possible, upon the basis of the common ownership of the means of production, distribution, and exchange, and the best obtainable system of popular administration and control of each industry or service": Party Constitution, Clause IV, section (4).

[22] Julian Critchley, a young Bow-Grouper elected M.P. for Rochester and Chatham in 1959, wrote: "The truth is . . . that Conservatives do not have political principles. They have prejudices guided by fact . . . . It is the belief that the most important thing in politics is the continuance of Conservative government, and that compromise is the means whereby this aim may be achieved, that makes the Tory Party so formidable": "Principles of Conservatism," *The Spectator*, December 1, 1961, pp. 810–11.

[23] Two clear instances are: the selection of Konni Zilliacus over Sir Frank Soskice at the Gorton division of Manchester in 1955, a victory for the Left (see p. 145); and the selection of Frank Tomney over W. T. Williams at North Hammersmith in 1955, a victory for the Right: *Times* (London), March 11, 1955, p. 4.

lists.[24] And we know that Transport House has vetoed the candidatures of some left-wingers and barred others from List B.[25]

Nevertheless, it is plain that ideological considerations have been decisive in relatively few Labour adoptions since 1945. Despite Labour's general lack of success in keeping its quarrels out of the press, almost no local Right-Left fights over candidatures have been reported. Moreover, a number of Labour officials (including a member of the NEC, a Transport House "civil servant," three area organizers, and several CLP agents, officers, candidates, and aspirants for candidature) all told the author that, since parliamentary discipline is so strong, most CLPs feel that how a particular aspirant stands on this or that policy question really matters very little. If adopted and elected, he will have to vote as the whip directs. They added that most CLPs, like most Conservative associations,[26] want to poll the maximum number of votes and are therefore concerned with the aspirants' personal qualities more than with the "correctness" of their views on the issues of the moment. And, as we shall see in Chapter 8, most trade unions choose the members of their parliamentary panels for their services to the union, not for their views on public policy.

Certainly a number of CLPs have adopted attractive right-wing candidates over less attractive left-wing rivals—and the reverse has also happened.[27] And while ideology has been a factor in many more Labour adoptions than Conservative, it has been decisive in only a small minority.

PERSONAL QUALITIES

Most GMC delegates, then, are concerned more with personal qualities than ideologies. What qualities do they seek? Much of what they say on this point sounds very much like what the Conservatives say: they want a man who speaks well in public, who will

---

[24] See pp. 159–60.

[25] See pp. 154–59, 161–64, 182–84.

[26] See pp. 96–97.

[27] An example of the former is Desmond Donnelly, who was supported by the Pembroke Labour party when he followed Aneurin Bevan and also when he opposed him: P. G. Richards, *Honourable Members* (London: Faber & Faber, Ltd., 1959), p. 22. An example of the latter is Ian Mikardo, a leading spokesman of the Left, who was adopted for the 1964 election by the Poplar Labour party, which is "a Right-wing party with a strong Roman Catholic Influence": Ian Waller, *Sunday Telegraph* (London), November 17, 1963, p. 4. See also R. L. Leonard, *Guide to the General Election* (London: Pan Books, Ltd., 1964), p. 95.

campaign hard, who will get on well with the CLP's workers, and who will have the maximum appeal to the constituency's particular brand of voters. Labour people often add a quality Conservatives rarely mention: they want a man who has given substantial service to the movement, whether in the party, a trade union, a co-operative society, or a socialist society.

There are other inter-party differences. For instance, religious prejudice, although not unknown in CLPs, is less common than in Conservative associations. The Nuffield general election studies show that Labour has had substantially more Jewish and nonconformist but somewhat fewer Roman Catholic candidates than the Conservatives.[28] According to some Labour officials, one rarely encounters anti-Semitism in the CLPs, but in some areas there is strong nonconformist feeling against Roman Catholics.[29]

Perhaps the most significant inter-party difference, however, is that Labour notions about desirable personal qualities vary more widely from place to place. The local party in a miners' seat may care only that the candidate be the choice of the local NUM branch.[30] Another party may prefer a sponsored candidate because he will solve their financial problems. Another may value its independence so much that it will not consider any sponsored nominee. Another—e.g., Ebbw Vale—may want a colorful figure from the Left to carry on the tradition of a former member. Another may want a respected local figure who will faithfully nurse the constituency and avoid attracting undue outside attention to himself or the CLP.[31] Another may want someone who seems likely to rise to ministerial rank. And so on.[32]

The characteristics of candidatures we reviewed earlier in this

---

[28] In 1959, for example, Labour had 41 Jewish candidates to the Conservatives' 9, 48 nonconformists to 8, but 20 Roman Catholics to 25: Butler and Rose, *The British Election of 1959*, p. 129.

[29] Liverpool was the instance most often mentioned.

[30] The author attended a selection conference in an East Midlands miners' seat in 1961, at which a predominantly right-wing GMC adopted a left-wing candidate because a majority were NUM members and he was the NUM's nominee.

[31] For example, when John Strachey, the shadow War Minister, died in 1963, the West Dundee Labour party resolved not to pick anyone like him as his successor. They felt that his neglect of his constituency duties had caused the steady decline in the party's local vote, and they determined to prevent any repetition. So they adopted a local man, Peter M. Doig, convener of the finance committee of the Dundee Corporation: *Times* (London), November 12, 1963, p. 7.

[32] Cf. T. E. M. McKitterick, "The Selection of Parliamentary Candidates: The Labour Party," *Political Quarterly*, XXX (July–September, 1959), 219–23.

chapter are the composite result of these differing preferences. Our data on educational and occupational backgrounds confirm the common impression that Labour draws most of its candidates from social strata different from those the Conservatives tap. They also suggest a pattern less widely understood: that most Labour local activists, like most Conservative, do not choose parliamentary candidates just like themselves; instead they choose men they think will make *better* candidates than themselves—better because they have more education, and have the skills and demeanor that better equip them to represent the party before the public. For they, like the Conservatives, know they are choosing the party's leaders.[33]

Inter-Constituency Movement of Candidates[34]

frequency of movement

The figures in Table 7.1 showed that of Labour candidatures in the general elections of 1951, 1955, 1959, and 1964, 42 per cent went to incumbent M.P.s, 34 per cent to newcomers, 10 per cent to non-incumbents standing again in constituencies they had previously lost; 14 per cent to non-incumbents standing in constituencies other than those they had previously lost; and under 0.5 per cent to former M.P.s. Hence only 14 per cent of the candidatures involved any movement between constituencies.

movement by incumbent m.p.s

During this period Labour had no counterpart of the two Conservative M.P.s who left one constituency for another even though redistribution had left their first constituencies unchanged.[35] But the boundary revisions of 1955, as we have seen, abolished a number of constituencies and renamed and substantially reshaped others. Twenty Labour M.P.s held seats thus affected. Of these, twelve moved to revised and renamed constituencies nearby, eleven were re-elected, and one (Maurice Webb) was defeated. Five (Dr. Edith Summerskill, W. R. Williams, W. T. Williams,

---

[33] In Chapter 8 we shall see that this attitude may be less characteristic of the minority of CLPs that choose union-sponsored candidates.

[34] Most of the material in this section is taken from the author's paper, "The Inter-Constituency Movement of British Parliamentary Candidates, 1951–1959," *American Political Science Review*, LVIII (March, 1964), 36–45.

[35] See p. 121.

Woodrow Wyatt, and G. W. Lloyd) moved to constituencies in other boroughs, four were re-elected, and one (Wyatt) was defeated in 1955 but elected in 1959. Two (George Porter and F. S. Cocks) did not stand again. And one (Sir Frank Soskice) did not stand in 1955, but was returned for Newport in the 1956 by-election.

One other Labour M.P., C. A. R. Crosland, sought a new constituency in 1955 because he believed that the boundary alterations of his South Gloucestershire seat had made it unwinnable. He moved to the Test division of Southampton, where he lost.[36] In 1959 he moved to Grimsby, where he won.

In short, seventeen of the twenty Labour M.P.s forced to move by the 1955 redistribution were adopted elsewhere and re-elected, fifteen in 1955, one in a 1956 by-election, and one in 1959. The party took good care of them.

EFFORTS BY DEFEATED M.P.S TO RE-ENTER PARLIAMENT

A former Labour M.P. who lost his marginal Midlands seat in 1959 told the author in 1962 of his search for a new and safer constituency:

I am looking for a new constituency because if I stay in X I am out of Parliament at least until the next general election. Also, of course, I would like a safer seat: when you are in a marginal seat like X you have to nurse it constantly, and that makes it impossible to give House business the attention it must have if you hope, as I do, to move to the front bench. I have been very careful to let the X Party's officers know I am looking for another seat, and they understand and sympathize. They have asked me to let them know definitely by the end of 1962 whether I will be their candidate again, and I have agreed to do so. No one resents an ex-M.P.'s looking for a better seat as long as he clears it with his CLP officers.

A lot of us in my position study the list of Labour M.P.s in their late sixties or seventies to see who are likely to retire at the next election. Then, at national and regional party meetings, we talk to the agents and officers of their parties to see whether or not they really do intend to retire. When we find out who is leaving, we get in touch with our friends in those parties and try to arrange for nominations. Then we visit the places and talk to as many ward committees, women's branches, and the like as we get invitations to.

It is important to be early in the field and get as much support committed in advance as you possibly can. There is nothing like a good head start. If you

---

[36] Ironically, his share of the poll in the Test division was smaller than that of his successor in South Gloucestershire, although both lost.

leave it all up to one brief appearance before a selection conference, you are taking a big risk.

Unless one has been hopeless, having been an M.P. is a big advantage. The delegates know who you are, and you have an initial prestige others lack. It isn't enough by itself, of course, but it helps a good deal.[37]

Eighty-six Labour M.P.s were defeated from 1950 to 1955, eleven of ministerial rank and seventy-five backbenchers. Of the eleven frontbenchers, nine shifted constituencies—seven were re-elected, two lost—and two did not stand again.[38] None stood again in the constituencies they had previously held and lost.

The seventy-five backbenchers did not fare so well: seven re-won the seats they had lost; thirteen stood and lost again in the same constituencies; four moved and won; eight moved and lost; and forty-three had no subsequent candidatures. However, former M.P.s did have an advantage over less experienced aspirants, as Table 7.12 shows.

For candidatures given to former M.P.s, the index of winnability was −35, compared with −69 and −76 for those given to persons with previous losses, and −76 for those given to new candidates.

Accordingly, while defeated Labour backbenchers did not fare so well as their frontbench colleagues, they received higher proportions of the more desirable candidatures than Labour candidates who had never been in the House. This supports the impression of the M.P. quoted above that in a contest for a desirable candidature having been in the House "isn't enough by itself, but it helps a good deal."

INTER-CONSTITUENCY MOVEMENT
BY OTHER CANDIDATES

In the Labour party, as in the Conservative, most inter-constituency movement was made by candidates who had never been M.P.s. As in Chapter 4, we shall analyze their movement by describing the subsequent electoral careers of the 342 Labour candidates who first stood and lost in the general elections of 1951 and 1955

---

[37] Some time after this interview, he was adopted for another, more promising constituency, and won the seat in the 1964 election. His former seat, however, remained Conservative in 1964.

[38] These figures include two ex-Labour M.P.s who later stood as Conservatives and won, Aiden Crawley and E. M. King.

TABLE 7.12

PREVIOUS ELECTORAL EXPERIENCE OF NON-INCUMBENTS RECEIVING LABOUR
CANDIDATURES, RELATED TO WINNABILITY OF CONSTITUENCY *

Winnability of Constituency	Former M.P.s	Two or More Previous Losses	One Previous Loss	First Contest
High	7%	4%	1%	5%
Medium	50	21	19	11
Low	42	73	77	81
Other	1	2	3	3
	100%	100%	100%	100%
Index of winnability	−35	−69	−76	−76
Number of cases	74	198	329	830

* The totals in Table 7.12 do not equal those given in the paragraph in the text preceding the table because they deal with different populations: the figures in the text include only M.P.s who lost in 1951 and 1955; the figures in Table 7.12 cover all candidatures from 1951 through 1964, and include all those given to former M.P.s regardless of when they lost their seats.

and who therefore had at least one general election and a number of by-elections in which they could have secured second candidatures.[39]

Of the 342, 51 per cent had no second candidatures, 19 per cent stood again in the same constituencies they had previously lost, 24 per cent moved to more promising constituencies, and 6 per cent moved to less promising or newly-formed constituencies. These are approximately the same proportions noted in Chapter 4 for the 350 Conservative first-time losers.

How did the Labour dropouts, stayers, and upward movers compare with each other and their Conservative counterparts?

1. Electoral Performance in First Candidature

In Chapter 4 we observed that Conservative first-time losers who had bettered their party's national average performance had fewer dropouts than those who had not, but that among the repeaters there was no significant relationship between electoral performance

---

[39] Note that the unit of analysis in this section is the individual candidate, not, as heretofore, the candidature.

TABLE 7.13

LABOUR CANDIDATES' ELECTORAL PERFORMANCE IN FIRST
CANDIDATURE RELATED TO SECOND CANDIDATURE

Second Candidature	Electoral Performance in First Candidature*			
	"Extra" Decrease	"Normal" Decrease	Increase	Other
None	58%	53%	38%	46%
In same constituency as the first	9	17	38	24
In constituency more favorable than the first	32	22	16	23
Other†	1	8	8	7
	100%	100%	100%	100%
Number of cases	85	161	39	57

* As in Chapter 4, electoral performance was measured by comparing the candidate's percentage of the poll in his first candidature with the Labour percentage in the same constituency in the preceding general election. Since in the elections of 1951 and 1955 the national swing away from Labour was 1.1 per cent and 1.8 per cent respectively, "extra" decrease means a decrease of 5.0 per cent or more, "normal" decrease means a decrease of 0.1 per cent to 4.9 per cent, and "other" means that no comparison is possible because the first candidature was in a newly-formed constituency or one in which no Conservative candidate stood in the preceding general election.

† In newly-formed constituency or constituency less favorable than the first.

in first candidature and the desirability of the second candidature. Table 7.13 shows a somewhat different pattern for Labour.

Table 7.13 shows that Labour first-time losers, like Conservative, had fewer dropouts among those who had bettered the party's national "par." But where most of the Conservatives' better performers moved on to more promising constituencies, most of Labour's made second tries in the same constituencies. This difference was not a reflection of a greater incidence of or special behavior by Labour local "flag showers": only 27 per cent of the Labour newcomers had local connections in their first constituencies, compared with 31 per cent of the Conservative. Moreover, the locals in both parties had almost exactly the same proportions of stayers and upward movers.

The difference is more likely related to the fact that the general decline in its vote in the 1950's left Labour fewer vacant promising constituencies than the Conservatives and hence fewer opportunities for upward movement.

2. *Age at First Candidature*

We noted in Chapter 4 that the Conservative first-time losers' ages at their first candidatures were significantly related to their subsequent electoral careers in only one respect: there were more dropouts in each successively older age group. The repeaters in each group, however, had approximately the same proportions of stayers and upward movers.

But among Labour's first-time losers, age was related both to rate of dropout and to movement by repeaters, as is evident in Table 7.14.

TABLE 7.14

LABOUR CANDIDATES' AGES AT FIRST CANDIDATURE
RELATED TO SECOND CANDIDATURE

Second Candidature	Age at First Candidature				
	21–29	30–39	40–49	50–59	60 and over
None	43%	47%	52%	61%	100%
In same constituency as the first	11	21	22	19	0
In constituency more promising than the first	43	26	20	10	0
Other	3	6	6	10	0
	100%	100%	100%	100%	100%
Number of cases	61	119	99	52	11

Table 7.14 shows not only more dropouts in each successively older group, but also more stayers and fewer upward movers. Accordingly, among Labour first-time losers even more than Conservative, age at first candidature was significantly related to subsequent electoral careers.

3. *Personal Connections in Constituency of First Candidature*

As we noted above, 27 per cent of the Labour first-time losers had personal connections in their first constituencies, compared with 31 per cent of the Conservatives. The dropout rates were nearly identical: 62 per cent of the Labour locals dropped out after their initial losses, compared with 63 per cent of the Conservative.

However, if age at first candidature is held constant, the ratio between dropouts and local connections persists for candidates over forty but disappears for those under forty—the reverse of the tendency observed earlier for Conservatives. This suggests that while Conservative associations drew their local "flag showers" mainly from younger persons, CLPs drew theirs more from older persons.[40] This is consistent with, although it hardly proves, the theory discussed previously that Labour more than the Conservatives values "service to the Movement" and calls upon its veterans rather than its novices to bear the party's burdens as well as to share its prizes.

4. *Education*

We noted above that the allocation of the more and less desirable Labour candidatures, unlike the Conservative, was not significantly related to the candidates' educational backgrounds. The same was also true of candidate movement: there were no significant differences among Labour's various educational groups in the proportions of dropouts, stayers, or upward movers.

CONCLUSION:
LABOUR'S PATHWAYS TO PARLIAMENT

During most of the period from 1945 to 1959 Labour's declining electoral fortunes restricted its aspirants to fewer and more clogged pathways to Parliament than those available to Conservative hopefuls. After 1959 a reverse trend set in, but during the whole postwar period the Labour pathway most commonly followed took a course quite different from its Conservative counterpart sketched at the conclusion of Chapter 4.

To begin with, at each general election an even higher proportion of Labour than Conservative safe and near-safe seats were preempted by M.P.s standing for re-election, partly because Labour had fewer safe seats to go around, partly because fewer Labour M.P.s retired voluntarily, and partly because Transport House provided M.P.s more protection than Central Office against being dropped by local parties.

Labour gave a somewhat higher proportion of its candidatures to aspirants who had fought previous parliamentary contests, in part

---

[40] See pp. 124–25.

because it had a larger pool of previous losers to draw on. But in sharp contrast with the Conservatives, Labour, despite the fact that it had fewer vacant candidatures in constituencies of high winnability, gave a far higher proportion of them to newcomers: 68 per cent to the Conservatives' 42 per cent. Accordingly, previous electoral experience was a promising, though crowded, pathway to a Labour candidature—but not to a Labour seat.

Labour candidates were generally older than Conservative. More had had experience in local government, but fewer had held party office. Despite the high proportion of vacant winnable seats going to newcomers, most Labour candidates, like most Conservative, fought their first contests in hopeless constituencies. Somewhat fewer Labour candidates than Conservative had personal connections in the constituencies for which they were adopted, and Labour's locals were a bit more concentrated than the Conservatives' in hopeless constituencies. Both parties had exceptionally high proportions of local candidates in the biggest cities outside London, and Labour's candidates in its miners' seats were mostly local men.

As we would expect, Labour drew its candidates from very different social strata than those supplying the Conservatives: Labour candidates had almost as much schooling as Conservative, but far fewer had attended public schools or Oxford or Cambridge; and while the Conservatives drew much more heavily than Labour from business and the professions, Labour drew much more heavily than the Conservatives from white-collar and manual workers.

Yet Labour candidates did not represent a cross-section of the general public or the working class. They were much more highly educated, many more held professional and white-collar jobs, and far fewer were manual workers.

Of the 830 new Labour candidates, 58 (7 per cent) won in their first tries, and the remaining 772 lost. The Labour first-time losers in 1951 and 1955 divided thereafter almost the same as the Conservative: just over half had no second candidature; and of the repeaters, slightly more than half were adopted in more favorable constituencies, slightly less than half stood again in the same constituencies, and only a small fraction moved to less favorable or newly-formed constituencies.

Labour's older first-time losers, like the Conservatives', dropped out at a higher rate than their younger colleagues; but, unlike the

Conservatives', Labour's older repeaters had more stayers and fewer upward movers than the younger ones.

Finally, Labour's first-time losers who bettered the party's national electoral par dropped out at a lower rate than those who did not; but most of these repeaters, unlike their Conservative counterparts, remained in the same constituencies rather than moving on to better ones.

Thus did Labour's pathways to Parliament parallel and diverge from the Conservatives'. Some of the differences stemmed from the disparity of the parties' electoral positions, others from their divergent ideologies and organizations, and still others from the dissimilarity of the social strata from which they drew their party workers and candidates.

Many of these differences are common knowledge. Less well known is the fact that most of the differences between Labour and Conservative candidatures were smaller than many of the differences between Labour's sponsored and unsponsored candidatures. These we shall consider in the next chapter.

Chapter 8 | *Sponsored and Unsponsored Candidatures: The Three Labour Parties*

Strictly speaking, every Labour parliamentary candidate is sponsored; that is, some organization affiliated with the party—a trade union, the Co-operative party, or a CLP—must formally undertake to pay part or all of his election expenses.[1] But a candidate not financed by either a trade union or the Co-operative party is commonly called unsponsored, since no direct financial benefit accrues to a CLP from his candidature.

In the general elections from 1951 to 1964, 47 per cent of the Labour candidatures by non-incumbents in the constituencies of high winnability went to sponsored candidates, as opposed to only 7 per cent in those of low winnability. Thirty-eight per cent of the Labour M.P.s elected in 1964 were sponsored by trade unions, 6 per cent by the Co-operative party, and the remaining 56 per cent were unsponsored.[2]

We shall conclude our analysis of candidate selection in the Labour party by describing the origins and present operation of union

---

[1] See p. 135.

[2] The comparable figures in 1951 were 37 per cent, 10 per cent, and 53 per cent; in 1955 they were 34 per cent, 10 per cent, and 56 per cent; in 1959 they were 36 per cent, 9 per cent, and 55 per cent.

and Co-operative sponsorship and by considering the similarities and differences among sponsored and unsponsored candidatures.

SPONSORSHIP BY TRADE UNIONS[3]

A BRIEF HISTORY

Trade unions sponsored parliamentary candidates long before the Labour party was founded. As early as 1874 unions nominated "workingmen's candidates" and paid their campaign expenses. After its establishment in 1900, the Labour Representation Committee (which became the Labour party in 1906) encouraged affiliated unions and socialist societies to sponsor and finance candidates, and by 1914 at least six unions did so regularly.[4]

The Party Constitution of 1914 stipulated that "a Candidate must be promoted by one or more affiliated Societies, which make themselves responsible for his election expenses."[5] At this time trade unions provided almost all the party's funds, workers, and votes, and so most Labour candidates and M.P.s were sponsored by by unions rather than by other affiliated organizations. The high-water mark of sponsorship came in the 1918 general election when of the 57 Labour M.P.s elected 49 were sponsored by trade unions and only 8 by the newly founded constituency Labour parties.[6]

In the 1920's the growth of the CLPs and the unions' heightened determination to conserve their funds for strikes increased the number of unsponsored candidates, but the sponsored continued to monopolize the winnable constituencies. The first open signs of discontent with sponsorship and demands for reform came in the late 1920's, when Sir Oswald Mosley was accused of having "bought" several seats for his followers.

The party's difficult circumstances in the early 1930's produced the first alterations in the system of sponsorship. The schism and ensuing electoral debacle of 1931 caused a sharp drop in the num-

---

[3] The ablest and most comprehensive treatment of this topic is Martin Harrison, *Trade Unions and the Labour Party since 1945* (London: George Allen & Unwin, Ltd., 1960), especially Ch. VI.

[4] *Ibid.*, pp. 262–63.

[5] Clause 6, section (4), paragraph 1, quoted in G. D. H. Cole, *A History of the Labour Party from 1914* (London: Routledge & Kegan Paul, Ltd., 1948), p. 76.

[6] W. L. Guttsman, *The British Political Elite* (London: MacGibbon & Kee, 1963), p. 236.

ber of winnable seats; in those that remained contests for adoptions increasingly resembled auctions in which CLPs bid for the support of wealthy trade unions. It was soon agreed that this tendency was dangerously unhealthy, and the 1933 annual conference adopted the first Hastings Agreement limiting the sums sponsoring organizations and individuals could contribute to constituency parties in connection with candidatures.[7]

As a result, the number of union-sponsored candidates dropped from 142 in 1931 to 130 in 1935. Since then the number has ranged around 130: 124 in 1945, 137 in 1950, 136 in 1951, 127 in 1955, 129 in 1959, and 138 in 1964.[8]

THE MACHINERY OF UNION SPONSORSHIP

1. *Choosing the Parliamentary Panels*[9]

Most trade unions maintain parliamentary panels—i.e., lists of persons they are prepared to sponsor if CLPs, with the unions' permission, adopt them as prospective candidates. Different unions choose their panels in different ways. The most common is a general ballot of the union's members, either by mail or by ballot at the union's annual conference. A few, for example, the Amalgamated Engineering Union (AEU) and the British Iron, Steel, & Kindred Trades' Association (BISAKTA), use weekend schools: the aspirants take examinations, write essays, and make speeches under the eyes of the unions' M.P.s. A few unions have no panels at all, but merely agree to sponsor an outstanding member if a CLP should adopt him.

The formal qualifications for inclusion on the panels usually include "holding a clean card" (i.e., having no undischarged obligations to the union) for a year and membership in the union for periods ranging from one to seven years. Many unions also impose an age limit of fifty-five, and some stop paying annual maintenance grants to a CLP's general funds when its sponsored M.P. passes the age of sixty-five.[10]

---

[7] The limits were increased in 1948 and again in 1957: see p. 136.

[8] Table 26 in Harrison, *Trade Unions and the Labour Party*, p. 265. The data for 1964 were generously supplied the author by Transport House.

[9] Cf. *ibid.*, pp. 279–85.

[10] For example, J. D. Murray, sponsored by the National Union of Mineworkers (NUM), was adopted and elected for the Spennymoor division of Durham in 1942 and

A solid record of service to the union and the movement constitutes the principal informal qualification. Most panels include only
men with fifteen to thirty years of union membership. Even so, a
union's most respected and able members are seldom included. The
reason is that most unions prohibit their permanent officials from
being M.P.s at the same time: they maintain that no one can satis-
factorily meet the demands of both posts. Forced to choose, most
senior trade union officers opt to remain with their unions; as Guttsman points out, "They have generally found real industrial power
preferable to possibly spurious and generally limited political
power."[11] Consequently, many sponsored M.P.s—especially from the
blue-collar unions—are men who did not quite make it to the top
of their unions, men for whom seats in Parliament are a kind of con-
solation prize.

Most unions reconstitute their panels after each election. But the
selectors are usually reluctant to strike off any holdover who
wishes to remain, and the names on the panels change only slowly
with deaths and occasional withdrawals.

2. *Drawing up List A*

List A, as we noted in Chapter 5, is composed of all those on the
unions' panels who have been accepted by the party's National Executive Committee. Like List B of the approved unsponsored candidates, it is made available on request to any CLP.

Occasionally the NEC has refused to accept a union nominee for
List A. Usually, however, it accepts them without investigation or
discussion; for, as a member of the NEC told the author, "most

---

for Durham North-West in 1950. In October, 1953, the Durham Miners' Association,
without bothering to notify the CLP, wrote Murray that he should stand down at the
next election. The reason given was that the association had passed a rule requiring all
their sponsored M.P.s to retire after reaching the age of 65, and Murray was 66. The
CLP officers were angered at being by-passed: one said, "This . . . savours too much
of dictatorship . . . [and] is causing serious concern among the rank and file who feel
they are the people who should choose the candidate for Parliamentary elections."
Murray complained that the rule was unfair, but agreed to stand down. In 1955 he
was replaced by John Ainsley, another NUM nominee: *Consett Chronicle*, October
22, 1953, p. 1; October 29, 1953, p. 1.

[11] Guttsman, *The British Political Elite*, p. 24. Cf. Harrison, *Trade Unions and the
Labour Party*, pp. 285–92.

unions are extremely annoyed if we even question the fitness of their nominees, let alone reject one. So we put them right on unless we get one, like Sam Goldberg, who just won't do at all."[12]

GRANTS TO CLPS

As we have seen, sponsoring a nominee means that the sponsoring union undertakes to contribute to the candidate's campaign expenses and to make maintenance grants to the CLP's general funds. The Model Rules require the sponsoring union's executive to give its consent in writing on a prescribed form, stipulating how much the union will contribute.[13] At present the Hastings Agreements set maxima of £350 on annual maintenance grants in borough constituencies and £420 in county constituencies, and allow the sponsor to contribute no more than 80 per cent of the campaign expenditures permitted by law.

By no means all trade unions contribute the full amounts allowed. The National Union of Mineworkers (NUM), for example, usually contributes only a fraction of the permitted maxima, and other unions negotiate the size of their grants with CLP executives.[14] Sometimes unions contribute more than the permitted maxima in order to "buy the seat"[15]—although rumors of seat-buying probably outrun the facts (see below).

Unions are not reckless with their money. For example, sponsorship usually ends if the candidate is defeated; as we shall see below, it is rarely renewed. Moreover, if a union nominee is adopted at the beginning of an election campaign and later defeated, his sponsor will contribute only to his election expenses and make no maintenance grant.

Even so, the unions' financial power gives them a considerable advantage in placing their nominees. How have they used it?

---

[12] The Sam Goldberg case is described above, p. 163.

[13] See pp. 135–36.

[14] Harrison, *Trade Unions and the Labour Party*, pp. 80–81.

[15] Harrison mentions some instances in which the Union of Shop, Distributive, and Allied Workers (USDAW) and the National Union of General & Municipal Workers (NUGMW) have paid "bonuses" in order to control adoptions. However, he concludes that "most unions' accounts lend little credence to allegations that *sub rosa* payments are made": *ibid.*, pp. 81–84.

PLACING UNION-SPONSORED CANDIDATES

1. *Safe* v. *Hopeless Constituencies*

In the general elections from 1945 to 1964, trade unions sponsored a total of 790 candidatures, of which 643 (81 per cent) won seats—a record of success explained largely by the fact that most were by incumbents standing for re-election in safe seats. But the unions also sponsored some non-incumbents. Table 8.1 compares

TABLE 8.1

SPONSORSHIP OF CANDIDATURES BY LABOUR NON-INCUMBENTS
RELATED TO WINNABILITY OF CONSTITUENCY

Winnability of Constituency	Sponsorship		
	By Trade Unions	By Co-op. Party	By CLPs
High	17%	7%	2%
Medium	32	25	14
Low	48	61	82
Other	3	7	2
	100%	100%	100%
Index of winnability*	−31	−54	−80
Number of cases	162	68	1,201

* Computed by subtracting the per cent in the high-winnability category from the per cent in the low-winnability category. The lower the index number the higher the proportion of the candidates in the category in the most desirable constituencies.

their distribution among the levels of winnability with that of the unsponsored in the elections from 1951 to 1964.

Union-sponsored non-incumbents, as Table 8.1 makes clear, were more concentrated in the winnable seats than the Co-operative-sponsored and much more than the unsponsored: their index of winnability was −31, compared with −54 for the Co-operative-sponsored, and −80 for the unsponsored.

But some unions insisted on safe constituencies more than others. This is evident in Table 8.2 which ranks the unions in order of the number of candidatures sponsored and shows the proportion of winning candidatures sponsored by each.

TABLE 8.2

CANDIDATURES SPONSORED BY TRADE UNIONS, 1945–1964 *

Sponsoring Union	Candida-tures Sponsored	Number Winning	Per Cent Winning
National Union of Mineworkers (NUM)	203	200	99
Transport & General Workers' Union (T & GWU)	112	96	86
Amalgamated Engineering Union (AEU)	73	50	68
National Union of Railwaymen (NUR)	62	50	81
Union of Shop, Distributive & Allied Workers (USDAW)	57	52	91
Transport Salaried Staffs' Association (TSSA)	56	40	71
National Union of General & Municipal Workers (NUGMW)	45	39	87
National Union of Agricultural Workers (NUAW)	17	7	41
Electrical Trades Union (ETU)	17	4	23
Amalgamated Society of Woodworkers (ASW)	16	12	75
Union of Post Office Workers (UPOW)	15	9	60
United Textile Factory Workers' Association (UTFWA)	14	9	64
Associated Society of Locomotive Engineers & Firemen (ASLEF)	13	12	92
British Iron, Steel & Kindred Trades Association (BISAKTA)	11	11	100
National Union of Boot & Shoe Operatives (NUBSO)	7	6	86
Other unions	72	46	64
Total	790	643	81%

* Adapted from Harrison, *Trade Unions and the Labour Party*, Tables 26 and 27, pp. 265 and 267.

The NUM sponsored almost twice as many candidatures as any other union and over a quarter of the total by all unions. All but three won seats.[16] Of the other most active unions, USDAW, T & GWU, and NUGMW also sponsored more winners than the overall "par" of 81 per cent; NUM's score was exactly "par"; and AEU and TSSA sponsored fewer winners than "par." The other unions ranged from 100 per cent winners (BISAKTA) to 23 per cent (ETU).

[16] One person received two of the NUM's three losing candidatures in this period: D. R. Llewellyn, a miners' agent for 15 years, member of the NUM's national executive and member of the Somerset County Council, was adopted for Wells in 1951 and lost. In 1955 he was adopted for North Somerset, and lost again. He received no further candidatures. The other was Alexander Eadie, who stood for Ayr in 1964 and lost with 47.8 per cent of the vote in a straight fight.

2. *Sponsoring Missions*

Table 8.2 shows that some unions—notably ETU, NUAW, UPOW, UTFWA, and AEU—sponsored a number of losing candidatures. Some, of course, were in marginal constituencies they expected to win, but a number were in safe Tory seats. Sponsoring candidates in hopeless constituencies is sometimes called "sending missions": a union contributes a candidate and funds to a CLP with no thought of winning, but to "show the flag," raise local party morale, and spread the socialist word to the ideological heathen.

Some examples of recent "missions": in 1951 the AEU sponsored P. C. McNally in Esher, where the Conservatives had a margin of 32 per cent in 1950; in 1959 the ASW sponsored G. E. Peters in Canterbury, with a Conservative majority of 33 per cent in 1955, and the ETU sponsored J. B. Urquhart in East Aberdeenshire, with a Conservative majority of 37 per cent in 1955; and in 1964 the Amalgamated Society of Woodworkers (ASW) sponsored Peter O'Grady in Ripon, with a Conservative majority of 40 per cent in 1959, and the T & GWU sponsored John Ellis in Wokingham, with a Conservative majority of 30 per cent in 1959.

Most unions which send missions prefer to pass their favors about: in the general elections from 1951 to 1964, only the UTFWA sponsored losing candidatures in the same constituency in as many as three elections.[17] The AEU sponsored losers in Rochdale in 1951 and 1955, but, with the help of Liberal interventions, won with Jack McCann at the 1958 by-election and in 1959. The AEU and TSSA sponsored two successive losers in each of four different constituencies, and five other unions did so in one constituency each. But the other 42 constituencies with union-sponsored losers in 1951 or 1955 had unsponsored candidates thereafter.

3. *Buying Seats*

Among Labour activists there is considerable talk of trade unions buying seats—i.e., capturing candidatures in safe constituencies by making lavish contributions to the CLPs. One hears such talk not

---

[17] The favored constituency was Clitheroe, which had Conservative majorities of 6 per cent in 1950, 14 per cent in 1951, and 12 per cent in 1955. The union sponsored Harold Bradley in 1951, and William Rutter in 1955 and 1959.

only by CLP members about unions in general, but also by some unions about others. And certainly seat buying was common when the Hastings Agreements were adopted in 1933.

How common is it today? Martin Harrison, who has made the most thorough study of the question, says that in most cases allegations of seat buying are difficult for an outside observer to verify or disprove.[18] Occasionally a CLP has refused to put any unsponsored candidate on its short list.[19] But on other occasions CLPs have begun by resolving to choose a sponsored candidate but ended by adopting an unsponsored one because of his superior performance at the selection conference or because they resented the unions' "flashing their money." Harrison concludes:

> Labour Party officials do not deny that some constituencies are venal—although some veteran officials put the proportion at no more than three in a hundred. The Party has not yet matched the Conservatives' success in banishing financial considerations from selection conferences. Even if a scandal can be avoided, the importance of finance in swinging nominations has declined, and seems likely to decline still further—to the detriment of the unions' representation in Parliament.[20]

In short, whatever may be the number of seats bought by trade unions since 1945, it is higher than any comparable number in the Conservative party—and yet not high enough to keep the unions from grumbling that too many of their nominees are being passed over in favor of middle-class intellectuals. We shall return to this complaint below.

SPONSORSHIP BY THE CO-OPERATIVE PARTY[21]

CO-OPERATIVE–LABOUR RELATIONS PRIOR TO 1946

In the Labour party's early years a few local co-operative societies affiliated directly with local trades councils, but most held aloof.

---

[18] Cf. Harrison, *Trade Unions and the Labour Party*, pp. 273–78.

[19] A recent example was that of Newark in 1963: despite the advice of the regional organizer, the CLP executive in this marginal Labour constituency decided to exclude all unsponsored nominees from the short list even though at least one had a number of nominations: *Daily Telegraph* (London), September 16, 1963, p. 1; *New Statesman and Nation*, September 20, 1963, p. 2.

[20] *Trade Unions and the Labour Party*, p. 278. Cf. Robert T. McKenzie, *British Political Parties*, 2nd ed. (London: Mercury Books, 1964), p. 554.

[21] Useful discussions of the organization of the Co-operative party and its relations with the Labour party are: Cole, *History of the Labour Party, passim.;* Jack Bailey,

A number of the co-operative movement's leaders strongly opposed any kind of direct affiliation with Labour: some were Liberals, others believed co-operation was more likely than state socialism to bring the New Jerusalem, and still others felt that direct political action was improper for a consumers' movement.

In 1917 the Co-operative congress, angered by new taxes imposed on co-operatives, voted to establish a Co-operative Representation Committee—obviously modeled on the Labour Representation Committee of 1900—"to secure direct representation in Parliament and on all local administrative bodies." Thus was founded the Co-operative party, which ever since has been affiliated but not identical with the Co-operative Union and subject to direction by the Co-operative Union's congresses. The new party put up several candidates in the 1918 general election, and elected one.[22]

The lone Co-operative M.P. joined the parliamentary Labour party, and an increasing number of co-operators pressed for a closer alliance or even complete fusion with Labour. In 1927, after considerable debate, the Co-operative congress ratified, by the narrow vote of 1,960 to 1,843, the Cheltenham Agreement. This was an arrangement negotiated with the Labour party in 1926 to establish a joint committee to consult on electoral matters, prevent Labour-Co-operative parliamentary and local contests, and arrange joint campaigns. Local Co-operative parties or councils were permitted to affiliate with CLPs, with voting rights corresponding to the affiliation fees they paid. And in national elections and in Parliament the Co-operative party was to be associated but not affiliated with Labour. This state of affairs continued until 1946.[23]

THE AGREEMENT OF 1946

Although neither Labour's nor the Co-operative party's leaders were altogether happy with the 1927 agreement, the troubles be-

---

"The Consumer in Politics," in Noah Barou, ed., *The Co-operative Movement in Labour Britain* (London: Victor Gollancz, Ltd., 1948), pp. 100–110; S. R. Elliott, *The English Coöperatives* (New Haven: Yale University Press, 1937), Ch. XIII; and *The Organisation of the Co-operative Party*, a pamphlet issued by the Co-operative party in 1953.

[22] Cole, *History of the Labour Party*, pp. 61–63.

[23] For the text of the Cheltenham Agreement, see *Report of the Thirty-Seventh Annual Conference of the Labour Party, 1927*, pp. 7–8.

setting both parties during the 1930's and the continuing resistance of many co-operators to closer affiliation with Labour prevented any serious effort to revise it until after the War. After their great victory of 1945, however, Labour's leaders pressed for a new and closer relationship with the Co-operative party. They encountered little resistance, and in 1946 a new agreement went into effect. It provided for:

(1) A joint committee of representatives from the NEC and the National Co-operative Union "to consider Parliamentary and Local Government Policy which would affect their mutual interests."

(2) A joint committee of representatives from the NEC and the Co-operative party to consider political organization and allied problems.

(3) Affiliation of local Co-operative *parties* to CLPs (the co-operative guilds and other auxiliaries were requested not to apply for local affiliations).

(4) "The Nomination of Parliamentary Candidates by the Co-operative Party to Constituency Labour Parties under the rules of the Labour Party."

(5) The signing by all Co-operative–sponsored candidates of a form containing this declaration:

> I accept nomination as a Parliamentary Candidate of the Co-operative Party running in association with the Labour Party. If elected to Parliament, I undertake to join the Parliamentary Labour Party and to accept and to act in harmony with the Standing Orders of the Parliamentary Labour Party for the time being in force.

(6) Such candidates would be designated "Co-operative and Labour Candidates."[24]

By this agreement the Co-operative party acquired a status comparable in many respects to a trade union's. It chose a parliamentary panel consisting of persons nominated by local Co-operative parties and approved by the party's national executive. Local parties were advised to be "on the lookout for possible Parliamentary seats," and to inform party Head Office if they found a good prospect. And if a CLP adopted a person on the Co-operative party's panel with

---

[24] The text is given in *Report of the Forty-Fifth Annual Conference of the Labour Party, 1946*, pp. 229–30.

Head Office's consent, the national party would make grants to the CLP's campaign and general funds.[25]

As noted above, since 1945 a number of trade unionists have complained that unions have not received their proper share of Labour candidatures in winnable constituencies. One cause, according to many, has been the competition from the Co-operators, who can match the unions' financial resources.

Three instances in particular incensed the unions. Morpeth, which had been a miners' seat for years, adopted Co-operative nominee W. J. Owen for the 1954 by-election. To replace Stanley Evans in safe Wednesbury in the 1957 by-election, the CLP passed over TSSA-sponsored Ray Gunter, a trade union member of the NEC, in favor of John Stonehouse, a director of the London Co-operative Society. And in 1958, when S. P. Viant, who had been the ASW-sponsored M.P. for West Willesden since 1935, announced that he would stand down at the next election, the CLP chose as his successor Co-operative-sponsored Laurence Pavitt over Mrs. Margaret McKay, the Trades Union Congress's officer for women's affairs, who was sponsored by the T & GWU.

By the mid-1950's, the unions' resentment of Co-operative competition grew into a demand for revision of the 1946 agreement so as to reduce substantially the number of Co-operative-sponsored nominees permitted.

THE AGREEMENT OF 1958

In February, 1957, the NEC called a conference of affiliated trade unions (but not Co-operative party representatives) to consider upward revision of the Hastings Agreements maxima. The union leaders seized the occasion to demand that the NEC do something about Co-operative competition. Two weeks later the NEC notified the Co-operative party that it was terminating the 1946 agreement, and suggested that a new one be worked out.[26]

A joint committee of representatives from the NEC and the National Policy Committee of the National Co-operative Union be-

[25] *The Organisation of the Co-operative Party,* pp. 13, 17, 25, 45.
[26] *Times* (London), February 28, 1957, p. 4.

gan negotiations. It soon became apparent that Labour hoped to persuade the Co-operators to agree to a gradual reduction of the number of Co-operative-and-Labour M.P.s from twenty to six. Not only did the Co-operators flatly refuse, but they sought popular support by leaking Labour's proposals to the press.[27]

The negotiations dragged on for over a year. Finally, in July, 1958, the terms of the new agreement were announced:

(1) The twenty Co-operative-sponsored M.P.s and ten Co-operative-sponsored prospective candidates already endorsed by the NEC would be permitted to stand at the next election as "Labour and Co-operative" candidates.[28]

(2) If any of the thirty withdrew, the NEC and the Co-operative party would consider whether he could be replaced by another Co-operative-sponsored candidate.

(3) After each general election thereafter the number of candidates the Co-operative party could sponsor would be reviewed by the NEC and representatives from the Co-operative Union.[29]

The 1959 general election was fought under this agreement, but it was reconsidered and revised afterward.

THE AGREEMENT OF 1960

In the 1959 general election Labour-and-Co-operative M.P.s were defeated at Barons Court, North-East Bristol, Cleveland, and Uxbridge, which reduced their total number to sixteen. In 1960 the NEC again met with Co-operative party representatives and negotiated a revision of the 1958 agreement in the light of the new situation. Its terms were:

(1) If the remaining sixteen Labour-and-Co-operative M.P.s wished to stand again at the next general election, their readoption would have the same protection as that of any other Labour M.P.[30]

(2) If the four defeated M.P.s and ten defeated non-incumbents wished to stand again in the same constituencies they had lost in 1959, the NEC would not oppose them, but they would have to take their chances in selection conferences without NEC assistance.

---

[27] Harrison, *Trade Unions and the Labour Party*, pp. 304–5.

[28] Note the reversal of the former order of the parties' names.

[29] The text is given in *Report of the Fifty-Seventh Annual Conference of the Labour Party, 1958*, pp. 254–55.

[30] See pp. 180–81.

(3) If any of these fourteen candidatures were lost by a Co-operative-sponsored nominee, the NEC and the Co-operative party would consult as to whether it could be made up in another constituency—although, as the *Times* political correspondent commented, "a Co-operative nomination for a more favourable constituency than the one lost would be unlikely to receive Labour Party approval."[31]

It now became the Co-operators' turn to complain. In 1961 the NEC refused to allow a Co-operative-sponsored nominee to compete for the candidature for the Glasgow Bridgeton by-election,[32] and later refused permission for a Co-operative nominee to compete at Tottenham, a constituency once held by a Co-operative M.P.[33]

In 1964, then, the Co-operative party was restricted to a maximum of thirty candidatures—in the sixteen seats they held and in fourteen other constituencies. A total of twenty-seven Co-operative-sponsored candidates actually stood. Fifteen were incumbents, all of whom were re-elected. Twelve were non-incumbents, of whom four won. As a result, the total number of Labour-and-Co-operative M.P.s increased to nineteen. But it was clear that even the maximum of thirty candidatures is not guaranteed forever. The NEC has evidently determined to spread most of the Co-operative-sponsored candidatures by non-incumbents in the future among all kinds of constituencies; it will not permit them to be concentrated in the constituencies of high winnability, as the Co-operators obviously would prefer.

The Co-operative movement's leaders are divided on their next move. Some argue that the consumers' interests are inseparable from the unions', and that division in the face of the capitalist enemy can only harm both; accordingly, they propose that the Co-operators abandon entirely their semi-independent political posture and affiliate with the Labour party nationally as well as locally. Others take the position that since trade unions and socialists represent producer interests, there is as great a need as ever for an independent organization to protect consumers. Many are so annoyed at union hostility and the NEC's recent restrictions that they advocate a complete break with Labour at all levels and the re-

---

[31] *Times* (London), May 6, 1960, p. 10.
[32] *Co-operative News* (London), August 19, 1961, pp. 1, 2, 16.
[33] *Times* (London), August 18, 1961, p. 4.

establishment of a truly independent Co-operative party. Still others oppose both extremes and suggest negotiating a more satisfactory agreement with Labour—e.g., accepting a top limit of twenty-four sponsored candidatures but having them unrestricted as to location and free from any special NEC veto.[34]

Whatever its future status, the Co-operative party's present position in sponsoring candidatures is analogous to that of a large and wealthy trade union—with two significant exceptions: it is not affiliated with Labour at the national level and makes no direct financial contribution to Labour's national operations; and it is restricted in both the number and location of its candidatures by the NEC.

CHARACTERISTICS OF SPONSORED AND
UNSPONSORED CANDIDATURES

The system of sponsorship has clearly caused considerable squabbling inside the Labour party. What difference has it made in the kinds of persons who have become Labour candidates?

We noted one significant difference in Table 8.1: only 48 per cent of the candidatures by union-sponsored non-incumbents were in constituencies of low winnability, compared with 61 per cent of those by Co-operative-sponsored, and 82 per cent of those by unsponsored.[35] The principal reason for this is clear: since 1945 the NEC has done all it can to have a Labour candidate in every constituency, and every CLP, no matter how large the local Tory majority, feels duty-bound to put up a candidate. Trade unions and the Co-operative party, on the other hand, feel no obligation to sponsor candidates in every seat or to divide their efforts equally between winnable and hopeless constituencies. As we have seen, except for supporting an occasional "mission," they sponsor candidatures only in constituencies they feel they have at least a reasonable chance of winning.

There are many other differences as well. To identify them, we shall compare the characteristics of the three types of non-incumbents filling Labour candidatures in the general elections of 1951, 1955, 1959, and 1964.

---

[34] For expressions of these points of view, see the *Co-operative News* (London), August 19, 1961, p. 9; *Times* (London), March 3, 1963, p. 6; and March 5, 1963, p. 11.
[35] See p. 226.

AGE

The data in Chapter 7 confirm the common impression that Labour candidates were generally older than Conservative.[36] However, Table 8.3 reveals that the biggest age differentials were not those between the two parties, but those within the Labour party.

TABLE 8.3

SPONSORSHIP OF CANDIDATURES BY NON-INCUMBENTS RELATED TO AGE

Age	Sponsorship of Labour Candidatures			Conservative Candidatures
	By Trade Unions	By Co-op. Party	By CLPs	
21–29	2%	6%	12%	12%
30–39	17	34	36	40
40–49	40	35	31	29
50–59	35	18	17	16
60 and over	6	7	4	3
	100%	100%	100%	100%
Number of cases	162	68	1,201	1,311

Table 8.3 shows that only 19 per cent of the union-sponsored candidatures went to persons under forty, compared with 40 per cent of the Co-operative-sponsored and 48 per cent of the unsponsored. At the other end of the scale, 41 per cent of the union-sponsored candidatures were by persons over fifty, compared with 25 per cent of the Co-operative-sponsored and 21 per cent of the unsponsored.

This discloses a pattern we shall encounter repeatedly in the pages ahead: the unsponsored Labour candidates more closely resembled their Conservative opponents than their union-sponsored Labour colleagues, with the Co-operative-sponsored falling between. The age differentials doubtless resulted mainly from the unions' general practice, noted above, of stocking their parliamentary panels largely with men who have given many years of faithful union service.

PREVIOUS ELECTORAL EXPERIENCE

In Chapter 7 we took note of the fact that a higher proportion of Labour than Conservative candidatures went to persons who had

---

[36] See pp. 198–99.

previously fought parliamentary contests.[37] If, however, we are correct in believing that trade unions generally value union experience more than any other, we should expect higher proportions of newcomers in the union-sponsored candidatures in the most winnable constituencies than in poor constituencies. Table 8.4 shows that this was the case.

TABLE 8.4

Sponsorship of Candidatures by Labour Non-Incumbents Related to Previous Electoral Experience, by Winnability of Constituency

Previous Electoral Experience	Sponsorship								
	By Trade Unions			By Co-op. Party			By CLPs		
	High	Medium	Low	High	Medium	Low	High	Medium	Low
First contest	(74%)*	44%	49%	(40%)	(41%)	41%	(64%)	39%	63%
One previous loss	(15)	17	23	(20)	(29)	35	(4)	28	22
Two or more previous losses	(7)	25	23	(40)	(24)	17	(16)	15	13
Former M.P.s	(4)	14	5	(0)	(6)	7	(16)	18	2
	100%	100%	100%	100%	100%	100%	100%	100%	100%
Number of cases	27	52	78	5	17	41	25	163	984

* Percentages in parentheses because of the small number of cases.

Despite the small number of cases in many of its cells, Table 8.4 shows that a higher proportion of union-sponsored than unsponsored candidatures went to newcomers in the most winnable constituencies. The Co-operative proportions varied little among the three winnability categories. Thirteen of the twenty union candidatures by newcomers in the best constituencies were by men sponsored by the NUM. All thirteen had long been active in NUM affairs; as a reward they were nominated by their local branches for candidatures in vacant miners' seats, adopted, financed by the union, and elected.

SEX

Only 2 per cent of the union-sponsored candidatures went to women, compared with 12 per cent of the Co-operative-spon-

---

[37] See pp. 195–96.

sored and 6 per cent of the unsponsored. These slight differences suggest, not that trade unionists were unusually prejudiced against women in politics, but rather that it was particularly difficult for women to rise to prominence in union affairs.

EXPERIENCE IN LOCAL GOVERNMENT,
CIVIC ORGANIZATIONS, AND PARTY OFFICE

In Chapter 7 we observed that a substantially higher proportion of Labour than Conservative candidatures went to persons who had held office in local government.[38] Table 8.5 shows that union-sponsored candidates accounted for most of the difference.

TABLE 8.5

SPONSORSHIP OF CANDIDATURES BY NON-INCUMBENTS RELATED TO EXPERIENCE IN LOCAL GOVERNMENT, CIVIC AND RELIGIOUS ORGANIZATIONS, AND PARTY OFFICE

Experience	Sponsorship of Labour Candidatures			Conservative Candidatures
	By Trade Unions	By Co-op. Party	By CLPs	
Local Government				
Some	64%	47%	45%	36%
None	36	53	55	64
	100%	100%	100%	100%
Civic or Religious Organizations				
Some	10%	3%	10%	7%
None	90	97	90	93
	100%	100%	100%	100%
Local or National Party Office				
Some	16%	16%	18%	26%
None	84	84	82	74
	100%	100%	100%	100%
Number of cases	162	68	1,201	1,311

Table 8.5 shows that the union-sponsored candidatures included a significantly larger proportion than the others of persons with experience in local government.[39] The Co-operative-sponsored and

---

[38] See p. 197.

[39] For example, 11 of the 17 NUM-sponsored candidatures went to persons who had served on local government councils.

unsponsored candidatures had higher proportions than the Conservatives', but the proportion of union-sponsored was by far the largest of the three Labour groups. Having served on a local council probably helped applicants win places on the unions' parliamentary panels. It may also have seemed to some CLPs an additional reason for adopting union nominees; for it was good evidence that they were more than union hacks put on parliamentary panels because they were not good enough for high union office.

The other intra-Labour differences are too small to make much of, but the substantially lower proportion of all Labour candidatures than Conservative going to persons who had held party office is consistent with the impression discussed previously that Labour activists value service to the movement, of which party work is only one variety and not necessarily the most important.[40]

EDUCATION

When we tabulate the candidatures according to formal schooling, as in Table 8.6, we see the most striking differences among the three Labour parties.

TABLE 8.6

SPONSORSHIP OF CANDIDATURES BY NON-INCUMBENTS RELATED TO EDUCATION

Education	Sponsorship of Labour Candidatures			Conservative Candidatures
	By Trade Unions	By Co-op. Party	By CLPs	
Elementary only and elementary plus	48%	9%	15%	3%
Secondary only and secondary plus	43	57	33	27
Secondary and university other than Oxbridge	5	18	28	14
Secondary and Oxbridge	3	6	9	6
Public school only	0	3	3	20
Public school and university other than Oxbridge	1	3	2	5
Public school and Oxbridge	0	4	10	25
	100%	100%	100%	100%
Number of cases	162	68	1,201	1,311

[40] See pp. 176, 197.

The differences in formal schooling were much greater between the union-sponsored and unsponsored Labour candidatures than between the latter and Conservative candidatures. For example, 48 per cent of the union-sponsored went to persons who did not go beyond elementary school, compared with 9 per cent of the Co-operative-sponsored, 15 per cent of the unsponsored, and 3 per cent of the Conservatives'. At the other end of the scale, only 4 per cent of the union-sponsored were filled by persons who had attended universities, compared with 31 per cent of the Co-operative-sponsored, 49 per cent of the unsponsored, and 50 per cent of the Conservatives'.

The differences between Labour's unsponsored candidatures and the Conservatives' in the social prestige of the schools attended were as great as the general inter-party gulf noted in Chapter 7: the former included far fewer persons with public school backgrounds (15 per cent to 50 per cent) and attendance at Oxford or Cambridge (19 per cent to 31 per cent). But, measured by years of schooling, the persons given Labour's unsponsored candidatures were educationally much closer to their Conservative opponents than to their union-sponsored fellow partisans. And once again, the Co-operative candidatures stood between the union-sponsored and unsponsored.

OCCUPATION

Since trade unions fill their panels with veteran union members, we should expect most of their candidatures to go to manual workers, white-collar workers, and trade union officials. On the other hand, the aspirants on Transport House's List B have a much wider occupational range. Accordingly, if the CLPs picked union-sponsored nominees because they were workingmen and thus appropriate representatives for the workingman's party, we should expect to see little difference in the occupational distributions of sponsored and unsponsored candidatures. But if the CLPs picked sponsored candidates more for the financial benefits they brought, we should expect the unsponsored group to show quite a different occupational distribution. Table 8.7 shows that the latter was clearly the case.

There were several sharp occupational differences among the

TABLE 8.7

Occupation	Sponsorship of Labour Candidatures			Conservative Candidatures
	By Trade Unions	By Co-op. Party	By CLPs	
Barrister	0.5%	3%	7%	13%
Solicitor	0	1	4	8
Journalist, publicist, author	2	8	8	5
Teacher	2	28	25	6
Chartered accountant	0	0	1	3
Civil engineer or surveyor	5	3	1	3
Doctor, dentist, clergyman, or other professional	0	1	4	3
Armed services	0.5	0	1	3
Company executive or director	0.5	3	6	25
Small business proprietor	2	9	4	8
Farmer	0.5	0	3	5
Civil servant	0.5	0	4	2
White-collar	23	16	17	9
Trade union official	20	9	3	0
Manual worker	43	4	9	3
Political organizer	0.5	6	1	1
Housewife	0	8	1	1
Private means	0	0	0	1
Student	0	1	1	1
Not ascertained	0	0	*	*
	100%	100%	100%	100%
Number of cases	162	68	1,201	1,311

* Less than 0.5 per cent.

three types of Labour candidatures. For example, 63 per cent of the union-sponsored went to manual workers and trade union officials, compared with 13 per cent of the Co-operative-sponsored and 12 per cent of the unsponsored. When we add white-collar clerical workers, we account for 86 per cent of the union-sponsored, but only 29 per cent of the Co-operative-sponsored, and 29 per cent of the unsponsored. On the other hand, the Co-operative parties and CLPs drew more heavily from school teachers than from any other occupational group: 28 per cent and 25 per cent respectively, compared with only 2 per cent of the union-sponsored.

There were also a number of significant differences between Labour's unsponsored candidatures and the Conservatives': Labour had fewer lawyers, company executives and directors, and many more school teachers, white-collar workers, and manual workers. But the most striking differences in Table 8.7, as in many other comparisons, were those between Labour's union-sponsored and unsponsored candidatures.

PERSONAL CONNECTIONS IN
THE CONSTITUENCY

We observed in Chapter 7 that somewhat fewer Labour than Conservative candidatures went to persons with personal connections in the constituencies for which they were adopted, but that Labour's locals were more concentrated than the Conservatives' in the high-winnability constituencies.[41] Table 8.8 shows that only the Co-operative-sponsored candidatures differed markedly from the Conservatives'!

TABLE 8.8

SPONSORSHIP OF CANDIDATURES BY NON-INCUMBENTS RELATED TO
PERSONAL CONSTITUENCY CONNECTIONS

Local Connections	SPONSORSHIP OF LABOUR CANDIDATURES			Conservative Candidatures
	By Trade Unions	By Co-op. Party	By CLPs	
Some	31%	22%	31%	32%
None	69	78	69	68
	100%	100%	100%	100%
Number of cases	162	68	1,201	1,311

Table 8.8 shows that the union-sponsored candidatures had nearly the same proportion of locals as the Conservatives' and the unsponsored, but the Co-operative-sponsored substantially fewer. The union figures, however, reflect the special placement policies of the most active sponsoring union, the NUM. Most trade unions are glad to sponsor members of their panels in any winnable constituency regardless of its location, and some, as we have seen, send occasional missions to solid Tory seats. The NUM follows a different policy: it

---

[41] See pp. 206–7.

is not interested in placing its candidates in any winnable constituency, but only in miners' seats. Accordingly, when a candidature in such a constituency becomes vacant, the NUM customarily lets its branches in the area choose a man. When they have, the union's national executive agrees to sponsor him. The branches almost always choose local men, and the national office encourages them to do so. Thus fifteen of the seventeen NUM-sponsored candidatures were by local men,[42] and the figures in the first column of Table 8.8 are biased accordingly. When the NUM candidatures are withdrawn, the number of union-sponsored candidatures by locally-connected persons becomes 36 out of 145, or 25 per cent—a figure which is lower than the proportion of locals among the unsponsored, but still higher than the proportion among the Co-operative-sponsored. Except for this one union's candidatures, in short, Labour candidatures generally included fewer locals than Conservative.

POPULATION TYPES OF CONSTITUENCIES

Labour's winnable constituencies are not spread as evenly across the country as the Conservatives'; they are concentrated mainly in the working-class areas of the larger cities and in those rural and semi-rural areas in which mining is the principal activity. Since, as we have seen, the trade unions and the Co-operative party confine their sponsorships mostly to winnable constituencies, we should expect the sponsored candidates to be more unevenly distributed than the unsponsored among constituencies of various population types. Table 8.9 confirms this expectation.

Table 8.9 shows that the union-sponsored candidatures were most heavily concentrated in the mining areas, the Scottish burghs, and the non-metropolitan urban areas. Co-operative-sponsored candidatures were largely confined to the urban and metropolitan areas. And the unsponsored candidatures, as we expected, were overrepresented in the rural areas, underrepresented in the mining areas

---

[42] According to the testimony of a party "civil servant," a typical procedure is that followed by the Durham Miners' Federation: each of, say, ten lodges in a constituency with a vacant candidature nominates a candidate, who by rule must be a local man. Each lodge then ballots to choose two from the original group of twenty—and each votes for its own man and for the weakest of his rivals. Hence the two weakest men usually get on the short list.

TABLE 8.9

POPULATION TYPE OF CONSTITUENCY RELATED TO SPONSORSHIP OF
CANDIDATURES BY LABOUR NON-INCUMBENTS

Sponsor	Population Type of Constituency									
	London	Other Metropolitan	Other Urban	Semi-rural	Semi-rural, Mining	Rural	Rural, Mining	Scot. Burghs	Scot. County	Ulster
Trade unions	8%	9%	14%	9%	(36%)*	6%	(50%)	23%	9%	0%
Co-op. party	6	9	6	5	(0)	2	(0)	6	1	0
CLPs	86	82	80	86	(64)	92	(50)	71	90	(100)
	100%	100%	100%	100%	100%	100%	100%	100%	100%	100%
Number of cases	60	89	660	119	11	305	18	53	99	17

* Percentages in parentheses because of the small number of cases.

and Scottish burghs, but otherwise were spread across the country evenly.

CONCLUSION: THE THREE LABOUR PARTIES
AND THEIR PATHWAYS TO PARLIAMENT

The Labour party began as a federation of trade unions and socialist intellectuals, and its two elements and their Co-operative associate, while maintaining high parliamentary cohesion and working together at elections, have from the beginning remained distinct—and in some degree of tension.

The Labour party's triangularity has manifested itself in many ways, not the least of which is its three distinctly different sets of parliamentary candidates. In the foregoing pages we have seen that in their ages, their experience in local government, their formal education, and their occupations, the persons filling the unsponsored Labour candidatures in the 1950's were much more like their Conservative opponents than their union-sponsored fellow partisans, while the Co-operative-sponsored candidatures occupied a middle position.

The sponsoring of candidates both results from and reinforces the union-nonunion-Co-operative divisions which have characterized—some say plagued—the party from its origins. The abolition of sponsorship would certainly not end the social, educational, occupational, and psychological tensions among the three elements. But the selection of candidates, particularly in the winnable seats, is one of the party's principal stakes of power, and conflict over adoptions is inevitable. Sponsorship tends to keep the conflict in the traditional battle-lines of union *v.* intellectuals, union *v.* Co-operatives, and union *v.* union. It clearly identifies the combatants, emphasizes their differences in interest and outlook, and produces victories and defeats.

Thus each of the three Labour parties, as we have seen, has periodically complained that it is not receiving its fair share of the party's M.P.s and candidatures—and will complain again. The continuing quarrel over candidatures is one of the factors which has made one side or another repeatedly raise the question of whether it—and the movement—would not be better off if the unions and/or the co-operative societies were officially independent of the party, as are their counterparts in the United States.[43]

That question lies outside the scope of this book. But it is clear that whether or not we may speak of three Labour parties in any strict sense, we must recognize that Labour has not one but three distinct pathways to Parliament.

THE TRADE UNION WAY

One who takes the trade union way typically leaves school at an early age and goes to work. He soon becomes an active and valued member of his trade union. With its encouragement and support, he is elected a Labour member of a borough or county council. After several decades of local government and union service, he becomes a candidate for a top office in his union, but is passed over. He is then put on the union's parliamentary panel and on Transport House's List A.

Then he or someone in another branch of his union learns of a CLP in a winnable constituency looking for a candidate, preferably sponsored. The branch of his union affiliated with the CLP nominates him, and he is adopted.

If he wins the seat, he will be readopted and sponsored until he wishes to retire or until his union forces him to retire because he is

---

[43] Cf. Harrison, *Trade Unions and the Labour Party*, Ch. VIII.

overage. If he loses his first parliamentary contest, the chances are 3 in 5 that he will receive no second candidature—perhaps because his union may not wish to sponsor him again and/or perhaps because he is unable to persuade another CLP to adopt him. If he manages to get a second candidature, the chances are 1 in 5 that he will be readopted in the same constituency and 1 in 7 that he will move to a more promising constituency.[44]

THE CO-OPERATIVE PARTY WAY

The typical aspirant who takes this way stays in school longer than his trade union colleague, and takes a white-collar job. He soon becomes active in the co-operative movement. Unlike some of his fellow co-operators, he comes to believe that political action is a valuable means for achieving the movement's ends, and so becomes active in the Co-operative party. His local party nominates him for the parliamentary panel, and the party's national executive approves. A local party affiliated with a CLP looking for a sponsored candidate nominates him, the NEC allows him to compete, and he is adopted.

If he wins his first contest, he is in the same strong position for readoption and continued sponsorship as any other sponsored M.P. If he loses, he has 1 chance in 2 of getting a second candidature but only 3 chances in 10 of moving on to a more promising constituency.

THE WAY OF THE UNSPONSORED

Well over half of Labour's candidatures are reached by this third pathway. A typical wayfarer attends a grammar or secondary modern school and goes on to a "redbrick" university. He takes a white-collar job and joins a white-collar union. He also joins the Labour party as an individual member, and becomes active in a ward committee or a socialist society. He applies for inclusion on List B, and is accepted by the NEC.

By talking to people at regional and national party meetings and by corresponding with others in between, he learns of some CLPs looking for candidates and not committed solely to sponsored nom-

---

[44] These and the odds given for the Co-operative-sponsored and unsponsored candidates are based upon the analyses of the subsequent candidatures of Labour's first-time losers in 1951 and 1955: see pp. 214–18.

inees. His friends in the CLPs' ward committees or the branches of his union nominate him. Or—especially in the hopeless constituencies—the CLP's executive asks him if he would like to be considered. In either case he is nominated, competes with others at the selection conference, and wins the candidature.

If he wins the seat, he, too, gains the standard security of readoption. If he loses, the chances are 1 in 2 that he will have a second candidature, 1 in 5 that he will be readopted in the same constituency, and 1 in 4 that he will be adopted in a more promising constituency. In short, he is somewhat more likely to make his way eventually to Parliament after an initial loss than his sponsored colleagues, although he may fight two or even three losing contests before he finally wins.

Thus while Labour's three pathways to Parliament have the same destination, they follow very different routes and are traveled by different kinds of people. The third pathway is followed most often and diverges considerably from that followed by most Conservative aspirants; but it diverges even more from Labour's other two routes. And this both results from and reinforces the party's triangular, federative nature.

| Chapter 9 | *The Recruitment of Liberal Candidates* |

The Electoral Context

The term "candidate selection," as we have seen, is generally used to denote the extralegal processes by which a political party decides whom it will put forth and support as its candidates for elective office.[1] In some respects it is a misleading label for the Conservative and Labour processes we have described in the preceding chapters: it implies that in every situation several aspirants actively seek the candidature, and the party selects the one it wants. Yet we have observed that each party is saddled with a number of constituencies in which everyone knows its candidates have no chance of being elected. Nevertheless, both parties feel they must put up candidates in almost all constituencies, however hopeless. Only thus, their leaders believe, can they sustain their local organizations' morale and claim to be truly national parties. So both regularly "show the flag" by nominating a number of candidates with no hope whatever of electing them.

Sometimes in some hopeless constituencies no aspirants at all come forward. When this happens, the local parties, perhaps with

[1] See pp. vii–viii.

national assistance, have to search for candidates rather than select them: that is, they have to persuade someone acceptable to make the hopeless fights.[2]

Even so, in most hopeless constituencies most of the time several aspirants *do* come forward and compete for the major parties' candidatures. In such a situation, of course, the local party's range of choice is considerably narrower than in a winnable constituency; but it can make a genuine choice, it can select a candidate.

Why would anyone compete for the Conservative candidature in, say, Hemsworth or Rother Valley, or the Labour candidature in, say, East Surrey or South Kensington? Certainly not because he hopes to be elected, but probably for one or more of several quite different reasons: he may hope to make contacts and develop skills that will help him in his business or profession; he may enjoy campaigning and the honor of being a parliamentary candidate; or he may feel a duty to his party to see that its flag is carried by someone presentable—*faute de mieux,* by himself.

He may also view a hopeless fight as a useful preliminary to being adopted in a winnable constituency. He knows that at each general election and at some by-elections his party has a number of vacant candidatures in winnable seats. No residence rule binds him, as it would in the United States, to his home constituency; he can stand anywhere. And he may hope that fighting a good fight in a hopeless constituency will give him the skills, experience, and reputation which will help him win a desirable candidature. Nor is this hope illusory: we learned earlier that almost a quarter of both the Conservative and Labour candidates who first stood and lost in 1951 and 1955 were later adopted in other, more promising constituencies.[3]

The Liberals, however, are in a very different electoral position, as Table 9.1 makes clear.

After their disastrous defeat in 1950, the Liberals contested far fewer constituencies and thereby reduced their forfeited deposits. Even after their recovery of the late 1950's and early 1960's, however, 15 per cent of their candidates in 1964 failed to win the one-eighth of the votes legally required to save their deposits; and in 83 per

---

[2] For some examples, see p. 170, footnote 8.
[3] See pp. 122–23, 214–15.

TABLE 9.1

LIBERAL CANDIDATES IN GENERAL ELECTIONS, 1950–1964

	General Election				
	1950	1951	1955	1959	1964
Total number of candidates	475	109	110	216	365
Constituencies fought by Liberal Candidates	76%	17%	17%	34%	58%
Share of national popular vote	11%	3%	3%	6%	11%
Candidates losing deposits	67%	61%	55%	26%	15%
Candidates' order of finish					
First	2%	6%	5%	3%	2%
Second	4	10	10	12	15
Third	94	84	83	85	83
Fourth	*	0	2	0	*
	100%	100%	100%	100%	100%

* Less than 0.5 per cent.

cent of the constituencies they contested, the Liberals finished third. They did better on all counts in 1964 than in 1959, but they still won only a small fraction (11 per cent) of the popular votes and an even smaller fraction (2 per cent) of the seats.

If anything, the figures in Table 9.1 overstate the Liberals' postwar strength; for of the five constituencies they won in 1951 and held in 1955 and 1959 in only one (Orkney and Zetland, held by Jo Grimond, the party Leader) did the Liberal face a Conservative as well as a Labour opponent in all three elections. In at least one constituency this was the result of a pact or tacit understanding with the Conservatives, according to which each party agreed to unite the anti-Labour vote by dividing the borough's two seats between them.[4]

---

[4] In 1950 both the East and West divisions of Bolton had three-cornered fights won by Labour. In January, 1951, the Liberals and Conservatives in Bolton agreed that the Liberals would not contest the East division and the Conservatives would stay out of the West division. Accordingly, in 1951 a Conservative won the East division and Liberal Arthur Holt won the West division. This arrangement continued in 1955 and 1959 with the same results, but dissatisfaction with it grew in both local parties. Before the 1959 election, the West Bolton Conservative association's executive decided to put up a candidate, but they were overruled by a general meeting of the association: *Bolton Evening News*, February 19, 1959, pp. 1, 7; February 21, 1959, p. 1; April 14, 1959, p. 5. Emboldened by their gains in post-1959 by-elections, the Liberals decided to contest the East division in the 1960 by-election. They failed to win the seat, and

We shall observe later that the Liberals' fortunes improved in the by-elections from 1958 through the end of 1963.[5] Our point here is that in the post-war period only a small fraction of the constituencies the Liberals chose to fight—to say nothing of those they passed up—were in any sense winnable, and most of those few were pre-empted by incumbent Liberal M.P.s.

Accordingly, a Liberal candidate who fought and lost had three possibilities: he could give up, try again in the same constituency, or move to another. Most chose the first: of the 85 Liberal candidates who first stood and lost in 1951 and 1955, 80 per cent did not stand again, compared to 54 per cent of the Conservatives and 51 per cent of the Socialists. If we apply the same criteria used earlier for the major parties, only 6 per cent of the Liberal first-time losers moved to more promising constituencies, compared with 23 per cent of the Conservatives and 24 per cent of the Socialists.[6] It is not surprising, then, that the nomination of Liberal candidates in all but a few instances resulted from searches rather than selections.

THE RECRUITMENT PROCESS[7]

THE ROLE OF THE NATIONAL AGENCIES

1. *Organization*

Like the Conservatives and Labour, the Liberals are organized into: a parliamentary party; a national federation of constituency

---

put an end to the Bolton pact. As a result both parties lost their seats: in two three-cornered fights in the 1964 general election the Conservative incumbent lost to a Labour candidate in the East division, and Arthur Holt lost to the Labour candidate in the West division.

[5] The Liberals were so encouraged by their post-1959 successes in by-elections that at one point they planned to put as many as 470 candidates in the field in the 1964 general election—almost as many as in 1950, and well over twice as many as in any election since 1950. By September, 1963, they had 420 prospective candidates already adopted and expected at least 50 more. Their losses in the 1964 by-elections dampened their optimism, however, and in the 1964 general election 365 Liberals actually stood.

[6] See Austin Ranney, "Inter-Constituency Movement of British Parliamentary Candidates, 1951–1959," *American Political Science Review,* LVIII (March, 1964), Table III, at p. 39. As we shall see later, what constituted a more promising constituency was different for the Liberals than for the major parties.

[7] The most comprehensive study of the post-1945 Liberal party is Jorgen S. Rasmussen, *Retrenchment and Revival: A Study of the Contemporary British Liberal Party* (Tucson: University of Arizona Press, 1964). See also Philip Skelsey, "The Selection of Parliamentary Candidates: The Liberal Party," *Political Quarterly,* XXX (July–September, 1959), 223–26. The present writer also gained valuable information from interviews in 1962 with Donald Wade, then the Chief Whip, and Thomas Nudds, the permanent secretary of the Liberal Central Association.

associations (reorganized and named the Liberal Party Organisation—LPO—in 1936), with an annual assembly, an elected council, an executive committee, and a staff of paid employees; and the Liberal Central Association (LCA), another office of paid employees working under the direction of the Leader and Chief Whip, whose chief administrative officer is the permanent secretary. The Liberal Party Committee, under the Leader's direction, meets from time to time, issues statements of party policy, and acts as a channel of communications between the LPO and the LCA. All four agencies are commonly, if somewhat inaccurately, referred to collectively as party HQ.[8]

2. *Recruiting and Vetting Potential Candidates*

Since the mid-nineteenth century the Chief Whip has been the party's principal national officer concerned with parliamentary candidatures. To assist him and to give the extraparliamentary organization a stronger voice, the party established in 1947 a five-man prospective candidates' committee drawn from the LPO and chaired by the Chief Whip. The committee was charged with recruiting and interviewing potential condidates so as to build up a list of approved candidates from which the constituency associations might draw. The LCA's permanent secretary became the committee's secretary, and has guided most of its decisions.

The committee was augmented after the 1950 election by a fourteen-man candidates' sub-committee, which in effect took over the parent committee's functions. Since then the sub-committee and the permanent secretary have encouraged likely prospects to apply for inclusion on the list and have vetted the applicants.[9] Each applicant completes a form giving biographical information and the names of at least two party members as referees. The permanent

---

[8] Rasmussen has the most complete account of the Liberals' complex national structure: *Retrenchment and Revival*, Chs. IV–V. For shorter accounts, see Robert T. McKenzie, *British Political Parties*, 2nd. ed. (London: Mercury Books, 1964), pp. 650–52; and Richard West, "Liberal HQ," *Time & Tide* (March 22, 1962), pp. 7–8. In 1963, according to R. L. Leonard, Liberal HQ had 25 administrative and 40 clerical employees, compared with the Conservatives' 132 and 203 and Labour's 78 and 89: *Guide to the General Election* (London: Pan Books, Ltd., 1964), Table 6, p. 47.

[9] "Vetting" in British usage is equivalent to "screening" in American: i.e., examining and evaluating the applicants' qualifications with a view to approving some and rejecting others.

secretary collects the referees' comments, talks to the applicant, and arranges for an interview by one of the sub-committee's several three-man panels composed of M.P.s and experienced parliamentary candidates. After the interview and a review of the referees' opinions, the panel recommends to the sub-committee either that the applicant be put on the list or that he be asked to try again later. The sub-committee's chairman recently estimated that about 80 per cent of those interviewed are included on their first try.

Professor Jorgen Rasmussen's explanation of why the remaining 20 per cent are turned down is illuminating:

> The chief reason for rejection of an interviewee is an insufficient knowledge of party policy. In an effort to obtain only those people who are so committed to Liberal principles as to be willing to sacrifice and fight for them, the secretary of the Liberal Central Association discourages any potential candidate who indicates he is interested in standing because he hopes to get into Parliament.[10]

The list of approved candidates and the permanent secretary's advice are available to any constituency association requesting them, but there is no obligation to choose only from among the persons on the list.

3. *The Absence of a National Veto*

By contrast with the two major parties, no Liberal national agency has the power to veto a candidature. Once a constituency association has formally adopted someone he becomes the official prospective liberal candidate whether party HQ approves or not. "The result," Rasmussen remarks, "is that it is not unusual for candidates to be adopted unknown to anyone at the national level."[11]

Indeed, the very thought of vetoing locally adopted candidates is most remote from Liberal HQ's concerns. Their job is to bring candidates in, not throw them out. They are, of course, concerned that the candidates be as personally attractive and politically reliable as possible; and occasionally, as we shall see, they raise questions with constituency associations as to whether a seat should be fought. But if an association has found a man it likes and will support—and whom it has persuaded to accept—Headquarters would almost never use a

---

[10] Rasmussen, *Retrenchment and Revival*, p. 212.
[11] *Ibid.*, p. 88.

veto even if it had one. The only centrally-imposed condition is that the candidate must undertake, if elected, to accept the party whip. Given the Liberals' electoral position, this means very little.

THE ROLE OF THE
CONSTITUENCY ASSOCIATIONS

The national agencies' funds are limited and the professional staff small. Burdened with such tasks as publicity, organization, research, and publications, the staff can afford to devote little time to recruiting candidates. Hence the job is left mainly to the consituency associations.[12]

1. *Organization*

Liberal constituency associations are organized much like Conservative. Anyone paying dues to an association or to an ancillary organization, such as the Young Liberals or Women Liberals, is a member. The members meet annually to elect officers and an executive committee, who conduct most of the association's business including the recruitment of candidates.

2. *Deciding Whether to Fight*

The choice of a selection procedure is left up to each Liberal association—not, as in the major parties, prescribed from above. Usually the association executive, in consultation with HQ, first decides whether to fight the seat. This is commonly the most difficult stage in the process, and has caused most of what disputes there have been in recent years between HQ and local associations. Sometimes local Liberals have decided to put up a candidate, while HQ has felt there was neither the money nor the organization for a respectable showing, and has tried to persuade the association to reconsider. But in this as in most other matters, HQ can only advise; the final decision is the local association's, and they have not always accepted HQ's advice.[13]

---

[12] *Ibid.*, pp. 86, 210–11; McKenzie, *British Political Parties*, p. 652. Basil Wigoder, the chairman of the party executive, stated: "We do not place our candidates. Our constituency associations grow up, get support and then want to fight elections. We encourage them and help them to find good prospective candidates": *Times* (London), September 11, 1963, p. 5.

[13] For example, in 1953 the Liberal association's executive in Holborn and St. Pancras

3. Recruiting the Candidate

After it has decided to fight a seat, an association executive usually appoints—or itself acts as—what is usually termed a screening committee but might more accurately be called a search committee. Working with the secretary of the regional federation,[14] and often in consultation with the permanent secretary at HQ, the committee decides what kind of person it wants and then tries to persuade someone suitable to accept the candidature. Usually it recommends only one name to the executive, although on occasion selection conferences similar to the major parties' have been held. In all cases the executive recommends a single person to a general meeting of the association, which adopts him as its prospective candidate.

Unlike the major parties, the Liberals place no restrictions on the financial contribution a candidate may make to the association's funds. The party's chronic poverty, indeed, compels most associations to ask their candidate to contribute what he can, and many have contributed sums ranging from £50 to £500.[15] No one, however, has ever been accused of buying a seat!

WHY CANDIDATES ACCEPT

Anyone offered a Liberal candidature in the 1950's and 1960's had many excellent reasons to decline. He had almost no chance of

---

South wanted to fight the by-election caused by the death of the Labour M.P. The national executive advised against it, on the ground that the local association was too weak to make an effective campaign. The local executive nevertheless resolved to fight, and HQ said that, while they would not hinder the candidate, they could not provide him with funds, speakers, or any other help. A dissident group in the association sought a court injunction to prevent the candidature, but their petition was denied. A number of Liberal associations around the country publicly criticized what they called "HQ's fight-only-where-the-deposit-is-safe" policy. At the election the Liberal candidate, I. J. Hyman, got 2 per cent of the votes and lost his deposit: *Times* (London), November 10, 1953, p. 2; November 14, 1953, p. 2; November 17, 1953, p. 4; *North London Press*, November 13, 1953, p. 1.

[14] The Liberals have ten area federations in England, two in Wales, and none in Scotland. They are, however, far less active than their counterparts in the major parties: for example, in 1961 only four maintained full-time professional secretaries. And, significantly, their professional staffs are responsible to the regional federations of constituency associations, not to HQ as in the major parties: Rasmussen, *Retrenchment and Revival*, pp. 86–87.

[15] Rasmussen, *Retrenchment and Revival*, pp. 209–10.

election. He had no better chance of later moving to a winnable constituency. If he accepted he was bound to contribute a good deal of time, energy, and money to a cause that was electorally hopeless.

Yet on 769 occasions a non-incumbent accepted a Liberal candidature. Why? The best available answers are provided by Professor Rasmussen's interviews during 1960–1961 with sixty-three post-

TABLE 9.2

LIBERAL CANDIDATES' REASONS FOR STANDING *

Reason	Number Giving Reason	Per Cent of Total†
Improving prospects for winning eventual seat in Parliament	44	70
Obligation to assist the party	33	52
Prestige of being a parliamentary candidate	31	49
Enjoyment of campaigning	23	37
Desire to promote Liberal principles	23	37
Obligation to community to participate in politics	10	16
Making social contacts	8	13
Improving personal skills	7	11
Not ascertained	5	8

* Adapted from Jorgen S. Rasmussen, *Retrenchment and Revival: A Study of the Contemporary British Liberal Party* (Tucson: University of Arizona Press, 1964), Table XXII, p. 233.

† The figures add up to more than 100 per cent because most respondents gave more than one reason.

war Liberal candidates. His summary of the reasons they gave for standing is presented in Table 9.2

Most of the reasons are not unexpected, and most proclaim goals which one could reasonably hope to achieve by accepting a Liberal candidature: fulfilling a party obligation to "show the flag" and a community obligation to participate in politics; enjoying campaigning; spreading Liberal ideas; and widening contacts and improving personal skills.

But, in the light of the Liberals' electoral prospects in the 1950's, the reason most commonly given is quite unexpected: 70 per cent stated that standing would help them eventually secure seats in Parliament! For example, one respondent "observed that standing where no immediate prospect of election existed was not pointless; one never knew what would happen. One might get a big vote and if that happened then next time he might get in."[16] Others explained "that they 'had to start somewhere' and a hopeless seat was as good as any for gaining experience. Frequently related to this attitude was the belief that if one did well in a poor seat he might then be able to obtain a seat with a greater potential."[17] In the electoral context of the 1950's and 1960's, such hopes surely demanded a remarkable degree of optimism—but a surprising number of Liberals managed it nevertheless. Indeed, "optimism" for the Liberals meant something different than for the major parties. A "seat with a greater potential" did not necessarily mean a winnable one or even one offering a chance of finishing second. It often meant simply a seat where a Liberal could save his deposit, or a seat in which a Liberal, by drawing an unexpectedly large share of the poll, could cause a national stir and help make the party seem an electoral force of growing significance.

CHARACTERISTICS OF LIBERAL CANDIDATURES IN GENERAL ELECTIONS, 1951–64

In our earlier analyses of Conservative and Labour candidatures we used a scale of "constituency winnability" based on the assumptions that the more winnable seats would attract more aspirants and give the local selectors wider ranges of choice, and that by comparing their choices with those made in the less winnable seats we could learn something about the kinds of persons who came forth and the criteria the selectors applied. However, this scale is not appropriate for analyzing Liberal candidatures: by its criteria, of the 769 Liberal candidatures by non-incumbents in the general elections of 1951, 1955, 1959, and 1964, none fall in the "high" category, only 23 (3 per cent) in the "medium" category, 387 (50 per cent) in the "low" category, and the remaining 359 (47 per cent) in the "other" group.

Yet, as Table 9.2 shows, the hope of eventual electoral success was a factor in most Liberals' willingness to stand, and presumably

---

[16] *Ibid.*, p. 222.
[17] *Ibid.*, pp. 222–23.

they regarded some constituencies as electorally superior to others. Accordingly, for our comparisons among Liberal candidatures we have devised a scale of constituency desirability using criteria different from those of the winnability scale used for the major parties.[18] And for our inter-party comparisons we shall use only the candidatures in the "low" categories on both scales so as to hold as constant as possible expectations of electoral success, however defined.

TABLE 9.3

DESIRABILITY OF CONSTITUENCY RELATED TO PREVIOUS ELECTORAL
EXPERIENCE OF LIBERAL NON-INCUMBENTS

Previous Electoral Experience	Constituency Desirability*		
	Medium	Low	Other
First contest	(49%)†	49%	76%
One previous loss	(21)	31	12
Two or more previous losses	(27)	20	11
Former M.P.s	(3)	0	1
	100%	100%	100%
Number of cases	97	313	359

* The categories are defined thus: "medium" means that in the preceding general election in the constituency a Liberal candidate finished second by any margin or third by a margin between 0.1% to 9.9 per cent behind the candidate who finished second; "low" means that in the preceding election a Liberal candidate finished third or fourth by a margin of 10% or more behind the candidate who finished second; "other" means that no Liberal contested the seat in the preceding general election.

† Percentages are in parentheses because of the small number of cases.

PREVIOUS ELECTORAL EXPERIENCE

In earlier chapters we noted that the most desirable candidatures by non-incumbents in both major parties went predominantly to persons who had fought previous elections, and that the newcomers were most heavily concentrated in the least desirable constituencies.[19] Table 9.3 shows that this relationship also held among the Liberals.

---

[18] For the criteria used for both scales, see the Appendix.

[19] This relationship is modified only by the tendency of the National Union of Mineworkers to sponsor new candidates in safe miners' seats: see Table 4.2, p. 94; Table 7.2, p. 196; and Table 8.3, p. 236.

The few cases in the "medium" category and the larger number in the "other" category make caution advisable in interpreting Table 9.3 and similar comparisons to follow. The table does suggest that, for the Liberals as well as the major parties, the more desirable candidatures went to the more experienced candidates. It also shows that the "other" candidatures, whose desirability was presumably less certain because there were no previous Liberal candidatures to judge by, had the highest proportion of new candidates.

We cannot definitively explain this relationship, but we can offer a speculation. We have seen that a number of Liberals accepted candidatures not necessarily expecting to win but still feeling that "you never know what might happen." A newcomer would seem more likely to feel this way than one who had been through the mill; the veteran would be more inclined to feel from experience that you know only too well what will happen. Moreover, the you-never-know attitude would be more natural in a constituency where no Liberal candidate had recently fought than in one where a Liberal had been crushed in the last election. It may be, in short, that for potential Liberal candidates "an optimist is one who believes the future is uncertain." If so, the veteran party warrior would be more willing to fight a contest he knows to be hopeless out of a sense of duty, while a newcomer would be more willing to take a flyer in a constituency of uncertain prospects.

The inter-party comparisons of the "low-desirability" candidatures shown in Table 9.4 are consistent with this conjecture.

TABLE 9.4

PREVIOUS ELECTORAL EXPERIENCE OF NON-INCUMBENTS
IN CANDIDATURES OF LOW DESIRABILITY

Previous Electoral Experience	Candidatures		
	Conservative	Labour	Liberal
First contest	67%	61%	49%
One previous loss	24	23	31
Two or more previous losses	8	13	20
Former M.P.s	1	3	0
	100%	100%	100%
Number of cases	771	1,103	313

Table 9.4 shows some sharp inter-party differences in the proportions of candidatures in hopeless seats undertaken by newcomers: the Conservatives had the most (67 per cent), Labour substantially fewer (61 per cent), and the Liberals much fewer than Labour (49 per cent). It seems more than coincidental that this is also the rank order of the three parties in electoral success and in the number of winnable constituencies to which a first-time loser in a hopeless constituency might move. It suggests that the major parties could persuade newcomers to undertake hopeless fights by offering them the real possibility of afterward moving to winnable constituencies. The Liberals could offer no such possibility, and so they had to depend on their party votaries to "show the flag" in constituencies where experience showed they had no chance.

AGE

Liberal candidatures displayed a relationship between age and desirability of constituency similar to those we have observed in the major parties: 42 per cent in the "medium" category went to persons under forty, compared with 46 per cent of those in the "low" category and 54 per cent in the "other" category.[20] Comparison of the three parties' "low" groups shows that the Liberals occupied a position between the two major parties: 54 per cent of the Liberals' hopeless candidatures went to persons under 40, compared with 58 per cent of the Conservatives' and 47 per cent of Labour's. Twenty-two per cent of the Liberals' and 23 per cent of Labour's went to persons over 50, compared with 17 per cent of the Conservatives'. This, too, suggests that Labour and the Liberals more than the Conservatives filled their hopeless candidatures with party veterans rather than ambitious young men.

SEX

Like the major parties, the Liberals gave more candidatures to women in the low-desirability constituencies (11 per cent) than in the medium (2 per cent). The comparable figures for both Conservative and Labour candidatures in the low-winnability constituencies were 6 and 7 per cent; whether the Liberals' inferior electoral position made them less inclined than the major parties to discriminate

---

[20] For the comparable age-to-winnability relationships among Conservative and Labour candidatures, see pp. 99–100, 200.

against women, or perhaps less able to indulge such prejudice, our data do not reveal.

EXPERIENCE IN LOCAL GOVERNMENT AND PARTY OFFICE

1. *Local Government*

During most of the post-war period Liberals found it almost as difficult to enter local councils as Parliament. Hence it is not surprising that only 11.5 per cent of the Liberal "lows" had held local office, compared with 37 per cent of the Conservative and 47 per cent of the Labour. The Liberal "mediums," on the other hand, had 15 per cent with local government experience and the Liberal "others" 17 per cent. Evidently, then, those who had had a taste of electoral victory were less willing or had less need to fight hopeless parliamentary contests than those who had not.

2. *Party Office*

The party's electoral position prevented Liberal activists from being elected to local councils but it encouraged them to hold party office: 42 per cent of the Liberal "lows" had held party office, compared with only 27 per cent of the Conservatives' and 18 per cent of Labour's. Moreover, the Liberals' "mediums" and "others" had even higher proportions of party officeholders (54 per cent and 48 per cent, respectively) than their "lows." The reason for the differences with the major parties is clear: in many constituencies the local Liberal associations for all practical purposes consist of handfuls of activists who not only accept party office but undertake most other party chores, including parliamentary candidatures.

EDUCATION

The marked intraparty educational differences we have observed in each of the major parties appear more blurred among Liberal candidatures. For example, 25 per cent of the Liberal "mediums" did not go beyond secondary school, compared with 34 per cent of the "lows" and 35 per cent of the "others." For university attendance, the proportions were, respectively, 67 per cent, 55 per cent, and 53 per cent. And for attendance at public schools they were 37 per cent, 39 per cent, and 31 per cent.

The most striking inter-party educational comparisons put the Liberals and Conservatives on one side and Labour on the other; for the

Liberal "lows" had more schooling than even the Conservative and as high or higher proportions attending the prestige schools. This is evident in Table 9.5.

TABLE 9.5

EDUCATION OF NON-INCUMBENTS IN CONSTITUENCIES OF LOW DESIRABILITY

Education	Conservative	Labour	Liberal
Elementary and secondary only	33%	54%	34%
Secondary and university other than Oxford or Cambridge	14	24	18
Secondary and Oxford or Cambridge	7	9	10
Public school only	18	3	11
Public school and university other than Oxford or Cambridge	6	2	4
Public school and Oxford or Cambridge	22	8	23
	100%	100%	100%
Number of cases	771	1,103	313

The Liberals' "lows," as Table 9.5 shows, had as much or more schooling as the other three parties: only 34 per cent did not go beyond the secondary level, compared with 33 per cent of the Conservatives', and 54 per cent of Labour's. Moreover, 33 per cent of the Liberals had attended Oxford or Cambridge, compared with 29 per cent of the Conservatives and 17 per cent of the Socialists. Even in attendance at public schools the Liberals almost matched the Tories, with 38 per cent to 46 per cent (by contrast with only 13 per cent of the Labour candidates). Thus by one major index of social class, the Liberals drew their candidates from the same strata as the Conservatives and quite different strata from all three segments of Labour.

OCCUPATION

A comparison of the occupations of the Liberal "lows" with those of their major-party opposite numbers, as in Table 9.6, provides further support for the generalization that Liberal and Conservative candidates came from the same ranks of British society.

The occupational distributions shown in Table 9.6 are almost the same for the Liberals and the Conservatives, and both differ markedly from Labour. Since there are no significant differences

TABLE 9.6

OCCUPATIONS OF NON-INCUMBENTS IN CONSTITUENCIES OF LOW DESIRABILITY

Occupation	Conservative	Labour	Liberal
Proprietor, managerial	38%	12%	29%
Professional	36	23	40
White-collar	19	46	26
Intermediate	3	3	4
Manual, wage-earning	4	16	1
	100%	100%	100%
Number of cases	771	1,103	313

among the various categories of Liberal candidates,[21] the conclusion indicated by Tables 9.5 and 9.6 is that the Liberals drew their candidates mainly from the middle and upper-middle ranks of British society in about the same proportions as did the Conservatives.

LOCAL CONNECTIONS

Unlike their major-party counterparts, officials in Liberal HQ testify that they prefer local candidates and urge local associations to approach outsiders only after they have exhausted the local possibilities. This policy, combined with the local associations' assumption of the main burden of recruitment, should result in a higher proportion of local candidates among Liberal "lows" than Conservative or Labour. However, our data show that only 29 per cent of the Liberals had local connections, compared with 32 per cent of the Tories and 30 per cent of the Socialists. But since this may be a product of the incompleteness of our data rather than the actual incidence of local connections,[22] we can report only that our information does not confirm (but also does not deny) our ex-

---

[21] Among the Liberals, the occupations receiving the highest proportions of "medium" to "low" candidatures were farmers, barristers, and solicitors, although the differences were too slight and based on too few cases in the "medium" category to make much of.

[22] The sources for identifying local connections for the candidates of all three parties were the short biographies in the *Times House of Common* volumes. Usually the entries for Liberal candidates are shorter and report less information than those for the major-party candidates, and it seems likely that as a result our figures understate the incidence of local connections among Liberal candidates substantially more than among Conservative or Labour candidates.

pectation of more locally-connected candidates among the Liberals than among Labour or the Conservatives.

Many of these contrasts become even sharper when we examine Liberal by-election candidatures.

LIBERAL CANDIDATURES IN BY-ELECTIONS

THE ELECTORAL CONTEXT

By-elections have been even more important for the Liberals than for the major parties. There are relatively few by-elections, and the considerable national publicity they attract enables the

TABLE 9.7

LIBERAL CANDIDATES IN BY-ELECTIONS, 1951–1963

	1951–1955	1955–1959	1959–1963	Total
Total number of by-elections	47	53	55	155
By-elections fought by Liberal candidates	17%	40%	85%	49%
Liberals losing deposits	88%	5%	4%	15%
Liberals' order of finish				
First	0%	5%	4%	4%
Second	12	33	36	34
Third	88	62	60	62
Fourth	0	0	0	0
	100%	100%	100%	100%

Liberals to exploit them far more effectively than general elections. Moreover, voters are more detachable from the major parties in by-elections when the fate of the government is not at stake. Hence the Liberals are likely to poll more votes than at general elections and their candidatures are correspondingly more desirable. Table 9.7 arrays some supporting evidence.

The Liberals' disaster in the 1950 general election[23] caused them to fight few by-elections in the early 1950's, and even in these they fared badly. After 1955, however, their fortunes improved; they

---

[23] They put up 475 candidates in the 625 constituencies; only 4 per cent finished second, 93 per cent third, and the remainder fourth or worse; and worst of all, two-thirds lost their deposits.

fought many more by-elections and did considerably better, reaching their high point in 1958 with the election of Mark Bonham Carter at Torrington. They fought most by-elections between 1959 and 1963, won Orpington from the Conservatives and held Montgomery in 1962, finished second in seventeen other contests, and lost only three deposits. Accordingly, in the post-war period by-elections provided the Liberals with their principal—many would say their only—opportunity to play a role of electoral importance.

THE RECRUITMENT OF
BY-ELECTION CANDIDATES

Like Central Office and Transport House, Liberal HQ has taken an exceptionally active part in the conduct of all phases of by-elections. When a vacancy has occurred, the Chief Whip has called together representatives of the LPO and the relevant constituency association and regional federation to discuss whether the seat should be fought. As in general elections, the final decision is up to the local association; but only rarely have they decided to fight against HQ's advice.[24]

In most by-elections, moreover, not only the permanent secretary and the candidates' sub-committee but often the Chief Whip and the Leader as well consult closely with the constituency and regional officers in recruiting the candidate. Although here, too, the final decision rests with the local association, rarely do they adopt persons HQ disapproves.[25]

---

[24] As in the Holborn and St. Pancras South episode in 1953: see above, footnote 13.

[25] This central-local consultation is far from being dictation by HQ, but it certainly departs from the party's usual decentralization in candidate recruitment. Sometimes it has caused local resentment. The best-known example is that of Torrington in 1958. When a vacancy occurred in this winnable constituency, the Liberals already had a local man as prospective candidate. However, the Torrington association and HQ managed to replace him with an outsider with a distinguished party name, Mark Bonham Carter. This stung some of the party faithful. For example, Alan Gibson, the prospective candidate for Falmouth and Camborne, publicly protested the switch, claiming that the candidate should have been "a west countryman capable of understanding the problems of the people of North Devon . . . . Thanks to the intervention, or so I suspect, of Liberal Party Headquarters in London . . . this has not been done . . . . If the Liberal candidate in Torrington were to lose his deposit it would serve him jolly well right": *Times* (London), March 4, 1958, p. 8. In fact, Bonham Carter won. Gibson later apologized to him and to Liberal HQ, and offered to resign his own candidature, but was told that no such gesture was called for.

THE CANDIDATES RECRUITED

Liberal candidatures should be more desirable at by-elections than general: the candidate receives much national publicity; he is doing a job the party values highly; and above all he has a better chance to finish high in the poll—perhaps even to win (remember Torrington and Orpington!).

If this is true, we should expect the Liberals' candidates in by-elections to differ significantly from those in general elections. Table 9.8, which compares the candidatures by non-incumbents in general elections from 1951 to 1959 with those in by-elections during the same period, strongly confirms this expectation.

Table 9.8 reveals a number of marked differences between Liberal candidates recruited for the two kinds of elections. The party fought a much lower proportion of hopeless constituencies in by-elections than in general elections. By-election candidates had considerably more previous electoral experience. They were older. Somewhat more had been elected to local councils. They had somewhat more schooling, and rather more had attended the prestige schools. Substantially more had identifiable local connections, although this may merely reflect the greater completeness of our information about Liberal by-election than general election candidates.

The most striking difference shown in Table 9.8 is in the proportions of Liberal candidatures filled by persons who had held party office: 40 per cent of those in general elections, compared with only 14 per cent in by-elections. This provides further confirmation for our conclusion that to fill their candidatures in the constituencies known by recent experience to be hopeless, the Liberals relied heavily upon devoted party veterans.

CONCLUSION

Despite their post-1958 electoral renaissance, the Liberals fought the 1964 general election as little more than an electoral guerilla force. They could harass the major parties by raids on the largest number of constituencies since 1950. And while it was not clear that doing so hurt one major party much more than the other, the sharp increase

TABLE 9.8

LIBERAL CANDIDATURES BY NON-INCUMBENTS IN GENERAL ELECTIONS
AND BY-ELECTIONS, 1951–1959

Desirability of Constituencies	Gen. Elect.	By-elect.	Previous Electoral Experience	Gen. Elect.	By-elect.
Medium	7%	17%	First contest	52%	10%
Low	47	24	One previous loss	28	56
Other	46	59	Two or more previous losses	19	31
	100%	100%	Former M.P.s	1	3
Number of cases	411	29		100%	100%
			Number of cases	411	29

Age	Gen. Elect.	By-elect.	Local Govt. Experience	Gen. Elect.	By-elect.
21–29	15%	7%	Some	10%	14%
30–39	31	21	None	90	86
40–49	31	45		100%	100%
50–59	18	24	Number of cases	411	29
60 and over	5	3			
	100%	100%	Party Office	Gen. Elect.	By-elect.
Number of cases	411	29			
			Some	40%	14%
			None	60	86
Education	Gen. Elect.	By-elect.		100%	100%
			Number of cases	411	29
No more than secondary	35%	28%	Local Connections	Gen. Elect.	By-elect.
Attended university	53%	59%			
Attended Oxford or Cambridge	31%	35%	Some	22%	45%
Attended public school	36%	38%	None	78	55
				100%	100%
Number of cases	411	29	Number of cases	411	29

in Liberal candidatures introduced an element of doubt welcomed by neither Labour nor the Conservatives—nor even by some Liberals.[26]

One thing was clear: the Liberals continued to recruit their candidates from the same ranks of society as the Conservatives. Hence whatever might be their impact on the Tories' chances in battle, the Liberals were a constant threat to their lines of supply.

---

[26] For example, in November, 1963, Lord Moynihan, who had been chairman of the Liberal national executive in 1949–1950, resigned from the party. His reason was that "the present intention of the party to put so many candidates in the field in the next election, the majority of them in Conservative-held seats, will have the effect of putting the Socialists into power . . . [and I] cannot consider a policy that virtually means supporting the Socialists against the Conservatives": *Times* (London), November 18, 1963, p. 6.

Another Liberal leader shared his views: John Holt, chairman of the Yorkshire Young Liberals and member of the Liberal party council, resigned as prospective candidate for Dewsbury in January, 1964, stating that "the danger of a Socialist Government has been immeasurably increased by those who have advocated the adoption of over 400 prospective candidates, many of them in vital marginal seats which are now practically a gift for Labour": *The Guardian* (London), January 14, 1964, p. 1.

Chapter 10 | Conclusions

One of this century's most influential writers on political parties has written:

> The nominating process . . . has become the crucial process of the party. The nature of the nominating procedure determines the nature of the party; he who can make nominations is the owner of the party. This is therefore one of the best points at which to observe the distribution of power within the party.[1]

If this view is correct, summarizing and reflecting upon what we have observed of the selection of parliamentary candidates should provide some insight into the nature of British parties and into the political and social environment in which they act. It may also furnish some grounds for judging whether British practices can and should be the model for other democracies to follow.

THE DISTRIBUTION OF POWER WITHIN THE PARTIES

PARLIAMENTARY v. EXTRAPARLIAMENTARY ORGANIZATIONS

In each of the three British parties we have studied the power to select parliamentary candidates is formally vested in extraparliamentary organizations. Constituency associations composed of

---

[1] E. E. Schattschneider, *Party Government* (New York: Farrar and Rinehart, Inc., 1942), p. 64.

rank-and-file party members select the candidates; and they are subject to certain formal controls by national party committees established by and responsible to the parties' national federations of constituency organizations.

These national committees, however, are manned by amateur part-timers who for the most part merely ratify decisions made by professional full-timers working with them. And the latter invariably reflect the wishes of the parties' parliamentary leaders. Accordingly, conflicts over candidatures between the parliamentary and extraparliamentary organizations have taken a mainly national-local form.

NATIONAL *v.* LOCAL ORGANIZATIONS

1. *Endemic Conflict*

Democratic political parties are first and foremost bodies for making nominations and contesting elections; the attainment of everything else they wish depends largely upon their success in these two basic activities. Consequently parties generally establish organizations for each area from which one or more significant public officials are elected. Wherever members of the national legislature are elected from sub-national, single-member constituencies —as, for example, in the United States, Canada, Australia, and New Zealand as well as in Great Britain—the leading parties establish organizations in most or all of the constituencies and form some kind of national federation of the local bodies. And the constituency organizations enjoy the power to select the candidates for their areas, and bear most of the burden of campaigning for their election. So it is in Britain.

In all such countries some conflict between the national and local organizations over candidate selection is endemic and stems from certain inherent differences in outlook. On the one hand, the national leaders view the candidature of any particular constituency as merely one local element in a much broader national operation, and they are concerned that it contribute to the national effort. For example, they want their national roster of candidates to be representative—that is, to include persons from all major segments of the society. They want some candidates in the winnable constituencies to have the talents and expertise needed to strengthen the parliamentary party. And they want candidates in all constituencies (but especially in the winnable ones) who can be counted on for loyal support of the party's national leaders and legislative program.

On the other hand, a constituency organization is likely to see its candidature from a mainly local perspective. Most of its activists are well aware that selecting the parliamentary candidate is their only opportunity to make a significant decision, as opposed to supporting (or registering futile protests against) decisions made by the national leaders. If they surrender even this power to national headquarters they accept completely the status of local servants of national masters. But in none of the three British parties are they willing to do so; rather, most are jealous of their prerogative to select the candidate and quick to resent any effort by the national leaders to interfere.

This does not mean that the local activists usually prefer candidates prone to attack the national leaders' legislative programs or defy the whips in parliamentary votes. Quite the contrary: most insist that their candidates give the national leaders loyal support both on the hustings and in the House. But it does mean that the typical constituency party looks, not for a candidate who will help round out the national roster, but rather for one who will poll the maximum vote in their particular constituency, work well and cordially with the local volunteers, and faithfully grace local fundraising and social affairs with his presence.[2]

Given these differences in interest and outlook, then, some national-local conflict over candidatures is inevitable.

2. *The National Organizations' Supervisory Powers*

Britain's national party organizations cannot afford to let their local affiliates select candidates entirely unsupervised. The structure of cabinet government makes any large-scale parliamentary defection disastrous for the government and extremely damaging for the opposition; and the national leaders of both feel they must have

---

[2] One by-product of the elimination of seat-buying in the Conservative party by the Maxwell Fyfe reforms (see Chapter 2) has been a noticeable increase in this attitude among the constituency associations. Many have come to feel that since they raise the money they have a right to pick a man who will give substantial local service. Some, as we have seen, deliberately choose candidates *not* likely to become ministers precisely because they are more likely to be active in constituency and association affairs.

weapons to prevent it. Accordingly, both major parties' national organs have acquired certain formal powers to supervise local selections.[3] Labour's powers are more elaborate, but the national headquarters of both parties exercise some control of local selection procedures, maintain lists of persons approved for candidature, consult with local leaders in the early stages of selection,[4] insist on more intensive consultation in selections for by-elections, and reserve the right to veto any locally adopted candidate, which effectively strips him of the official party label. Underlying all these powers is their weapon of last resort: the power to disaffiliate constituency organizations from the national federation and to expel individual recalcitrants from the party.

3. The Limitations of National Control

One of this book's principal findings is that the national organizations' actual influence over candidate selection is substantially weaker than their formal supervisory powers allow. For example, their placement power is extremely weak in selections for general elections: rarely are they able to persuade a particular local association to adopt a particular individual, and in most instances any obvious effort to do so is likely to kill his chances altogether. Moreover, they are unable to persuade local selectors to adopt more candidates of certain types, as witness Conservative Central Office's failure to get more women and trade unionists adopted in winnable constituencies. Our evidence indicates that Transport House and Liberal HQ have somewhat more influence on selections for by-elections than for general elections, but Central Office does not have even this advantage.

For another example, the impressive formal veto power has in fact played a negligible role in Conservative selections and only a minor one in Labour's (Liberal HQ has no such power). The

---

[3] Liberal HQ has not; but it seems reasonable to suppose that if the Liberals were to win enough seats to form or overthrow a government, they would strengthen their national supervision of local candidate selection. Indeed, in Chapter 9 we noted a few small steps already taken in this direction in recent years.

[4] The national offices' regional agents and organizers play especially prominent roles in these consultations, in large part because their local connections are usually as strong as their national obligations.

Standing Advisory Committee on Candidates has directly vetoed only one locally adopted candidate since 1945, and not only did his constituency association stand by him but he almost won the seat. Moreover, on several occasions Central Office has *as a matter of principle* refrained from vetoing the readoption of M.P.s who have disobeyed or resigned the whip—the stated principle being that the selection of candidates is the constituency associations' affair, not Central Office's.

To be sure, Labour's Right-dominated NEC has vetoed ten locally adopted left-wing candidates and, through its regional organizers, blocked others short of adoption. But the NEC has acted only when it was confident the CLP would have to accept its verdict because an officially approved candidate would outpoll the vetoed candidate if he stood as an independent. In most situations where circumstances were less favorable, the NEC endorsed left-wing candidates, restored the whip to dissident left-wing M.P.s, and otherwise avoided direct tests of strength it might not win with left-wing CLPs.

In short, Labour has the most formal central control of the three parties and has used it the most; the Conservatives have somewhat less and have used it very little; and the Liberals have little central power or influence. Thus we may conclude that while British national party organizations play distinctly more active roles than their American counterparts in the selection of candidates for national offices, the great majority of the choices have been made in "law" and in fact by the constituency organizations.

The Selection of Candidates by Constituency Organizations

who does the selecting?

In Conservative and Labour constituency organizations candidates are formally chosen by large elected councils representing the local dues-paying members. But the councils choose from among alternatives on short lists prepared by much smaller screening committees of one sort or another. Thus while the final answers are given by the councils, the questions are framed and the ranges of choice fixed by the screening committees. Short listing is to the selection process what candidate selection is to the electoral process:

the stage at which most aspirants are eliminated and the *kind* of candidate to be chosen is decided.[5]

Despite the enthusiasm for intraparty democracy often proclaimed, particularly in the Labour party, the screening committees usually consist of eighteen to twenty of the local parties' leading activists and are often dominated by one or two officers. While they rarely recommend short lists containing only the name of the one person they prefer, they usually recommend lists containing no names of persons they strongly disapprove. So they have more to say about who shall be selected than any other party element, local or national.

In part, of course, this is simply the British instance of a general tendency in western democracies toward the control of candidate selection by small groups of dedicated insiders working within the formal framework of decisions by large masses of party workers or supporters.[6] But in Britain it is reinforced by the secrecy in which candidate selection, like most other party business, is conducted. Such secrecy makes control by insiders much easier than if all party members knew and could publicly dispute the claims of all the aspirants.[7] The secrecy is sustained by a belief widespread in Britain that political parties are private associations, like clubs or gardening societies; and most Britons feel that a private association should be allowed to make its decisions and settle its internal disputes entirely out of the public gaze.

FACTORS AFFECTING THE RANGES OF CHOICE

The short listers, then, fix the selectors' ranges of choice. But the short listers' own ranges of choice are limited by how many aspirants come forward to seek the candidature. The number, variety, and quality of the aspirants varies widely from one constituency to another, and is related to at least the following three factors.

---

[5] Most Liberal constituency associations seek candidates rather than select them, and their small search committees are comparable to the major parties' screening committees.

[6] This tendency operates even in the hostile environment created for it by the direct primaries in the United States: cf. V. O. Key, Jr., *Politics, Parties and Pressure Groups,* 5th. ed. (New York: Thomas Y. Crowell Company, 1964), pp. 394–95. For its operation in continental European parties, see Maurice Duverger, *Political Parties,* trans. Barbara and Robert North (New York: John Wiley & Sons, Inc., 1954), pp. 141–42.

[7] As is often the case in the United States: cf. Key, *Politics, Parties, and Pressure Groups,* p. 453.

1. *Incumbency*

In all three parties it is presumed that an incumbent M.P. who wishes to stand again must be readopted, and this presumption is rarely overborne. Accordingly, if a constituency party is known to have an M.P. who intends to stand again, the party's hopefuls look elsewhere.

2. *Winnability of the Constituency*

Around 90 per cent of each party's candidatures in its safe seats are pre-empted by incumbents. The remaining 10 per cent attract many more aspirants than the marginal constituencies,[8] and the latter in turn draw better than the hopeless constituencies. Consequently the selectors in the most winnable constituencies have their pick of a large number and variety of aspirants, while those in the least winnable sometimes find they have no volunteers at all and have to seek a candidate rather than select one.

3. *Upward Political Mobility*

By the criteria of constituency winnability we have used, 59 per cent of the Conservatives' candidatures by non-incumbents in the period 1951–1964 were in hopeless constituencies; for Labour the figure was 77 per cent, and for the Liberals almost all. Yet in most instances the Liberals had to search for party veterans to "show the flag" without hope of victory, while most Conservative and Labour local parties with no better prospects of immediate electoral success had several aspirants and were able to select rather than seek their candidates. The reason for this discrepancy is clear: the absence of a residence rule for M.P.s allows a candidate to stand anywhere, and to move from one constituency to another in successive elections. Many major-party aspirants to Parliament believe that the *cursus honorum* begins with fighting a good fight in a hopeless constituency and ends with being adopted for a safe seat. And in this period, indeed, many Conservative and Labour losers did move on to more promising constituencies after good showings in

---

[8] The only significant exception is a vacant "miners' seat" in the Labour party, which is often pre-empted by the nominee of the National Union of Mineworkers almost as surely as an incumbent pre-empts a candidature, although, as we saw in Chapter 8, the NUM has lost some of its seats in recent years.

their first tries. Most Liberal losers, on the other hand, dropped out after their initial defeats mainly because there were very few more promising constituencies they could move to. In short, the possibility of upward political mobility often gives the major parties' selectors in hopeless constituencies wider ranges of choice than they would have if Britain, like the United States, required its parliamentary candidates to be residents of the constituencies in which they stand.

THE CHOSEN FEW

1. *Assets and Liabilities*

We have assumed that the constituency organizations in the most winnable constituencies consider larger numbers and wider ranges of aspirants than those in the least winnable, and that by comparing the characteristics of the non-incumbents adopted in each category we could learn something of what the local selectors regard as assets and liabilities for candidature. The most significant differences found were as follows:

Previous Candidatures. In all three parties persons who have fought previous parliamentary contests are markedly overrepresented in the most winnable constituencies, and newcomers are equally overrepresented in the least winnable. So having already been a candidate seems to be a substantial asset for moving to a winnable seat.

Age. In all three parties each older age group from the twenties through the forties wins a higher proportion of the most desirable constituencies than the next younger group; among the Conservatives, but not Labour, the proportion declines for those in their fifties, still more for those in their sixties, and even more for those in their seventies. Labour candidates are generally older than Conservative or Liberal, although most of the difference reflects the much higher average age of Labour candidates sponsored by trade unions.

Sex. Central Office expresses much more concern than Transport House with the local selectors' prejudice against women candidates; but both parties give about the same small fraction (5 and 7 per cent) of their candidatures to women. The Liberals have a slightly higher proportion of women, but they can rarely afford to be as selective as the major parties.

Local Connections. Despite the absence of a local residence rule and the presumed centralization of British politics, almost a third of the Conservatives' candidatures by non-incumbents and over a quarter of Labour's have gone to persons with personal connections in the constituencies for which they were adopted. However, local connections seem to be an advantage in some constituencies but not in others: the preference for local candidates in both parties is most marked, not in the rural areas as one might expect, but in the ten largest English, Welsh, and Scottish cities outside London—and, for Labour only, in the mining areas where the National Union of Mineworkers dominates most selections.

Education. Neither Labour nor Liberal candidatures show any significant relationship between education and constituency winnability. Education as measured by years of schooling is little more significant in the allocation of Conservative candidatures. But education measured by the social prestige of schools attended is highly related to the distribution of Conservative candidates among the more and less desirable constituencies: persons who have attended public schools are heavily overrepresented in the best constituencies, while persons who have not fight a disproportionate number of hopeless constituencies. University attendance, on the other hand, makes little difference: the public-school-and-Oxbridge candidates have done no better than the public-school-only group; and the secondary-and-Oxbridge group have done no better than the secondary-and-no-university group.

Occupation. One of the most striking differences between the two major parties is in the occupational groups which win the highest proportions of the best candidatures: civil servants and farmers are favored by the Conservatives, while trade union officials and political organizers do best with Labour—members of the ruling "establishment" and of old county families for the Tories, and full-time servants of the movement for the Socialists.

Ideology. By all accounts the aspirants' general political ideologies and specific views on the issues of the moment play almost no role in the selection of Conservative and Liberal candidates. Both factors have been somewhat more prominent in Labour selections because of the sharp and persistent factional fight between Left and Right. But even so, ideological considerations have been decisive in only a minority of Labour selections, and left-wing CLPs have often chosen right-wing candidates and vice versa.

Personality.   Activists in all three parties testify that the greatest asset an aspirant can have is the right kind of personality or character. Some of the specific qualities mentioned are common to all the parties: skill at public speaking, ability to get on well with people (especially with local party workers), a willingness to serve the local organization as well as the national party, and so on. But the parties' images of the ideal candidate also differ in several significant respects. Most Conservatives speak of wanting a man of character—solid, loyal, dependable in a tight spot, not flashy or brilliant. Most Socialists, on the other hand, speak of wanting a dedicated servant of the movement. But to most trade unionists this means a man who has worked with his hands, served his union faithfully, and accumulated the seniority that entitles him to parliamentary candidature. To most individual CLP members it means an intellectual who has proved his devotion to certain causes—nationalization, racial equality, nuclear disarmament, equal educational opportunities, or whatever. And to most Co-operative party members it means a man who has worked faithfully in the co-operative movement. Hence the "three Labour parties" we spoke of in Chapter 8.

2. *Candidates, Party Members, and Party Voters*

Labour voters and party workers are drawn mainly from the lower-middle and working classes, while Conservative and Liberal voters and workers include much higher proportions from the middle and upper ranks of British society.[9] These differences are paralleled by differences between the parties' candidates, although the differences *within* the Labour party are even wider than those between Labour and its opponents.

However, no party's roster of candidates is a representative cross-section of its voters or workers. The candidates are generally of higher social status; they have substantially more formal schooling; more by far have attended high-prestige schools; and they hold

---

[9] See Jean Blondel, *Voters, Parties, and Leaders* (London: Penguin Books, Ltd., 1963), Chs. 3–4; and R. R. Alford, *Party and Society* (Chicago: Rand McNally & Company, 1963), Ch. 6.

mainly business, professional, or white-collar jobs, while many more of their voters and party workers are manual laborers. Socially, then, each party's candidates do not represent its rank-and-file; rather they occupy a considerably higher level in the party hierarchy. As Guttsman well sums it up:

> If we ascend the political hierarchy, from the voters upwards, we find that at each level—the membership of political parties, party activists, local political leaders, M.P.s, National Leaders—the social character of the group is slightly less "representative" and slightly more tilted in favour of those who belong to the middle and upper levels of our society. Ability and availability, deference and assumed superiority contribute to this pattern at each level. For major politicians are initially made by minor politicians and the "political leaders in miniature" who man the local party Executives and Management Committees tend to choose as candidates men who are like themselves or who are socially above them.[10]

This social gap between party leaders and party workers and voters is not unique to Britain; it appears to some degree in all western democracies no matter how class-identified may be their political parties ideologically.[11] There are good reasons why it does. Most candidate selectors do not intend to choose the aspirant most like themselves for the honor of candidature; rather they try to choose the aspirant most likely to make the best candidate—one who will work the most effectively with the local organization and appeal most strongly to the local voters. The selectors know that a good candidate needs, among other things, time away from his job to campaign, an ability to express himself well in public, and a reputable position in society. And in Britain as elsewhere, persons in the upper reaches of the educational-occupational scale are more likely to have these advantages than those in the lower.[12]

Thus in social status, personality, and outlook the parliamentary candidates of all three British parties, like their counterparts in other democracies, resemble each other more closely than they resemble their respective supporters. They may not constitute a rul-

---

[10] W. L. Guttsman, *The British Political Elite* (London: MacGibbon & Kee, 1963), p. 27.

[11] Cf. D. R. Matthews, *The Social Background of Political Decision-Makers* (Garden City, L.I.: Doubleday & Company, Inc., 1954), Chs. 3–4; and Max Weber, "Politics as a Vocation," *Essays in Sociology*, translated and edited by H. H. Gerth and C. W. Mills (New York: Oxford University Press, 1946), Essay IV.

[12] Cf. Duverger, *Political Parties*, pp. 158–62.

ing class in the traditional sense, but they are certainly a political élite.

CANDIDATE SELECTION IN THE BRITISH SYSTEM

CONTRIBUTION TO COHESION

We noted in Chapter 1 that the parliamentary cohesion of British parties is the trait most admired by those who would make them models for all democratic parties; for party solidarity in parliamentary votes is a necessary if not sufficient condition for enabling the voters to hold the majority party collectively responsible for how the government is run.

Why do British M.P.s almost always obey their party whips while American congressmen often disregard theirs? Is it, as some have suggested, because American national party leaders have no effective control over the local selection of legislative candidates while British leaders do?

Our findings indicate that central *control* of candidate selection makes only a minor contribution to British party cohesion, for it simply is not very strong. No party's national organization can place particular candidates or types of candidates wherever it wishes. The Conservatives' SACC has the power to veto local adoptions, but almost never uses it. Labour's NEC has used its veto more often, but only a minority of the party's rebel M.P.s and dissident candidates have been disciplined in this manner.

Since 1945, in fact, far more M.P.s in both major parties have been disciplined by their constituency organizations than by national officers. The Maxwell Fyfe reforms made the Conservative associations financially independent of their candidates and M.P.s, and many local leaders have come to feel that disciplining the local M.P. is their prerogative. The result, in McKenzie's words, is that "if the independently-minded Conservative M.P. now has little to fear from the Whips in Parliament, he may have a good deal to fear from the scorpions in the constituency associations."[13] Many CLPs who refuse all sponsored candidates have developed similar notions.

Moreover, neither party's constituency organizations have been

---

[13] Robert T. McKenzie, *British Political Parties,* 2nd. ed. (London: Mercury Books, 1964), p. 633.

inclined to deny their M.P.s readoption for just *any* kind of parliamentary deviation. Indeed, they have smiled benignly on M.P.s who deserted the national leaders' middle positions for more extreme versions of the parties' traditional ideologies: witness the absence of local attacks on the Bevanite rebels in the Labour party and on the Conservative right-wing Suez rebels. On the other hand, the local parties have usually denied readoption to M.P.s who abandoned the leaders' position for one nearer the opposition's: witness the fierce local attacks on the Labour M.P. who supported the Suez intervention in 1956 and on the Conservative M.P.s who opposed it.

Yet even though the national leaders cannot force them to do so, the local parties voluntarily continue to adopt candidates who, when elected, dutifully vote as the whips direct. Hence although the *de facto* local control of candidate selection in Britain resembles the *de jure* local control in the United States much more closely than is commonly supposed, it does not produce parliamentary parties of nearly so low cohesion as those in Congress.

Why? The fundamental answer lies in the fact that British constituency parties are not local in the same sense as American state and local parties. They are manned by activists primarily loyal to the national parties' leaders and causes. Each is established for an essentially national purpose: to elect a Member of Parliament. Everything else it does is subordinate to that purpose. And its activists know that when their M.P. takes his seat he cannot be an independent operator like an American Senator or Representative; he can only be a member of the government team or the opposition team. If he defies the whip he can only embarrass his (and their) team; he cannot change the course of governmental policy except by helping the other side to win or keep power. Most local activists feel that giving aid and comfort to the opposition is the most grievous of political sins. Hence, as we have seen, they are far more prone than the national leaders to deny readoption to an M.P. who, by defying the whip, supports the other party's position.

In short, the national leaders do not need to control local candidate selection in order to maintain party cohesion in Parliament; the local activists do the job for them. To be sure, the national leaders cannot force the local parties to adopt candidates with the personal attributes needed to round out national rosters, and this may deprive them of some talent they need in the House. But this does not affect their ability to muster their M.P.s in the proper lobby whenever they wish. Thus local control in the British system has very different results from local control in the American.

SELECTION, CONSTITUTION, AND SOCIETY

The British way of selecting parliamentary candidates is both shaped by and helps to sustain the whole constitutional and social system in which it operates. Its principal procedural traits, as we have seen, are the making of decisions by small groups of insiders in a framework of formal responsibility to wider but less active circles, the remolding of formal rules by informal understandings, and the veil of secrecy drawn against prying outsiders. These same traits generally characterize decision-making in the parliamentary parties, cabinet, civil service, business corporations, and trade unions as well. So it is in no sense a strange or un-British way of doing things.

Moreover, the candidates it produces come mainly from the public school aristocracy, the grammar school meritocracy, Oxbridge, and the trade unions—institutions which also supply most of the country's economic, religious, and educational leaders.[14] As—but only as—the sources of leadership in other areas of British society change, so will the sources of parliamentary candidates change.

The selection process thus seems well suited to a political system which requires each legislator to be first and foremost a good party man, whether minister, potential minister, or "lobby fodder." It would be highly unsuitable, if not downright subversive, for a system in which a legislator is expected to be an independent spokesman for his constituency first and a party man second.

So when an outsider manages a few glimpses into "the secret garden of British politics" he sees nothing shameful or even surprising; he sees the same political and social flora and fauna that have flourished elsewhere in British soil for a long time. How they might prosper—and mutate—in other soils and other climates is another question.

---

[14] This point is thoroughly documented by Guttsman, *The British Political Elite,* especially Ch. XI.

APPENDIX

INDEX

APPENDIX

Materials and Methods Used for the
Statistical Analysis of Characteristics of
Candidates and Constituencies

Information about Candidates

1. *Non-Incumbent and Incumbent Candidates*

Dr. David Butler of Nuffield College, Oxford, has collected biographical information about all the candidates standing in the general elections of 1951, 1955, 1959, and 1964, and has summarized some of their characteristics in his studies of those elections. He generously gave the author full access to this rich body of data, and the author supplemented it with comparable information from the volumes of the *House of Commons* series published by the *Times* (London) and the candidates' biographies issued by the three parties.

For each candidate at each election the following items were punched on IBM cards: year of election, party, whether elected or defeated, age at the time of the election, sex, declared religion (so little useful information on this subject is published that no attempt has been made to analyze it), marital status, previous contests and their results, previous membership on local government councils, previous activity in nonpartisan civic and religious organizations, previous offices held in local or national party organizations, previous candidatures in the constituency being contested or in other constituencies, level of formal education, public school (if any) attended, university (if any) attended, occupation, ministerial experience, personal connections in the constituency being

285

contested, sponsoring organization (for Labour candidates only), and sponsoring union (for Labour candidates only).

2. *First-Time Losers in 1951 and 1955*

For those candidates who stood for the first time and lost in the general elections of 1951 and 1955, the following additional information was punched in the cards recording their first contests: performance in first candidature (see Chapter 4 for the definition of the categories used); subsequent candidatures, if any; election of second candidature; changes in personal characteristics between first and second candidatures; identification number of second constituency (see below); party area of second constituency; population type of second constituency; personal connections in second constituency; comparison of winnability of first and second constituencies; performance in second candidature; outcome of second candidature; third candidature, if any.

3. *Classification of Occupations*

For the general occupational classes used in Tables 4.7, 7.7, and 9.6, the following occupations were included:

Proprietor, managerial: company executive or director, small business proprietor, farmer, private means.

Professional: barrister, solicitor, journalist, author, publicist, chartered accountant, civil engineer, surveyor, doctor, dentist, clergyman, armed services.

White-collar: teacher, civil servant, clerical, political organizer.

Intermediate: housewife, student.

Manual, wage-earning: manual worker, trade union official.

INFORMATION ABOUT CONSTITUENCIES

1. *General*

The *Times House of Commons* volumes list the election returns in each constituency for each election. The Conservative and Unionist Central Office's pamphlet, *Party Organisation,* and the Labour party's published reports of its annual conferences in the four election years indicate the party areas or regions in which each constituency was located.

2. *Classification as to Winnability*

In the general elections of 1951, 1955, and 1959 the Conservatives lost a total of seven seats. Six of these had been held by margins ranging from 0.6 per cent of the popular vote to 2.2 per cent. The seventh, North Devon, had been won by a margin of 14.6 per cent in 1955 but lost to a Liberal by a margin of 0.9 per cent in 1959—a "swing" so much greater than all the others that it seemed best not to let it fix the limits of a winnability category.

During the same three elections Labour lost fifty-eight seats. Among those in which direct inter-election comparisons are possible because unaffected by the entry or exit of third candidates, the previous Labour majorities had ranged from 0.1 per cent to 8.8 per cent.

In the light of these considerations, the winnability categories for the two major parties were defined as follows:

Result in preceding general election	*Con.*	*Lab.*
Conservative won by 4.0% or more	High	Low
Conservative won by 0.1% to 3.9%	Medium	Medium
Labour won by 0.1% to 8.9%	Medium	Medium
Labour won by 9.0% or more	Low	High
Election won by party other than Conservative or Labour; newly-formed constituency	Other	Other

Since Labour did substantially better in the 1964 general election, an analysis of candidate selection after 1964 should modify these categories to take account of Labour's improved prospects. But for the period 1945–1964 the definitions given above seem the most appropriate.

3. Classification of Liberal Candidatures

For reasons given in the text (pp. 257–58) the foregoing scale of constituency winnability was not used for the analysis of Liberal candidatures. A scale of "constituency desirability" was substituted, employing the following criteria:

Medium: in the preceding general election the Liberal candidate finished second, or finished third 0.1 per cent to 9.9 per cent behind the candidate finishing second.

Low: in the preceding general election the Liberal candidate finished third or fourth by 10 per cent or more behind the candidate finishing second.

Other: the constituency had no Liberal candidate in the preceding general election.

4. Classification as to Population Type

This was done in part according to the criteria used by S. E. Finer, H. B. Berrington, and D. J. Bartholomew in their *Backbench Opinion in the House of Commons, 1955–59* (London: Pergamon Press, 1961), pp. 156–57. The definition of each category was:

Urban: constituencies in which less than a third of the population lived in rural districts.

Semi-rural: constituencies in which between a third and a half lived in rural districts.

Rural: constituencies in which more than half lived in rural districts.

Semi-rural-mining and rural-mining: constituencies in the second and third categories in which mining was the predominant industry.

London, Scottish burghs, Scottish counties, and Ulster: all self-explanatory.

Other metropolitan: Birmingham, Bristol, Leeds, Liverpool, Manchester, Sheffield, Cardiff, and Swansea.

5. *Items Punched*

For each constituency at each election the following items were punched: an identification number (from 1 to 625 for 1951, and 1 to 630 for 1955, 1959, and 1964) based on the order of listing in the *Times House of Commons* volumes, 1951–1959; the difference between each party's percentage of the poll and its leading rival's percentage of the poll in the general election immediately preceding the general election in question; the party organizational area or region in which the constituency was located; the constituency's classification according to the urban-rural classification described above; and the constituency's winnability according to the set of categories described above.

Analytical Procedures

The simpler distributions and calculations were performed by the author and his research assistants on IBM 083 and 101 machines. The larger and more complex manipulations were run on the IBM 1401 high speed electronic computer of the Statistical Service Unit of the University of Illinois and on the CDC 1604 high speed electronic computer of the Numerical Analysis Laboratory of the University of Wisconsin.

Since the nature of the data permitted measurement along nominal scales only for most variables, the author employed only nonparametric statistical tests, notably the chi-square test and the contingency coefficient: see Sidney Siegel, *Nonparametric Statistics for the Behavioral Sciences* (New York: McGraw-Hill Book Company, Inc., 1956), *passim;* and Hubert M. Blalock, Jr., *Social Statistics* (New York: McGraw-Hill Book Company, Inc., 1960), Chs. 2, 15, 16

INDEX